# The Globalisation of Indian Business

Consolidation activities such as mergers and acquisitions (M&As) have been one of the major strategies adopted by Indian firms to withstand global competition. M&As experienced a substantial increase in value and volume during the post-liberalisation era, facilitated by the presence of foreign subsidiaries in the Indian market as well as competitive pressure on domestic firms. The increased foreign investment through M&As brought new dimensions to the fore such as the implications on technological performance, efficiency, and more importantly, competition in the Indian market.

*The Globalisation of Indian Business: Cross Border Mergers and Acquisitions in Indian Manufacturing* provides an in-depth analysis of these issues, specifically aiming to understand whether the M&As strategies helped the firms to achieve their desired objectives in terms of improvement in technology, efficiency and market power in the context of the increase of M&As in India, using appropriate statistical and econometric techniques.

The book is of additional importance in the context of the recently implemented Competition Act, replacing the thirty-year-old Monopolies and Restrictive Trade Practices Act (MRTP) in India. The new Act aims to maintain competition and protect consumers' interests without harming that of the producers'. Based on the analysis, broadly, the study cautions the regulators to rethink the efficiency defence argument and become more vigilant on the creation of monopolies. On the other side, it suggests firms should reconsider their post-merger integration strategy since consolidation has not led to a sustainable increase in market share of the surviving firms.

**Beena Saraswathy** is Assistant Professor at the Institute for Studies in Industrial Development (ISID), New Delhi. She has completed MPhil in Applied Economics and Doctoral Degree in Economics from Centre for Development Studies, Thiruvananthapuram, Kerala (Jawaharlal Nehru University, New Delhi). Before joining ISID, she had been working with Indian Council for Research on International Economic Relations (ICRIER) and Competition Commission of India (CCI) under the Ministry of Corporate Affairs (MCA), Government of India (GOI). Her research interests include market competition, mergers and acquisitions, the pharmaceutical industry, business groups in India and contemporary development issues.

# Routledge Studies in the Economics of Business and Industry

# The Globalisation of Indian Business

## Cross Border Mergers and Acquisitions in Indian Manufacturing

**Beena Saraswathy**

Routledge
Taylor & Francis Group

LONDON AND NEW YORK

First published 2018 by Routledge

2 Park Square, Milton Park, Abingdon, Oxfordshire OX14 4RN

52 Vanderbilt Avenue, New York, NY 10017

*Routledge is an imprint of the Taylor & Francis Group, an informa business*

First issued in paperback 2019

*British Library Cataloguing-in-Publication Data*
A catalogue record for this book is available from the British Library

*Library of Congress Cataloguing-in-Publication Data*
Names: Saraswathy, Beena, author.
Title: The globalisation of Indian business: cross border mergers and acquisitions in Indian manufacturing / Beena Saraswathy.
Description: Abingdon, Oxon; New York, NY: Routledge, 2018. | Series: Routledge studies in the economics of business and industry | Includes bibliographical references and index.
Identifiers: LCCN 2017032213
Subjects: LCSH: Consolidation and merger of corporations—India. | Manufacturing industries—India. | International business enterprises—India.
Classification: LCC HD2746.55.I4 S273 2018 | DDC 338.8/8954—dc23
LC record available at https://lccn.loc.gov/2017032213

ISBN: 978-1-138-74027-3 (hbk)
ISBN: 978-0-367-88851-0 (pbk)

Typeset in Times New Roman
by codeMantra

*…..bhadre Narayana…hare Krishna….*

# Contents

# List of figures and tables

**Figures**

**Tables**

# List of abbreviations

| | |
|---|---|
| AIC | Akaike Information Criterion |
| BoD | Board of Directors |
| CA | Competition Act |
| CCI | Competition Commission of India |
| CL | Competition Law |
| CMIE | Centre for Monitoring Indian Economy |
| CSO | Central Statistical Organisation |
| ES | Efficiency Seekers |
| FDI | Foreign Direct Investment |
| FERA | Foreign Exchange Regulation Act |
| GoI | Government of India |
| HHI | Herfindahl Hirschman Index |
| IPRs | Intellectual Property Rights |
| LLF | Log Likelihood Function |
| LR test | Likelihood Ratio test |
| M&As | Mergers and Acquisitions |
| MC | Marginal Cost |
| MIC | Monopoly Inquiry Commission |
| MNC | Multi National Companies |
| MRTP Act | Monopolies and Restrictive Trade Practices Act |
| MRTPC | Monopolies and Restrictive Trade Practices Commission |
| MS | Market Seekers |
| MTPs | Monopoly Restrictive Practices |
| OFT | Office of Fair Trading |
| PCM | Price Cost Margin |
| PMI | Post Merger Integration |
| R&D | Research and Development |
| RS | Resource Seekers |
| RTPs | Restrictive Trade Practices |
| SEBI | Securities and Exchange Board of India |
| SS | Strategic Asset Seekers |
| UV | Utility Vehicles |
| VCE | Variance Component Estimation |

# Preface

Like the global scenario, the Indian corporate sector too experienced a boom in mergers and acquisitions led restructuring strategies especially after liberalization, which is mainly due to the increasing presence of subsidiaries of big MNCs here as well as due to the pressure exerted by such strategies on the domestic firms. Besides, many MNCs realised the fact that the Indian market is a big consumer base to meet their desired objectives such as market creation, efficiency enhancement, strategic assets creation etc. Thus, the entry into the Indian market is unavoidable. Mergers, acquisitions and similar other strategies are an easy way of accessing the big Indian market without much cost of time and effort compared to the Greenfield mode of entry. The book examines whether the M&As strategy helped the firms to achieve their desired objectives in terms of improvement in technology, efficiency and market power in the context of the increasing M&As in India, using appropriate statistical and econometric techniques.

Briefly, the following observations emerged. The analysis on technological performance reached the conclusion that the cross-border firms are becoming more technology import intensive, while the domestic firms have increased their spending on in-house R&D creation. Whether this increased spending leads to higher efficiency has been further analysed using Stochastic Frontier Production Function along with the inefficiency effects and found that in majority of the cases, efficiency is declining after getting into M&As. In order to examine the impact of consolidation activities on market power creation, we have used various techniques including disappearance rate, survival probability and concentration ratios and noticed that there has been a high degree of disappearance of firms through mergers in various sectors, and in those sectors the possible impact on market concentration is also high. However, this increased degree of influence is not helping the surviving firms to sustain their market share in the long run. This may be due to the absence of synergies creation after consolidation. We have also made an attempt to bring out the importance of prost merger integration in deciding the outcome of consolidation strategies.

Based on the analysis, broadly, the study cautions the regulators to rethink the efficiency defense argument and become more vigilant on monopolies creation. On the other side, it suggests the firms to reconsider their post-merger integration strategy since consolidation has not led to a sustainable increase in market shares of the surviving firms. The study also discussed the policy implications arising from the analysis, in the background of current Competition Act.

Being a beginner in the field of research, coupled with the specific nature of the topic, I had to depend on many for fulfilling this work. My sincere thanks to each one of them. This work is the updated version of the Doctoral thesis submitted to the Centre for Development Studies (CDS), Thiruvananthapuram. My heartfelt thanks to my supervisors Prof. P. Mohanan Pillai and Dr. P.L Beena; Prof. K.K Subrahmanian, Prof. Sunil Mani, Prof. K. Pushpangadan, Prof. N. Shanta, Prof. K.N Harilal, Prof. K. Joseph and all other teaching and non-teaching staffs at CDS; Prof. Chalapati Rao, Dr. Reji K. Joseph, Prof. Ranganathan, Prof. S. K Goyal, Director- Prof. Murthy, Dr. Satyaki Roy, and all other faculties at Institute for Studies in Industrial Development for providing all kinds of support and encouragement. My engagement with the Competition Commission of India helped a lot in understanding M&As from the ground level. I have also benefitted greatly from the comments received during various paper presentations made based on the study. The names of Prof. K. L Krishna, Dr. Vijayabaskar, Prof. Padmini Swaminathan, Prof. Biswanath Goldar, Prof. Kaliyappa Kalirajan, Dr. Bhandari, Dr. Parameswaran, Prof. N.S. Siddharthan are to be mentioned here. My special thanks to Routledge. Also I remember the love and support from all my family members and Vedavid Aneesh. The book may be of special interest to all those who are interested in the Indian M&A scenario.

## Previous publication acknowledgements:

*Chapter 3:*

Revised version of the (i) CDS Working Paper No.434, "Cross-border Mergers and Acquisitions in India: Extent, Nature and Structure", July, 2010 and (ii) chapter in the book "The Economic and Social Issues of Financial Liberalisation: Evidence from Emerging Countries" Reddy, Krishna (ed), Bookwell Publishing, New Delhi, pp. 26–40, 2013.

*Chapter 5:*

Revised version of the Indian Council for Research on International Economic Relations (ICRIER) Working Paper No. 299, "Production Efficiency of Firms with Mergers and Acquisitions in India", New Delhi, June 2015.

*Chapter 6:*

Revised version of the Institute for Studies in Industrial Development (ISID) Working Paper No. 188, "Impact of Mergers on Market Competition in the Indian Manufacturing: An Assessment", March 2016.

# 1   Introduction

Mergers and acquisitions (hereinafter M&As) are one way of achieving the objectives of business and corporate strategies. The corporate sector all over the world is restructuring its operations through different types of consolidation strategies[1] like M&As in order to face challenges posed by the new pattern of globalisation, which has led to the greater integration of national and international markets. The intensity of such operations is increasing with the deregulation of various government policies as a facilitator of the neoliberal economic regime. Earlier also the firms were widely using consolidation strategies, but one of the striking features of the present M&As scenario is the presence of a large number of cross-border deals. The intensity of cross-border operations recorded an unprecedented surge since the mid-1990s, and the same trend continues (World Investment Report, 2000). Earlier, foreign firms were facilitating market expansion strategy through the setting up of wholly owned subsidiaries in overseas markets (Jones, 2005), which has now become a 'second best option' since it involves much time and effort that may not suit to the changed global scenario.[2] Getting into cross-border M&As (hereinafter CM&As) became the 'first-best option' to the leading firms and others depended on the 'follow-the-leader' strategy.[3]

The Indian corporate sector too experienced such a boom in M&As that led restructuring strategies especially after liberalisation; this is due to the increasing presence of subsidiaries of big Multinational Corporations (MNCs) here as well as due to the pressure exerted by such strategies on the domestic firms. Besides, many MNCs realised the fact that the Indian market is a big consumer base to meet their desired objectives. Thus, the entry is unavoidable. They found that resorting to mergers, acquisitions and similar strategies is an easy way of entry into Indian market without much cost of time and money. In order to facilitate globalisation, the Indian government also implemented various policies which marked a paradigm shift in the operation of the domestic firms as it removed the patronage enjoyed by the domestic firms under the assumptions like Infant Industry argument and opened them for the free play of market forces. More importantly, globalisation reduced the product life cycles, and the firms began to bring out new products quickly to the market as compared to the past. Computer aided manufacturing helped to reduce the time needed for production. Shortened product life cycles meant high R&D intensity, and this has to be recouped before the technology becomes obsolete, which becomes especially important if a rival firm 'wins-the-race' to innovate a new generation product (Levin et al., 1997 as in Narula, 2003). These circumstances again prompted firms to engage in various kinds of agreements to reduce the high risk associated with innovation and to become successful through the sharing of tangible and intangible assets. These issues are equally important for the domestic deals in the present scenario. Given this broad context, the present study is an attempt to analyse the changing nature of foreign investment in the form of M&As. The second section of this chapter discusses, why firms are crossing borders through M&As and the third section will be dealing with the opportunities and challenges from such deals. The fourth section is an attempt to explore the issues emerging from the new pattern of internationalisation of Indian firms, and the subsequent sections discuss the data and methodology, objectives and chapter scheme of the study.

## 1.1  Why firms are crossing borders?

When we look at the business history, we can see at least four types of growth strategies were adopted by the firms. Firms started with domestic production and began to export to the foreign markets, the establishment of subsidiaries in overseas market was the third stage, and as a fourth phase, firms started to make an association with the foreign firms in the overseas market either through joint ventures or through acquisitions instead of establishing subsidiaries.[4] The increasing magnitude of investment through CM&As and its emergence as a major component of Foreign Direct Investment (FDI) even in the case of developing countries such as India demand us to think why firms are engaging in cross-border consolidations[5] instead of establishing subsidiaries or to engage in export-oriented growth. Answering this requires us to merge the prime objectives of foreign investment with that of M&As. We have observed that in many cases, the objectives of foreign investment are achieved through consolidation in an easier way, which is the reason behind the increasing importance of cross-border consolidation strategies. In this section, we shall try to bring together the two issues mentioned above, why do firms invest abroad and what makes M&As, a preferred mode to other strategies.

Behrman (1972) distinguished four major types of foreign investors based on the underlying motives, which later adapted and extended by Dunning.[6] They are (1) resource-seekers, (2) market-seekers, (3) efficiency-seekers and (4) strategic assets or capability-seekers. Presently, firms have multiple objectives, and they fall under more than one of these categories. We shall discuss each of these categories and try to incorporate, how M&As enable to achieve the desired objectives of each of these categories of investors.[7]

Resource Seekers are the firms investing abroad for obtaining specific resources at lower prices. They are either prompted by the nonavailability of these resources in the home market or lower prices prevailing in foreign locations compared to their home country. Resources include physical resources, skilled and semi-skilled labourers, technological capabilities, marketing and managerial expertise and organisational skills. The Strategic Asset Seekers are the firms, which try to sustain or enhance their international competitiveness or weaken that of other firms through acquiring the assets of foreign corporations. Their major motive is to add to the existing product portfolios rather than to exploit the marketing and other types of synergies. The Market Seekers, as the name suggests, seek new markets in order to expand and strengthen their operations outside the home country. Multinational Enterprises (MNEs) may consider it necessary to have a physical presence in leading markets served by its competitors and construct production units and research centres there. This will enable them to adapt their products to the local needs and to indigenous resource and capabilities,[8] which is essential to compete with the local firms. Hymer (1960) argued that local firms have better information about the economic environment of their country than do foreign firms and foreign firms should possess countervailing capabilities in order to overcome this (Calvet, A.L., 1981). Moreover, subsidiaries in foreign locations will help to reduce the production and transaction cost to a great extent compared to export from home market.[9] Efficiency Seekers (Rationalised FDI) tries to operate more efficiently by deriving economies of scale and scope and by reducing risk. They are mainly aiming to take advantage of different factor endowments, cultures, institutional arrangements, economic systems and policies and market structures by concentrating production in a limited number of locations. There are two types of Efficiency Seekers. First is to take advantage of the availability and cost of traditional factor endowments in different countries and the second is to take advantage of economies of scale and scope.

Most of these categories will be able to achieve their objectives through M&As in a better way compared to Greenfield investment, which will take much more time and effort. The Resource Seekers who are more interested in getting the physical and labour resources at cheaper rates will be better off through M&As compared to Greenfield investment since they will be able to use the already established resources of the partner firm. They can access the local firm's cheap labour and such other resources. The case of Strategic Asset Seekers is almost the same as the Resource Seekers. They can very well strengthen or diversify their product portfolio through acquiring the brands of their partner and make the firm more competitive.

Regarding the other two types of investors i.e. the Market Seekers and Efficiency Seekers, the advantages of market power and efficiency creation through M&As are well established since both categories of firms are aiming at the creation of economies of scale and scope and thereby market power. If they are following Greenfield mode of entry, major advantages to them are the expansion of their market to a foreign country. Whereas if they are entering a foreign market through M&As, they can achieve this objective with less cost and effort compared to the new entry. They can also access and share the already established market and avail critical resources of an established firm in a better way. They can not only achieve the benefits of large scale of operation but also reduce many expenses such as marketing, advertisement, distribution, R&D etc. through avoidance of duplicate expenses since consolidation allows the sharing of common resources compared to the pre-consolidation period. The effect of cutting R&D expenditure would be substantial since it will save much time and effort and it can be used more efficiently. Moreover, from a firm's point of view, they can raise the market power to a large extent through the reduction of the number of firms in the industry and the expansion of their operation, which enable them to have a say in the determination of prices. The major advantages to the Efficiency Seekers and Market Seekers from consolidation can be discussed with the help of the simple model developed by Williamson (1968).

If consolidation is taking place in a perfectly competitive market, assuming both the consolidating firms are producing their previous level of output, the cost of production will decline compared to that of the pre-consolidation period (i.e. $C_0 > C_1$) through increasing efficiency. With the reduced cost of production, the firm has three options. One is to sell their product at the previous level of price ($P_0$), second at a reduced price ($P_1$) and third at a higher price ($P_m$) using their increased market power.[10] In the first case, there will not be any change in prices and the firm will get profit ($\Pi_0$). In the second case, the firm can capture the entire market through a small marginal reduction in prices. Under the third case, allowing for an increase in the market power of the firm and restricted entry, the firm can set the prices at a profit maximising the level of a monopolist, say $P_m$, which will enable them to achieve a higher level of profit given the cost of production, $C_1 < C_0$. The consumers will be harmed due to the price hike.[11] The net welfare impact depends on the trade-off between cost saving due to consolidation and the deadweight loss arising out of monopoly pricing. The difference between these two has been an evergreen topic of debate in M&As literature. Williamson (1968) favoured the net efficiency gains and said, 'even then the cost differential is too low; the net benefits will offset the losses'. We will be discussing it again in Chapter 5.

Thus, from the above discussion, it follows that M&As is a better solution for firms, which want to internationalise their operations quickly, which is captured in Figure 1.1. As we discussed earlier, globalisation induced the disappearance of national borders. Now the firms are facing international competition even within the domestic boundaries due to the opening of the markets. It necessitates firms to strengthen themselves in the home market too, in the absence of it; they may be wiped out in the acute competition. Thus, on the one side, various policy changes are pushing firms to engage in

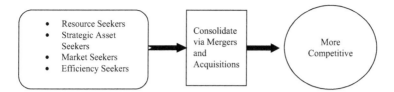

*Figure 1.1* Investors choice of consolidation.
Source: Authors compilation.

consolidation strategies, whereas on the other hand consolidation strategies are acting as a pull factor for the challenges arising out of policy changes.

### 1.1.1 The policy aspects

Broadly, there are three sets of major regulations faced by the firms under the present global scenario. They are, Corporate Law including Competition Law (CL), Intellectual Property Rights (IPRs) and Sectoral Policy Regulations. Amongst this, the Competition Law aims at enhancing consumer welfare through maintaining competition. IPRs give temporary monopoly for the owners of innovation, which is expected to enhance the innovation incentives of the innovating firms. The third set of regulations that is sectoral policies also aims at the consumer welfare, but the policy changes according to the welfare implications of different sectors. The policy makers are facing a dilemma whether to allow big firms to get into M&As and permit them to undertake costly innovations, or to restrict them on the grounds that it can lead to concentration of market power in the hands of a few big firms. If they allow, it can be argued that M&As will enhance consumer welfare in future with the introduction of better quality products at lower prices through engaging in innovation facilitated by consolidation as well as the enhancement of efficiency through synergy creation. On the other hand, it can also lead to the monopolisation of innovation and the consequent rise in prices, which will adversely affect the welfare of consumers in the long run. Thus, the central task with the regulators is to ensure maximum consumer surplus without harming that of producers'. Towards achieving this goal, most of the competition authorities relied on fixing a maximum ceiling limit for M&As; beyond this limit, the firms have to get prior permission from the respective authorities. Needless to say, the fixing of the ceiling raised several questions regarding the extent of the ceiling, which would have its impact on the market structure and performance. This limit varies from country to country due to the differences in the legal, economic and social framework existing in different countries. However, there are preliminary discussions going on for evolving an *International Competition Policy* for the global economy in the context of increasing global integration and reducing national boundaries (Utton, 2008; Dhall, 2007).

## 1.2  Opportunities and challenges from consolidation

The increasing extent of M&As raised many opportunities as well as challenges especially regarding the fulfilment of the desired objectives of firms through M&As such as technological performance, market expansion, efficiency enhancement and so on. These questions become more crucial for cross-border deals since it involves a 'nationality' element. The following section deals with some of these aspects.

### *1.2.1 Technological performance of developing economies*

As Bresman and Nobel (1999) have pointed out, '...we have grown from an age in which the most important resource was capital into an age in which the most critical resource is knowledge.... Those who have gained a competitive edge over their rivals have increasingly done so through innovative recombination of knowledge. There is evidence suggesting that the winners in tomorrow's market place will be the masters of knowledge management...' Mastery of knowledge management assists an organisation in its pursuit of innovative and entrepreneurial growth strategies that are critical to the organisations' survival (Nanaka and Takeuchi, 1995; Greenberg and Guinan, 2004). As mentioned earlier, due to the rapid pace of technological development and the shortened product life cycles, firms can no longer wait for the organic growth. Instead, they began to rely on other strategies such as mergers, acquisitions, strategic alliances etc.

Acquiring firms headquartered in other countries can provide various kinds of support for the acquired firms' innovation (Hitt and Pisano, 2004). For example, it enables the acquiring firms to make use of the already available technology elsewhere in the world rather than spending time and capital for re-inventing it. Consolidation enables the acquiring firms to have access to the acquired firms' innovation capabilities and new products in the pipeline. Thus, both the acquired and acquiring firms can internalise the technological capabilities. Compared to the domestic deals, the learning opportunities are expected to be higher in the case of cross-border deals due to the coming together of firms from different nations and the differences in the level of skills. The developing countries may be more benefited from this since they are so eager to get modern technologies from foreign multinationals in order to upgrade their technological capabilities and being part of the competitive global economy (Kabiraj and Marjit, 2003). Vermeulen and Barkema (2001) argues that the exploitation of the firms' knowledge through Greenfield ventures creates path dependence and that eventually produces organisational inertia in a firm, whereas CM&As broaden the knowledge base of the firm and decreases the organisational inertia (as in Shimizu and Vydyanadh, 2004). Knowledge spillovers become particularly important in the case of highly technology-intensive sectors[12] such as pharmaceutical industry, automobile, chemicals etc. The creation of mega-sized firms through

M&As also helps the domestic firms to undertake big innovation projects, which is key for their success in the international market. Here again, the dilemma between the size and efficiency creation comes in and thereby the question of net welfare arises. In short, the CM&As provide better opportunities to the firms to share the already available knowledge across the globe and to use the existing resources more effectively for further development of innovation.

Nevertheless, the major challenge in the innovation creation through CM&As depends on the absorptive capacity of the firms, because a minimum level of initial capacity is inevitable to absorb the externally acquired information (Narula, 2003), which many of the developing country firms lack. Schoenberg's (2001) study of knowledge transfer by the European acquirers found that the limited absorptive capacity along with the poor relationship between the acquirer and the target and the ambiguity regarding the nature of knowledge to be transferred are making barriers in the knowledge spillover process (as in Greenberg and Guinan, 2004). Greenberg and Guinan (2004) emphasised the need for proper integration in order to develop trust and shared identity which is a key to the successful working of firms belonging to different origins. Moreover, the quality of technology transferred through cross-border deals compared to the direct investment is another major issue (Mattoo and Saggi, 2001).

### 1.2.2 Efficiency-concentration trade-off

Getting into M&As enable firms to increase efficiency through deriving economies of scale[13] and scope (Ansoff and Weston, 1962). Economies of scale arise since the fixed cost of production is largely invariant to the volume of production, and thus, the average cost falls as the volume of production increases. Likewise, indivisibility may be existing in non-production costs associated with marketing, distribution, storage etc., before getting into M&As, which can be better utilised. Whereas, the scope economy arises when the total cost of producing and selling several products by a multi-product firm is less than the sum of the cost of producing and selling the same products by the individual firms specialising in each of those products; for example, the cost of R&D, use of a single brand name for selling several products, usage of common distribution counters etc. When the firms consolidate its business through M&As, both the acquiring and acquired firms can use their common distribution and marketing outlets and reduce the wastage of overlapping expenditure. Thus, getting into M&As are expected to enhance the productivity and efficiency of the firms through deriving various kinds of synergies as well as sharing of assets which has been widely discussed in the literature by various scholars.

However, M&As has been historically opposed since it is likely to enhance the market power and thereby involves a risk of price hike in concentrated oligopolistic industries (Bain, 1956; Modigliani, 1969 as in Pitelis, 2003). On the other hand, the proponents of efficiency effects of mergers argued that *ceteris paribus*, the increased concentration resulting from mergers leads to cost reductions, which allows increased margins. A third view emerged is that in many cases, M&As simultaneously produces efficiency gains through reducing the cost of production and some increase in the monopoly power which may manifest itself in higher prices, which raises the question of trade-off (Williamson, 1968; CEC, 1989; as in Kay, 1993); this has become a serious debatable issue in the merger literature, and it continues to be so. Nevertheless, the industrial structure and the degree of competition in each sector depend on the prevailing competitive rivalry, threat of new entry, relative bargaining power of the buyers of the firms' output, relative bargaining power of the seller of the firms' inputs and the availability of substitutes[14] (Porter, 1985, 1998). The recent upsurge in CM&As further complicates the situation, as it is likely to create global monopolies with the help of their already established subsidiaries all over the world. Globalisation also provided greater opportunities to create hard core cartels with international reach (Evenett, 2003). From the firm's point of view, the cross-border investment brings in integration challenges since both firms belong to different countries with different cultures. In the words of Kay (1993), *'it is difficult enough to marry together two different firms in the same country without an added complication of different cultures, language, legal systems and political conventions ... and there is every reason to suppose that the emerging wave of cross-frontier mergers is likely to be even problematic than are single nationality amalgamations'*.

## 1.3  Emerging issues

From 1990 to 2014, around 40 percent of world FDI came through the route of M&As. In India, it is nearly 20 percent.[15] Though the share of CM&As in developing countries is less compared to the developed nations, it is in the process of change. Compared to Greenfield investment, the significance of CM&As in FDI is increasing gradually (Saraswathy, B., 2016a). However, the developing countries are still depending on FDI to fill the shortage of capital to finance their developmental activities. From the above discussion, it is clear that the changing mode of foreign investment from Greenfield to M&As again raised concerns[16] such as, to what extent the CM&As are resulting in knowledge creation and the development of the innovation efforts, in-house investment in Research and Development and innovation, managerial know-how, impact on market competition and thereby consumer welfare, consequences on employment opportunities,[17] sectoral issues from CM&As, shareholders' value creation, corporate governance issues and so on.

In this context, it is to be mentioned that the implications of consolidation through domestic deals are also equally important as that of cross-border deals. The domestic firms are engaging in consolidation for a very long period and are also facing acute competition not only from the foreign firms but also from the domestic counterparts. This led them to involve in consolidation strategy, to face competition in and outside the domestic walls effectively. The above mentioned concerns are equally important for them. Therefore, it is important to understand whether these firms could earn the expected synergies by engaging in M&As strategy. These issues deserve special attention in the context of the newly implemented Competition Act too. The following are the already explored issues in the Indian merger literature.

### 1.3.1  Important issues covered in the Indian literature on M&As

In the absence of a long-time series database,[18] many studies have tried to understand the nature, structure and consequences of M&As in India through building their own databases from different secondary sources of information. As it can be seen from Table 1.1, most of the studies were focusing on the nature, extent and causes of M&As and the consequence of it especially the financial performance of the firms. Although these studies are based on different sample sizes and period of analysis, they reached similar conclusions about the nature and structure of M&As in India. Some of the observations based on these studies are the following.

M&As in India was dominated by horizontal type rather than vertical, that is, firms in the same industry group are consolidating. In this regard, Kumar (2000a) observed that out of the 256 MNEs-related deals, only three could be classified as vertical. The number of related M&As was higher as compared to the unrelated M&As. Our study on M&As in the Indian pharmaceuticals industry also reached similar observations (Beena, S., 2006). Further, we have found that in general, medium- and large-sized firms are going for M&As. Similarly, the number of group mergers constitutes a major part of it. Many of the Indian firms are acquiring firms or making alliances with firms outside India. Domestic firms rather than foreign firms dominate mergers, whereas, in the case of acquisitions as well as strategic alliances, foreign firms are getting more involved. The involvement of foreign firms is increasing in recent years (Kumar, 2000) due to the drastic changes in policies. There are only a few studies, which attempted to investigate the M&As involving foreign firms in India. Kumar (2000) studied the pattern of MNE related M&As in India during April 1993–February 2000 using a sample of 256 MNE related M&As. The study found that CM&As has become an important conduit for FDI flows in India. During 1997–1999, about 40 percent of the FDI inflows in India took the form of CM&As rather than Greenfield investment. In this study, all except three deals covered were horizontal in nature. This study raised several issues in the context of the current scenario. Beena (2004) compared the performance of foreign- and domestic-owned acquiring firms during 1995–2000 using 31 foreign and 84 domestic owned firms and found that the profitability performance of the firms in both groups showed a statistically significant downward trend during the post-merger period. Beena (2014) dealt with various issues such as the financing of M&As, overall competition and overseas acquisitions.

*Table 1.1* Selected studies on M&As in India

| Study | Period | Sample Size | Major Objective/s and Observation/s |
|---|---|---|---|
| Basanth (2000) | 1991–1997 | 252M & 145A | Nature, causes and distribution of M&As by broad industry group; MNCs have used consolidation to get access to strategic resources and market entry; In general firms are using it to expand their capacity. |
| Beena, P.L. (2000) | 1990–1991 to 1994–1995 | 109 Acquiring firms | Role of acquisitions in the growth of assets of acquired firms and sources of financing of growth; Acquisitions helped to make asset growth only in one-fifth of the sample of firms studied. Merger was not a route to growth, which was dominantly financed through resources acquired from buoyant share market. |
| Kumar (2000) | April 1993– February, 2000 | 256 M&A (MNE related) | Motivating factors behind M&As by MNEs and industrial composition of such activity; The study found that a considerable proportion of the deals were intended to expand the market; buying local partners and group restructuring was also considerable extent. |
| Beena, P.L. (2004) | 1995–2000 | 115 M&A (31 MNE) | Determinants and impact of it on the performance; Decline in the overall performance of the firms involved in M&As. Increase in HHI in the industries which experienced high incidence of M&As. |
| Agarwal and Bhattacharjea (2006) | 1973–1974 to 2000–2001 | 1795 M | Industry level factors in merger activity; Argued the clustering of merger activity, which may be indicating the response to the industry shocks; Following the 1991 MRTP amendments, firms started deals within the industry and business group with an expansionary motive. |
| Manthravadi, P. and Reddy (2007) | 1991–2003 | 96 M | Operating performance and its relationship with the relative firm size; Relative size difference does make some difference in the performance. |
| Manthravadi and Reddy (2008b) | 1991–2003 | 68 M | Operating performance and found sectorwise, there are differences in performance. |
| Manthravadi and Reddy (2008a) | 1991–2003 | 96 M | Operating performance for different types of deals and found there is no significant change in performance due to the type of mergers. |
| Beena, P.L. (2008) | 1990–2005 | 115 M&A (31 MNE) | The average performance of acquiring firms was relatively better than that of the manufacturing sector as a whole. Does not find any significant improvement in performance during the post-merger period compared to the pre-merger period. |

Source: Compiled from different studies.

There are studies at the sectoral level, which examined the performance of firms after entering consolidation. For example, Kaur (2010) examined the determinants of acquisitions in the Indian drugs and pharmaceutical industry for the period 1993–1994 to 2002–2003. The study examined why some firms acquire and why some others are getting acquired. The study found that better performing and high leveraged firms have higher chance to become acquired. Regarding acquiring firms, market share and efficiency play a positive role, while high leverage has a negative role in making acquisition their growth strategy. Similarly, Vyas et al. (2012) analysed the consolidation activity in the pharmaceutical sector during 2001–2010 and found that firms undertaking M&As are larger in size compared to the other firms. Further, the study observed that around 6 percent of the firms participating in M&As have a foreign affiliation, which has a positive impact on the firm's decision to participate in M&As. Mishra and Chandra (2010) examined the performance of firms entering into consolidation in the Indian pharmaceutical industry and observed that the M&As does not have any significant impact on the profitability of the firms in the long run, which may be due to the resultant X-inefficiency and new entry of firms into the market. Beena, S (2008) examined the post-merger performance of surviving firms in the pharmaceutical industry and found that the overall performance of the firms is improving after consolidation. The study further found that the performance of the firms entering consolidation is far better than that of the non-merging firms. And consolidation is contributing significantly to the market power of the surviving firms in the pharmaceutical industry.

There are also a few studies which examined the overseas acquisition scenario of the Indian firms. Pradhan (2007), Nayyar (2007) and Kumar (2008) explored the overseas acquisition of Indian firms, basically the nature, extent and structure of it. Beena (2011) examined the financing pattern of the overseas acquiring firms and found that Indian acquiring firms mobilised large funds through an external source, even though the retained profit was substantial for these firms. These firms could also raise funds from the capital market; however, borrowings remain as the major contributor to the external financing.

It can be noted from the foregone discussion that the existing literature on M&As especially the CM&As in India has not debated on most of the issues surrounding the consolidation activities discussed earlier even though there is a myriad of literature on M&As in the international context. Given the increased intensity of CM&As in India during the post liberalisation era, the present study is an attempt to examine the implications of CM&As on technological performance, production efficiency and market competition in the Indian manufacturing sector. Overall, the study is done in a comparative framework involving domestic and cross-border deals, taking their pre- and post-merger period performance, wherever it is possible. Broadly, it is done for the two-digit level of Standard Industrial Classification. Further, the pharmaceutical industry[19] is taken separately due to its special importance in the M&As scenario. Due to the extreme importance of disaggregated level of analysis in the case of market concentration, we have analysed it at the product level for two industries. Overall the study is limited to the two-digit level due to the less number of deals in many of the industries.

The study consists of eight chapters. After introducing the context and the issues in the first chapter, the second chapter discusses the basic concepts and policy issues in the context of globalisation. The third chapter gives a comparative picture of the nature and structures of cross-border deals vis-à-vis the domestic deals. The fourth chapter investigated the impact of CM&As on productivity and efficiency by comparing it with the domestic M&As and that of the pre-merger period. The fifth chapter attempts to find out the role of CM&As in changing the level of concentration in various sectors in a comparative perspective. The sixth chapter tries to understand the technological performance of cross-border and domestic deals. The seventh chapter provides one line of explanation to our findings. Specifically, it deals with some dimensions of governance issues, especially the role of post-merger integration in the success of deals. And the eighth chapter concludes the major findings and draws some policy inferences.

## Notes

1   In this study, we are dealing with only two consolidation strategies, i.e., mergers and acquisitions.
2   Otherwise the next best firm will bring out the product and reap the profit (World Investment Report, 2000).
3   'Follow-the leader strategy' is developed by Knickerbocker (1974).
4   All four strategies are in operation now. But the entry of each strategy was of this order. The policy changes were also facilitated in shaping this order.
5   In this study, we have used the term 'consolidation' to indicate mergers and acquisitions only.
6   See Dunning (1993) for a detailed discussion.
7   Dunning also discussed about Escape Investment, Support Investment and Passive Investments.
8   Such as raw materials, human resources and skills etc.
9   It will depend on the distance of foreign location.
10  It depends on the number of firms in the industry, elasticity of demand etc., which are assumed to be constant.
11  Since the firms were not getting profit (normal profit only) prior to merger.
12  Interestingly, these sectors are experiencing more number of cross-border deals globally.
13  Economies of scale is defined as the cost reduction in producing a product from increasing the scale of its production in a given period (Sudarsanam, 2004).
14  This theory is criticised due to its static nature.
15  See Chapter 3 for a detailed discussion.
16  See Lall (2002), Kumar (2000b).
17  Greenfield FDI always create new jobs, whereas acquisition of multiple units and their mergers may make a number of jobs such as those in marketing, finance, administration and other overheads redundant (Kumar, 2000).
18  See Chapter 3 for further discussion on data.
19  It comes under the four digit level classification.

# References

Agarwal, M. and Aditya, B. (2006). Mergers in India: A Response to Regulatory Shocks. *Emerging Markets Finance and Trade,* 42(3), pp. 46–55.

Ansoff, H.I. and Weston, J.F. (1962). Merger Objectives and Organizational Structure. *The Quarterly Review of Economics and Business*, 2(3), p. 49.

Beena, P.L. (2004). *Towards Understanding the Merger Wave in the Indian Corporate Sector: A Comparative Perspective.* Working Paper No. 355. Thiruvananthapuram: Centre for Development Studies.

Beena, P.L. (2008). Trends and Perspectives on Corporate Mergers in Contemporary India. *Economic and Political Weekly,* 43(39), pp. 48–56.

Bresman, H., Birkinshaw, J. and Nobel, R. (1999). Knowledge Transfer in International Acquisitions. *Journal of International business Studies,* 30(4), pp. 439–462.

Evenett, S. (2003). *The Cross-Border Mergers and Acquisitions: Wave of the Late 1990s.* Working Paper 9655. Cambridge: National Bureau of Economic Research.

Greenberg, D. and Guinan, P.J. (2004). Mergers and Acquisitions in Technology Intensive Industries: The Emergent Process of Technology Transfer. In: A.M. Pablo and M. Javidan, eds., *Mergers and Acquisitions: Creating Integrative Knowledge*. UK: Blackwell Publishing.

Hitt, M. and Pisano, V. (2004). Cross-Border Mergers and Acquisitions: Challenges and Opportunities. In: A.M. Pablo and M. Javidan, eds., *Mergers and Acquisitions: Creating Integrative Knowledge*. UK: Blackwell Publishing.

Jones, G. (2005). *Multinational and Global Capitalism from 19th to the 20th Century.* UK: Oxford University Press.

Kumar, N. (2000a). Mergers and Acquisitions by MNEs: Patterns and Implications. *Economic and Political Weekly,* 35(32), pp. 2851–2858.

Kumar, N. (2000b). Multinational Enterprises and M&As in India: Patterns and Implications. RIS DP# 5–2000.

Lall, S. (2002). *Implications of Cross Border Mergers and Acquisitions by TNCs in Developing Countries: A Beginners Guide.* QEH Working Paper Series-QEHWPS88. Available at: www3.qeh.ox.ac.uk/RePEc/qeh/qehwps/qehwps88. pdf. Accessed on 11th October, 2015.

Manthravadi, P. and Vidyadhar, A.R. (2007). Relative Size in Mergers and Operating Performance: Indian Experience. *Economic and Political Weekly,* 42(39), pp. 3936–3942.

Manthravadi, P. and Vidyadhar, A.R. (2008a). Type of Merger and Impact on Operating Performance: The Indian Experience. *Economic and Political Weekly,* 43(39), pp. 66–74.

Manthravadi, P. and Vidyadhar, A.R. (2008b). Post-Merger Performance of Acquiring Firms from Different Industries in India. *International Journal of Finance and Economics,* 22, pp. 193–204.

Mishra, P. and Tamal, C. (2010). Mergers and Acquisitions and Firms' Performance: Experience of Indian Pharmaceutical Industry. *Eurasian Journal of Business and Economics,* 3(5), pp. 111–126.

Narula, R. (2003). *Globalisation and Technology: Interdependence, Innovation Systems and industrial Policy.* UK: Cambridge Polity Press.

Pitelis, C. (2003). Privatisation, Regulation and Domestic Competition Policy. In: G. Wignaraja, ed., *Competitiveness Strategy in Developing Countries: A Manual for Policy Analysis*, pp. 239–273.

Shimizu, H. and Vydyanadh, P. (2004). Theoretical Foundations of Cross-Border Mergers and Acquisitions: A Review of Current Research and Recommendations for the Future. *Journal of International Management,* 10, pp. 307–353.

Siegel, D.S. and Simons, K.L. (2006). *Assessing Effects of Mergers and Acquisitions on Firm Performance, Plan Productivity and Workers: New Evidence from Matched Employer Employee Data.* Rensselaer Working Papers in Economics.

Sudarsanam, S. (2004). *Creating Value from Mergers and Acquisitions: The Challenges, An Integrated and International Perspective.* Pearson Education.

World Investment Report (2000). *Cross Border Mergers and Acquisitions and Development.* New York and Geneva: UNCTAD.

# 2 Concepts, evolution and policy points

In this chapter, our attempt is to understand the major concepts relating to M&As, which are relevant for our study. Subsequently, we will be discussing about a brief historical overview about the merger waves swept the US and UK, which is followed by a section on the government intervention in the form of changes in antitrust policies over time; in the fourth section, we will focus on the deal shaping process and the legal framework prevailing in India.

## 2.1 Concepts of mergers and acquisitions

The Company Secretaries of India (2008) Handbook on Mergers, *Amalgamations and Takeovers* defines various concepts on M&As as follows. A merger is *an arrangement whereby the assets of two (or more) companies become vested in, or under the control of one company (which may or may not be one of the original companies), which has its shareholders all or substantially all, the shareholders of the two companies.* Thus, in a merger, one of the two existing companies merges its identity into another existing company or one or more existing companies may form a new company and merge their identities into the new company by transferring their business and undertakings including all other assets and liabilities to the new company. The shareholders of the disappeared company will have the substantial shareholding in the new company. For them, shares will be exchanged in accordance with the swap ratio,[1] as prescribed by all or the majority of shareholders of both companies in their separate general meetings and as sanctioned by the court.

Amalgamation is *a legal process by which two or more companies are joined to form a new entity, or one or more companies are to be absorbed or blended with another as a consequence the amalgamating company losses its existence and its shareholders become the shareholders of the new company or amalgamated company.* Thus, a new company may come into existence, or an old company may survive while amalgamating company may lose its existence. The terms mergers and amalgamations usually used interchangeably and denote the situations, where two or more companies keeping in view their long-term business interests, combine into one economic entity to share risk and financial rewards. However, in a strict sense, a merger is the fusion of two companies. Amalgamation is an arrangement for bringing the assets of the two companies under control of one company, which may or may not be one of the original companies.

Acquisition or Takeover means the *acquiring control over another company, usually by buying all or a majority of its shares. A transaction or a series of transactions by which a person acquires control over the assets of a company is generally known as a takeover.* These are the business transactions, whereby an individual or a group of individuals or a company, either directly by becoming owners of those assets or indirectly by obtaining control of the management of the company. On the other hand, an arrangement whereby the assets of the two companies vest in one is known as a merger. In the Indian context as well as globally many of the studies are carried out without making a distinction between M&As, especially for analysing the financial performance since both are the tools to achieve similar ends.

Based on the products/services offered there are three types of deals. They are horizontal, vertical and conglomerate deals. The horizontal deals involve *the joining of two or more companies which are producing essentially the same products or rendering the same or similar services or their products and services directly compete in the market with each other.* Horizontal deals are viewed with special attention since it can lead to greater market power creation. In the case of horizontal deals, there is greater scope for deriving economies of scale and scope since they are operating in the similar product market. In the case of vertical deals, firms in buyer seller relation, producing and exporting firms etc. It is also expected to reduce the multiple expenses and result in more efficient operation. Vertical deals create competition concern when they practice market foreclosures. A conglomerate deal is a *merger involves coming together of two companies in different industries, that is, they may be engaging in completely unrelated businesses.* They are not horizontally or vertically related. The government regulations are mostly applied to the horizontal and vertical deals since they involve the overlapping products/services or vertical relations, which are having comparatively more threat to market competition,[2] Takeovers are classified into friendly and hostile based on the nature of negotiation process. Former is done through negotiations between the two parties, and the latter is done without having any mutual understanding between the parties. The acquirer silently and unilaterally follows the effort to gain control against the wishes of the existing management. It is also called 'takeover raids' or 'hostile takeover bids'.

Cross-border deals are the deals involving foreign firms. It can be classified into two, i.e. cross-border purchases and cross-border sales. Cross-border purchases include the purchase of a foreign firm by an

Indian firm whereas those of sales are the purchase of an Indian firm by a foreign firm. Purchases will result in outflows whereas sales will create FDI inflows.

## 2.2 Mergers and acquisitions in history: the case of USA and UK

Most of the initial merger studies were dealing with the first three merger waves occurred in the USA and four waves in the UK. It is not surprising that the antitrust policy formulations in these countries were also done in accordance with the merger activity.

The US has a long history of merger waves compared to any other country, that may be the reason why the merger regulations in the US has also undergone substantial changes over time. It is estimated that around 1800 firms disappeared and approximately 71 formerly competitive industries converted into virtual monopolies during the first merger wave, which started at the end of the nineteenth century (1890s) and lasted until 1905. This wave is described by Stigler (1950) as the *Merger for monopoly*. This wave was mainly due to the absence of rigid merger regulations. The Sherman Antitrust Act, 1890 was aiming to prohibit any contract that limited the trade between different states and countries, but it was not designed to deal with M&As. The Sherman Act addressed only issues relating to the substantial monopoly power and generally did not apply to stock for stock mergers. Consequently, the government passed the Clayton Act, 1914, in order to 'arrest the creation of trusts, conspiracies, and monopolies in their incipiency and before consummation'. It encouraged firms to form oligopolies rather than monopolies; this resulted in the second merger wave in the 1920s; the firms were reaping the benefit out of it. An estimated 12000 firms disappeared during this wave. This wave is known as *Merger for oligopoly*. However, the Great Depression of 1930 marked the end of this wave. This wave considered to be much smaller compared to the first wave since the asset involved is less than 10 percent compared to the first wave, which was over 15 percent. Again the Celler-Kefauver Amendment to the Clayton Act of 1914 was made in 1950 to deal with the anticompetitive mergers, occurred in the 1940s, which made the horizontal deals unattractive, and gradually conglomerate deals began to emerge; this constituted the third wave from the mid-1950s. This wave marked a shift in the business composition towards greater diversification. It is considered to be the *Merger for growth*. This wave ended due to the economic downturn as a result of the oil price hike and inflation of 1973 (Owen, 2006; Utton, 1971; Sudarsanam, 2004). All these three waves occurred during the economic prosperity, and rapidly rising stock market levels and each merger peaked almost with the stock market and then receded with the following economic recession (Sudarsanam, 2004). Most of the merger studies of US emerged in this broad context. The fourth wave of mergers occurred during the mid-1980s. This wave consists of two waves, mergers as well as divestitures. Divestitures constituted around 20–40 percent of the merger activity, which means that the firms were trying to simultaneously expand and downsize their operation in line with their competitive advantage. This wave ended by 1989 (Sudarsanam, 2004). Thus, this wave can be called the *Wave of divestitures*. The fifth wave started in the initial 1990s clearly 1993 onwards to 2000. It can be considered as the *Mother of all waves* since the value involvement is of gigantic proportions. This wave was prompted by the need for more competitive advantage to face acute competition in the wake of a more open market.

According to Owen (2006), there were four merger waves in the UK. First wave is considered to be a very small in the 1920s, which was mainly the result of the increased spending on production technologies immediately after the First World War, led to increased productivity and profit and further to a spate of M&As. Studies point out that it ultimately resulted in increased concentration in many sectors of the manufacturing industry. Government passed the Monopolies and Restrictive Practices Act, 1948. The real powerful merger wave occurred in the 1960s, which peaked in the year 1972. This was partly due to the policy of the government to enable big firms to compete in the international market. The passing of Monopolies and Mergers Act, 1965 prohibited all mergers, which are detrimental to the public good. However, mergers were encouraged for the creation of internationally competitive firms. Around 20 percent of the firms participated in mergers during this time. Conglomerate mergers began to grow (Owen, 2006). It is in this context that the merger studies, especially dealing with the implications of it on the market structure and efficiency creation emerged in UK. Most of the studies concentrated on the first and second waves.

### 2.3  Government intervention: merger regulations in India

As discussed in the previous chapter, broadly, there are three sets of regulations faced by the firms. They are, Corporate Law including Competition Law, Intellectual Property Rights (IPRs) and Sectoral Policy Regulations. Amongst this, the Competition Law aims at enhancing consumer welfare through regulating competition. IPRs give temporary monopoly for the owners of innovation, which is expected to enhance the innovation incentives of the innovating firms. Sectoral policies also aim at the consumer welfare, but the policy changes according to the welfare implications of different sectors. These issues become particularly important in the context of the global integration and increasing number of cross-border deals.[3] The recent buoyant surge in cross-border deals prompted many nations to set up merger review laws. According to White and Case (2001), 65 countries around the world has merger review laws in 2000 and among them, 30 have been enacted since 1990 (as in Evenett,

2003). As of now around 100 nations adopted competition law. Currently, the discussions are in progress regarding the integration of TRIPs provisions in the context of competition law.

### 2.3.1 The competition law

Competition Law (CL) is the major merger control measure all over the world. CL is an economic law, and it deals primarily with the economic behaviour of the agents. It is a subset of the Competition Policy (CP), which includes all the policies aiming at maintaining competition in the market, consumer welfare and efficient operation. The major objective of the Competition Law is to maintain competition and restrict the factors hindering competition. It is based on the assumption that consumer welfare will be highest under competition than under monopoly, where the possibility of X-inefficiency[4] is high. However, firms used to restrict competition through different types of strategies such as collusive agreements to fix prices and output, exploitative and exclusionary measures and use mergers and such forms of agreements to enhance the market power. Here arises the need for legal devices to restrict such anticompetitive practices (Dhall, 2007). CL all over the world has three substantive provisions. They are the prohibition of (a) anticompetitive agreements, (b) abuse of dominance and (c) anticompetitive mergers. CL also possesses supplementary objectives such as enhancing free trade and the distribution of market power. There has been a dilution of public sector monopoly under the era of global integration, which led to the opening of previously reserved areas for the private sector, which further led to the need for a much more cautious approach towards private monopoly. It is also true that the public-sector monopoly should also be viewed with concern. That may be the *raison d'être* for the inclusion of this under the purview of competition authorities in many such economies. In India, the Monopolies and Restrictive Trade Practices (MRTP) Actwas dealing these issues, which has been replaced with the Competition Act, 2002. The provisions of the Competition Act relating to anticompetitive agreements and abuse of dominance were notified on 20th May, 2009,[5] while provisions regarding combinations (M&As) were notified on 1st June 2011 onward. Here our focus is on the third provision.

#### 2.3.1.1 Anticompetitive merger regulation

Irrespective of the nations of origin, merger control measures in the CL face a trade-off between efficiency enhancement and monopoly creation. Competition regulators are responsible for preserving the possible positive effects of a merger such as increased innovative efforts of a resultant large firm, improved efficiency through economies of scale and scope, which will have cost reducing effects in future. Nevertheless, it has also another very important function of keeping the market competition active, which is important for the welfare of the consumers. Thus, there is no need to worry about a merger if it leads to a reduction in the price of relevant products or if it enhances the quality of the products. One major difference between merger control measures and other forms of anticompetitive provisions dealt by the competition authorities is the *ex-ante* nature of regulations, that is the outcome of merger is expected in future and not at the time of regulating it. The inclusion of merger regulations in their CL was done years after the implementation of original CL in countries like European Union (Dhall, 2007).[6] This is partly due to the fact that mergers become a concern to the regulators only in the later period when compared to the other restrictive practices such as cartels, collusive behavior, abuse of dominance, etc. since the occurrence of merger was in a very nascent stage during the initial years of implementation of CLs in those countries.

### 2.3.2 Paradigm shift in government policies in India

The evolution of competition law in India has been discussed in detail by Kumar, A (2007). The first CL in India is the MRTP Act, 1969, which was the result of the recommendations of Monopolies Inquiry Committee (MIC) appointed by the government to inquire into the extent, causes and consequences of economic concentration in India. The committee found that economic concentration in India is a serious matter and a substantial number of industries experience a high-level of concentration. The MIC found the existence of both monopoly restrictive practices (MTPs) as well as restrictive trade practices (RTPs). Very high levels of concentration were found in some sectors, which are essential for the ordinary consumers. Public sector and agricultural sector were excluded from the purview of this. MIC limited the scope of merger control to mergers involving dominant enterprises, which is the one with at least one-third of a share in production, supply or distribution of goods, that is applicable when the asset limit exceeds Rs. 10 million. The firms have to submit their expansion proposals to the commission, and the approval would then be deemed to be given if no decision is reached within 30 days.[7] The government appointed "High-Powered Expert Committee on Companies and MRTP Act" (Sachar Committee in 1977) to make appropriate changes to the MRTP Act and Companies Act. This committee pointed out that the effective administrative power to MRTP Commission is an essential factor for the success of its implementation.

Meanwhile, the announcement of New Industrial Policy in July 1991, marked a paradigm shift from an era of greater control to the free play of market forces and the attitude towards FDI became less stringent. The Government set up Securities and Exchange Board of India Act (SEBI), 1992 which was responsible for framing guidelines and rules regarding many aspects of corporate behaviour. In November 1994, SEBI issued Guidelines for Substantial Acquisitions of Shares and Takeovers widely referred to as 'Takeover Code 1994'. But due to the lacunas and loopholes of the Code, to deal with the complexity of the situation, Justice P.N. Bhagwati Committee appointed by the Government, which revised the Code and adopted by SEBI in February 1997 (Kumar, (2000a) and Kumar (2000b)), which mainly aimed at protecting the interest of minority shareholders. These regulations were further amended periodically. In 2001, a review of the Takeover Regulation of 1997 was carried out by the reconstituted Bhagwati Committee, which submitted a report in May 2002. Takeover Regulations of 1997 have been amended 23 times (Achuthan Committee Report on Takeover Regulations, 2010). It was in the context of the increased number of deals, and the changed global scenario that the Achuthan Committee was appointed with an aim to provide a transparent legal framework to facilitate takeover activities. Consequently, the New Takeover Code (NTC) became effective on 22nd October 2011 following the report submitted by the Achuthan Committee on 19th July 2010. According to the NTC, the acquirer can acquire up to 24.99 percent shares or voting rights in a listed company in India provided the acquirer is not taking over the control of the company. If this limit is crossing 25 percent, the acquirer is required to make an open offer to acquire at least 26 percent shares from the existing public shareholders of the target. Further, the acquirer holding 25 percent or more voting rights in the target company can acquire additional shares or voting rights to the extent of 5 percent in any financial year, up to the maximum permissible non-public shareholding limit (generally 75 percent). If the acquisition exceeds 5 percent in any financial year, triggers an open offer obligation.

Meanwhile, it was also recognized that in the changed economic scenario, the existing MRTP Act is not adequate to handle antitrust issues, which forced the Government to appoint another committee in October 1999, known as SVS Raghavan Committee (High-Level Committee on Competition Policy and Law) to recommend essential changes in the policy especially in the context of the economic reforms of the 1990s. The recommendations of this committee marked a paradigm shift in the anti-trust regulations existing in India. It recommended the need for setting up a new competition law and a competition authority, which are essential to prevent the anticompetitive practices that reduce welfare. Competition law is essential to maintain economic freedom. The committee recommended to incorporate merger control measures in the new Competition Law. The new regulation gives importance to the *rule of reason*[8] approach compared to *per se rule*. After considering the recommendations of this committee, the government enacted the Competition Act, 2002 in January 2003. The Competition Act states in its preamble, "*An Act to provide, keeping in view of the economic development of the country, for the establishment of a commission to promote, sustain competition in markets, to protect the interest of consumers and to ensure freedom of trade carried on by other participants in markets in India and for matters connected therewith or incidental thereto*". However, certain provisions in the Competition Act has been questioned again, and it was subsequently amended by the Competition (Amendment) Act, 2007. In accordance with the provisions of the Amendment Act, the Competition Commission of India (CCI) and the Competition Appellate Tribunal have been established.[9] The provisions of the CA relating to anticompetitive agreements and abuse of dominance were notified on May 20, 2009,[10] while the provisions regarding the mergers and acquisition were notified from 1st June 2011.

According to the CA, *no person or enterprises shall enter into a combination, which causes or is likely to cause an appreciable adverse effect on competition within the relevant market in India and such a combination shall be void.* It also requires the proposed merger parties to submit notice to the CCI in the prescribed form disclosing all the details of the proposed combination and have to remit the fee within thirty days of—(1) the approval from the board of directors of the enterprises or (2) execution of any agreement or other document regarding the combination. Further, no combination shall come into effect until 210 days have passed from the day on which the notice has been given to the CCI. The permission from the CCI is required if the value involvement of the combination belongs to the following category (see Table 2.1). Here the 'group' means two or more enterprises which, directly or indirectly are in a position to—(a) exercise 26 percent or more of the voting rights in other enterprise or (b) appoint more than 50 percent of the members of the board of directors in the other enterprise; or (c) control the management or affairs of the other enterprise.

The commission, with a view to making the filings simpler, exempted certain categories which are less likely to create an adverse effect on competition. Consequently, now there is no need for filing a notice in respect of mergers and amalgamations between parent and subsidiary and wholly owned entities of a group. Similarly, acquisitions that are less than 25 percent of the shares or voting rights of a company on cumulative basis are also exempted. The intra-group mergers/amalgamations involving a holding company and its subsidiary wholly owned by the enterprise belonging to the same group are also exempted from the filing of the notice (Government of India, 2012).

*Table 2.1* Revised thresholds for combination regulations

| Level | In India (in Rs Crore) | | In India and Outside | | | |
|---|---|---|---|---|---|---|
| | Asset | Turnover | Asset | | Turnover | |
| | | | Total | Minimum Indian Component | Total | Minimum Indian Component out of Total |
| Enterprise | >2000 | >6000 | >$1 billion | Rs. 1000 crore | >$3 billion | Rs. 3000 crore |
| Group | >8000 | >24000 | >$4 billion | Rs. 1000 crore | >$12 billion | Rs. 3000 crore |

Source: Revised Thresholds, Competition Commission of India, Government of India, 2016.

However, the policy has been criticised on the ground that there has not much provision to deal with the foreign monopoly and collusive behaviour created by the big MNCs and to control them separately. Along with this, various sectors of the economy are opened for foreign investment. All this helped the foreign firms to enter into the big Indian market through mergers, acquisition and alliances in order to fulfil their market expansion strategy.

## 2.4 The deal shaping process

Bruner (2004) mentioned 11 steps for undertaking a deal (see Figure 2.1). They are (1) Planning, search and the identification of the target, (2) Contacting the target: Depends on the size of the target, either the CEO or vice president, development officer or operating manager will contact the target firm. The target firm's CEO has two options. Agree or not agree. If s/he is not agreeing, the buyer can go for either "bear hug"[11] or "hostile tender offer"[12] (see the Figure 2.2). (3) Confidentiality of the agreement and related documents: the target gives all documents regarding the company to the buyer under the condition that it will be kept confidential. Otherwise, it will help the target's competitors to get crucial information regarding the

*Figure 2.1* The deal making process.
Source: Compiled from Bruner (2004).

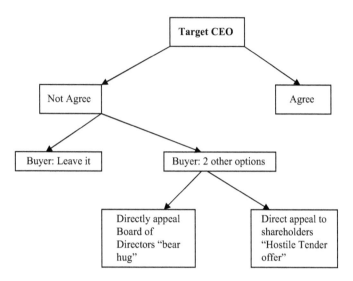

*Figure 2.2* Processing the deal: acquirer's options.
Source: Compiled from Bruner (2004).

company. Along with this, the *exclusive agreement and standstill agreement* is formed. The first, binds the target from discussing with other firms for transaction for a limited period of time. The conditions of which either side of the firm withdraws from the agreement are also mentioned. Through the second agreement, the buyer commits not to purchase shares of the target for a limited period of time, since the confidential documents are transferred to the buyer. (4) Term Sheet and Letter of Intent: It is a non-binding summary of the terms of the deal that will provide the basis for the definitive agreement, (5) Due Diligence and Negotiation of a Definitive Agreement. Due Diligence becomes the vital step, and thereby an in-depth analysis of the target is undertaken. Target also allows this due to the confidentiality agreement signed earlier and because of the desire to conclude the deal. (6) Affirmative Vote by the Board of Directors (BoD): The definitive agreement requires the affirmative vote from the BoD of both the firms. If a vote of shareholders is required, then the BoD can only say that they approve the deal. Usually, by this stage, the merger negotiations are disclosed to the public and regulators. (7) Disclosure to the Public and Regulators: Securities regulation and court decisions require firms to disclose to shareholders news about events that are material and probable. (8) Anti-trust Filings and Permission: In order to get permission to consummate the deal, getting permission from the anti-trust authorities are essential. (9) Informing the Shareholders and Gaining an Affirmative Vote: Getting permission from the shareholders of both the companies are essential. Usually, the firms issue a merger prospectus that informing the shareholders about the deal and a proxy statement that requests their votes in favour of the deal. It is usually scheduled for 3–6 months after the announcement of the definitive agreement. The outcome of the voting is typically known within days of the meeting. (10) Closing: At the closing, two sides document that they have met the representations, warranties and covenants outlined in the agreement. Payment is made, and the ownership is assumed by the buyer. (11) Post merger Integration: The success of the deal depends heavily on the proper post-merger integration of the firms. In order to facilitate that, the integration process ideally starts at the time of signing the agreement.

### 2.4.1 *Procedure for undertaking M&As in India*

In India, the process of mergers and acquisitions are court driven. Though the process can be initiated by both the parties to the combination, the effective implementation of it requires sanction from the High Court. The Companies Act, 1956 consolidate the provisions related to mergers, acquisitions and other related issues of compromises, arrangements and reconstructions. The statutory provisions relating to mergers and amalgamations are contained in sections 390 – 396A of the Companies Act, 1956. The procedure is complete only after getting the approval from the court under Section 394(2) and takes effect when such orders of court filed with Registrar of Companies.[13] The companies are required to get the approvals from: (1) the Board of Directors of both the companies should approve the scheme of amalgamation. The scheme of amalgamation includes all the important matters regarding a merger such as the effective date of amalgamation, the share exchange ratio, the expense of amalgamation and the management structure under the new scheme. (2) Stock exchanges where it is listed at least one month prior to filing it with the High Court, (3) Shareholders/creditors' permission is *sine qua non* for court's sanction. The scheme of the merger is to be approved by the majority, in number representing three-fourth of the value of creditors/members concerned. When the deal is approved by all concerned, a petition is presented to the court for sanction. The court sanctions it if it is satisfied with the fairness and justice. The Parliament passed the Companies Act, 2013 and received the assent of the President of India on 29th August, 2013. As per the new Act, the provisions related mergers are covered in Sections 230 to 240, which is yet to be notified. Until recently, the takeover procedures of listed companies were governed by the Takeover Code 1997.[14] With effect from 23rd October, 2011, SEBI repealed the Takeover code 1997 and introduced the New Takeover Code, 2011. The new Takeover Code has been the outcome of the Takeover Regulations Advisory Committee under the chairmanship of Mr. C. Achuthan, which was constituted to review the Takeover Code 1997 as discussed in section 2.3.2. The Takeover Code regulates both direct and indirect acquisition of shares, voting rights and control over the target firm.

In addition to the above, the Competition Commission of India assess mergers, acquisitions and other form of agreements to ensure that the deal is not likely to create any adverse effect market competition in the relevant geographic market and relevant product market in India, as per the provisions of the Competition Act, 2002, which is discussed in section 2.3.1.

In this chapter, our attempt has been to portray the concepts, policy points as well as the deal shaping process based on the existing literature. In the next chapter, we shall try to bring out the questions regarding the extent of M&As in India in the background of the global scenario, and the overall nature and structure of the deals.

## Notes

1 Swap ratio is the rate at which one company's shares are equated with the other companies' shares.
2 There are also some other types of mergers such as cash merger, defacto merger, downstream merger, upstream merger, short-term merger, triangular merger, reverse merger. We are not dealing with those deals separately in this study. Please see The Company Secretaries of India (2008) *Handbook on Mergers, Amalgamations and Takeovers* for detailed discussion.
3 Hereafter by cross-border deals, we mean cross-border mergers and acquisitions (CM&As), and by deals, we mean mergers and acquisitions (M&As).
4 X-inefficiency is the term used by Leibenstein, which says that under conditions of monopoly, firms may not be producing the maximum possible output from a given level of input due to the absence of competitive pressures, which creep in some 'organizational slack'.
5 For more details, see the official website of the Commission: www.cci.gov.in; accessed on 21st February 2016.
6 European Economic Community (EEC), the enforcement authority of EU CL incorporated competition law into the treaty of Rome in 1957. Merger regulations added in the year 1989 only.
7 Along with this, FERA, 1973 imposed a general limit of 40 percent on foreign ownership in Indian companies.
8 Rule of Reason approach takes into account both the adverse and beneficial effects of the deal.
9 It has been formally announced by the Finance Minister during its Budget Speech for the financial year 2009–2010.
10 For more details, see the official website of CCI, www.cci.gov.in/index.php. Accessed on 8th October 2012.
11 It is a technique one step short of a hostile takeover. The merger offer is sent directly to the Board of Directors (BoD), bypassing the CEO. Typically, the financial offer warrants serious considerations by the BoD. They appoint a special committee, excluding the CEO (Bruner, 2004).
12 A Tender offer invites the target company shareholders to submit (that is tender) their shares to the buyer in return for the offered payment. It is judged hostile when the target management and board are opposed to the deal (Bruner, 2004).
13 Please see the official website of Ministry of Corporate Affairs, Government of India and The Company Secretaries of India (2008) *Handbook on Mergers, Amalgamations and Takeovers* for more details.
14 Please see Takeover Code (1997) and the New Takeover Code (2011) for details.

# References

Bruner, R.F. (2004). *Applied Mergers and Acquisitions*. UK: John Wiley & Sons.

Company Secretaries of India (2008). *Handbook on Mergers, Amalgamations and Takeovers*. New Delhi: ICSI.

Dhall, V. (2007). *Competition Law Today: Concepts, Issues and the Law in Practice*. New Delhi: Oxford University Press.

Evenett, S. (2003). *The Cross-Border Mergers and Acquisitions: Wave of the Late 1990s*. Working Paper 9655. Cambridge: National Bureau of Economic Research.

Government of India (2012). Fair play. *The Quarterly Newsletter of Competition Commission of India*, vol. 1, April–June.

Kumar, A. (2007). Evolution of Competition Law in India. In: V. Dhall, ed., *Competition Law Today: Concepts, Issues and Law in Practice*. New Delhi: Oxford.

Kumar, N. (2000a). Mergers and Acquisitions by MNEs: Patterns and Implications. *Economic and Political Weekly*, 35(32), pp. 2851–2858.

Kumar, N. (2000b). Multinational Enterprises and M&As in India: Patterns and Implications. RIS DP# 5–2000.

Owen, S. (2006). *The History and Mystery of Merger Waves: A UK and US Perspective*. Working Paper No. 2006-02. Australia: The University of New South Wales.

Securities and Exchange Board of India (1997). Takeover Code: (Substantial Acquisition of Shares and Takeovers) Regulations, Government of India.

Securities and Exchange Board of India (2011). Takeover Code: (Substantial Acquisition of Shares and Takeovers) Regulations, Government of India.

Stigler, G.J. (1950). Monopoly and Oligopoly by Merger. *The American Economic Review*, 40(2), pp. 23–34.

Sudarsanam, S. (2004). *Creating Value from Mergers and Acquisitions: The Challenges, An Integrated and International Perspective*. Pearson Education.

Utton, M.A. (1971). The Effect of Mergers on Concentration: UK Manufacturing Industry 1954–1965. *The Journal of Industrial Economics,* 20(1), pp. 42–58.

White, and Case (2001). Survey of Worldwide Antitrust Merger Notification Requirements. Washington DC.

# 3 Cross-border deals

## Extent, nature and structure

### 3.1 An overview of global scenario

Cross-border transactions can be classified into two, i.e. cross-border purchases and cross-border sales. Cross-border purchases include the purchase of a foreign firm by an Indian firm whereas those of sales are the purchase of an Indian firm by a foreign firm. Purchases will result in outflows whereas sales will create FDI inflows. During the 1990s[1] itself, the developed countries are dominating both the sales as well as the purchases of cross-border transactions. However, there is a gradual decline in the share of developed countries over time due to the entry of many multinational firms from developing countries in an unprecedented manner along with the existing Multinational Companies (MNCs) search for new markets. In 1990, 86 percent of the purchases and 90 percent of the sales were made by the firms operating in developed countries, and the corresponding figures for 2009 are 66 and 82 percent respectively in 2014, purchases made by developed countries further declined to 57, and that of developing countries increased to 38 percent. Similarly, the value of sales also decreased to 69 percent for developed countries, and that of developing countries increased to 30 percent.

Interestingly, out of the overall cross-border *purchases* the share of two continents such as Europe and North America constituted 73 percent of the deals in 1990 and their dominance has been continuing. However, their share got reduced substantially to around 61 percent in 2009 and 42 percent in 2014. The share of North America remained far behind that of Europe till 2009; afterwards, the share of North America started to outweigh Europe (33 and 8 percent respectively in 2014). Notably, Asia region started with mere 6 percent, which increased to 24 percent and 34 percent respectively in 2009 and 2014. Much of this increase is visible after 2007.

Europe and North America are the top *sellers* of firms in the world with 84 percent of the transactions in 1990 i.e., similar to what we have seen in the case of cross-border purchases. Here the share of Europe was 44 percent, and that of North America was 41 percent. Moreover, in terms of sales, the share of Europe remained higher than that of North America, the next highest seller, in all the years except 2008. The share of Asia is substantial especially since the mid-2000s, which indicates that the firms in these regions are getting more responsive to cross-border transactions as a way of further expansion. One of the major reasons for this may be the pro-market policy adopted by the Governments in this region.[2] For Asia, it is important to note that the difference between purchases and sales was positive until the mid-1990s mainly due to the regulations prevailed, which witnessed negative trend later owing to the drastic shift in policies to attract foreign direct investment (FDI). This trend is again reversing since 2004 onwards, which may be indicating the strong presence of MNCs from this region in cross-border purchases.

When we take the cumulative value of all deals during 1990–2014, USA and UK are the top purchasers in the world with a share of around 30 percent of all purchases. The same trend continues for sales too, but here USA tops with 24 percent and that of UK's share is only 16 percent (see Table 3.1). One of the facilitating factors for Europe was the creation of European Union and the consequent break down of nationalistic barriers as the continent moved to a unified market structure with a common currency; companies began to see their market as all of Europe and more (Gaughan, 1999). The top ten purchasers in the world owns more than 70 percent of the value of purchases and the top ten sellers in the world constitute more than 73 percent of the value of sales. As per the 2014 estimates, 94 percent of the purchases are undertaken by the top 10 purchasers. Out of this, the USA remains as the individual top buyer (22 percent), whereas China is the top seller (13 percent). Further, Hong Kong, China is also emerging as a top purchaser (15 percent) as well as seller (8th seller with 4 percent sales share). Thus, like the case of overall FDI, some countries succeeded in attracting investment through mergers and acquisitions (M&As) route.[3] This national difference may be due to the favorable policies prevailing in these countries which help the firms to undertake deals easily.

Like the global trends, there has been a concentrated picture in the Asian case also. During 1990–2014, the top ten countries from Asia constituted 8 percent of the global value of cross-border M&A sales and 16 percent of the global purchases. The recent estimates are even more skewed. In 2014, the value of sales of top 10 Asian countries was 24 percent of the global sales and 46 percent of the global purchases. Needless to say, the significance of the top 10 countries within the Asian continent is much higher than that of global figures. It is clear that the value of purchases is far ahead of the sales figures. Amongst this, bulk of the purchases is made by Hong Kong, China (15 percent), Japan (11 percent) and China (10 percent). Likewise, China (13 percent), Hong Kong, China (4.3 percent) and Japan (2 percent) top the list of sales in 2014 (see Table 3.2). India (1.5 percent) ranks fourth position in this regard. In this year, India's purchase value was $1084 million (0.27 percent).

China is the second dealer in terms of purchase (10 percent) and first in sales (13 percent). India invested $94604 million during 1990–2014 for purchasing foreign firms and got $64747 million through sales (see Table 3.2).

Table 3.1 Top 10 purchasers and sellers in the world, 1990–2014

| | | 1990–2014* | | | 2014 | | |
|---|---|---|---|---|---|---|---|
| Rank Cum (1990–2014) | Economy | 1990–2014 Value (Mn$)* | Share (Percent) | Rank 2014 | Economy | 2014 Value (Mn$) | Share (Percent) |
| **Purchases** | | | | | | | |
| 1 | United States | 1518202 | 17.4 | 1 | United States | 86812 | 21.8 |
| 2 | United Kingdom | 1095175 | 12.6 | 2 | Hong Kong, China | 58959 | 14.8 |
| 3 | France | 716673 | 8.2 | 3 | Canada | 46739 | 11.7 |
| 4 | Germany | 560162 | 6.4 | 4 | Japan | 44985 | 11.3 |
| 5 | Canada | 538355 | 6.2 | 5 | China | 39580 | 9.9 |
| 6 | Japan | 402322 | 4.6 | 6 | Germany | 29490 | 7.4 |
| 7 | Switzerland | 362999 | 4.2 | 7 | Luxembourg | 23172 | 5.8 |
| 8 | Netherlands | 358424 | 4.1 | 8 | Singapore | 16674 | 4.2 |
| 9 | China | 285352 | 3.3 | 9 | France | 16586 | 4.2 |
| 10 | Spain | 267844 | 3.1 | 10 | Ireland | 10496 | 2.6 |
| 17 | India | 94604 | 1.1 | 39 | India | 1084 | 0.3 |
| | World | 8721091 | 100.0 | | World | 398899 | 100.0 |
| | Top 10 | 6105507 | 70 | | Top 10 | 373493 | 94 |
| **Sales** | | | | | | | |
| 1 | United States | 2061001 | 24 | 1 | China | 52415 | 13.1 |
| 2 | United Kingdom | 1381579 | 16 | 2 | United Kingdom | 33462 | 8.4 |
| 3 | Germany | 662192 | 8 | 3 | Canada | 33296 | 8.3 |
| 4 | Canada | 510849 | 6 | 4 | France | 27704 | 6.9 |
| 5 | Netherlands | 403759 | 5 | 5 | Spain | 23424 | 5.9 |
| 6 | France | 352394 | 4 | 6 | Australia | 21183 | 5.3 |
| 7 | Australia | 290868 | 3 | 7 | Switzerland | 20068 | 5.0 |
| 8 | Spain | 263722 | 3 | 8 | Hong Kong, China | 17070 | 4.3 |
| 9 | China | 243968 | 3 | 9 | Italy | 15315 | 3.8 |
| 10 | Italy | 198829 | 2 | 10 | Germany | 15034 | 3.8 |
| 23 | India | 64747 | 1 | 11 | India | 5892 | 1.5 |
| | World | 8721091 | 100 | | World | 398899 | 100.0 |
| | Top 10 | 6369161 | 73 | | Top 10 | 258971 | 65 |

Source: Calculated from UNCTAD, 2017.

Table 3.2 Cross-border M&A sales and purchase of top 10 Asian countries, 1990–2014

| | 1990–2014 | | | 2014 | | | |
|---|---|---|---|---|---|---|---|
| Rank cum (1990–2014) | Economy | 1990–2014 Value Mn$ | Global Share (percent) | Rank 2014 | Economy | 2014 Value Mn$ | Global Share (percent) |
| *Purchases* | | | | | | | |
| 1 | Japan | 402322 | 4.6 | 1 | Hong Kong, China | 58959 | 14.8 |
| 2 | China | 285352 | 3.3 | 2 | Japan | 44985 | 11.3 |
| 3 | Hong Kong, China | 211127 | 2.4 | 3 | China | 39580 | 9.9 |
| 4 | Singapore | 132452 | 1.5 | 4 | Singapore | 16674 | 4.2 |
| 5 | India | 94604 | 1.1 | 5 | UAE | 7964 | 2.0 |
| 6 | United Arab Emirates | 92092 | 1.1 | 6 | Korea, Republic of | 3928 | 1.0 |
| 7 | Malaysia | 56303 | 0.6 | 7 | Qatar | 3796 | 1.0 |
| 8 | Korea, Republic of | 54493 | 0.6 | 8 | Philippines | 3211 | 0.8 |
| 9 | Saudi Arabia | 41156 | 0.5 | 9 | Kuwait | 1414 | 0.4 |
| 10 | Qatar | 38759 | 0.4 | 10 | Taiwan Province of China | 1387 | 0.3 |
| | Top 10 | 1408659 | 16.2 | | Top 10 | 181898 | 45.6 |
| | World | 8721091 | 100.0 | | World | 398899 | 100.0 |
| *Sales* | | | | | | | |
| 1 | China | 243968 | 2.8 | 1 | China | 52415 | 13.1 |
| 2 | Japan | 104081 | 1.2 | 2 | Hong Kong, China | 17070 | 4.3 |
| 3 | Hong Kong, China | 101627 | 1.2 | 3 | Japan | 6997 | 1.8 |
| 4 | Turkey | 79462 | 0.9 | 4 | India | 5892 | 1.5 |
| 5 | Singapore | 73340 | 0.8 | 5 | Singapore | 4736 | 1.2 |
| 6 | India | 64747 | 0.7 | 6 | Korea, Republic of | 3843 | 1.0 |
| 7 | Korea, Republic of | 48483 | 0.6 | 7 | Turkey | 2045 | 0.5 |
| 8 | Indonesia | 27480 | 0.3 | 8 | Philippines | 922 | 0.2 |
| 9 | Malaysia | 23542 | 0.3 | 9 | Indonesia | 814 | 0.2 |
| 10 | Taiwan Province, China | 20925 | 0.2 | 10 | Kuwait | 629 | 0.2 |
| | Top 10 | 703032 | 8.1 | | Top 10 | 95363 | 23.9 |
| | World | 8721091 | 100.0 | | World | 398899 | 100.0 |

Source: Calculated from UNCTAD, 2017.

The value involved in China is much higher compared to that of India. Both India and China are exhibiting fluctuating trend in the value of cross-border transactions throughout. Both the countries started with a very low pace of transactions during the late 1980s and picked up during the 1990s. Post 1990s onwards both countries are active in sales, whereas the purchases started in a noticeable manner since post-2000s. In the case of sales, for most years, China remained far higher compared to India. Recently (the mid-1990s onwards) both countries are involved in cross-border transactions in an unprecedented manner. India ranks as the 5th largest purchaser and 5th seller in the Asian region; whereas China ranks first in sales and second in purchases in the year 2014. The significance of China in cross-border transactions further increases when Hong Kong is added to it.

### 3.1.1 Greenfield FDI vs. Brownfield FDI

A country can invest in another country either through the setting up of new firms i.e. making fresh investment or through making investments in an already established firm i.e. through M&As route. The first case is called Greenfield investment whereas the latter is Brownfield investment.[4] Since the 1990s, more than 20 percent of the world's FDI came through M&A route.[5] In some years its share was very high; for example, in 2000 it constituted 70 percent of the FDI; moreover, the year 2000 registered a record FDI of $1,363,215 Million, which again crossed later and 2007 experienced the highest value of FDI inflows, i.e. $1871702 Million. M&As had been a major driver of the FDI throughout and as a result the FDI graph follows the M&A waves (see Figure 3.1).

Despite the recent surge in cross-border deals, the Indian cross-border M&As scenario is still in a nascent stage (see Figure 3.2). Initially, its share was only 2 percent of the FDI inflows, which reached 17 percent in 2014.

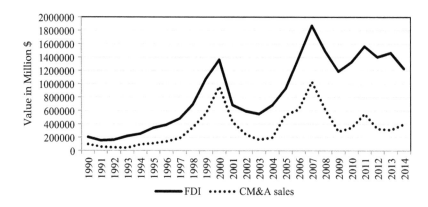

*Figure 3.1* World FDI inflows and cross-border flows.
Source: Calculated from UNCTAD Database, 2017.

From 1990 to 2014, it constituted around 20 percent of the FDI inflows in the country. Even though the share of Greenfield investment dominates almost the entire period, the contribution of cross-border M&As was also high in some years, for example, in the year 1999 it was 49 percent, and in 2011 it was 35 percent. In 2006, it registered 25 percent (see Table 3.3). It is evident that in general, the absolute value of Brownfield FDI in India has been moving in line with that of the global trends. That is, whenever there is a hike in the share of world brownfield investment, the Indian brownfield investment is also moving in same direction. However, there are slight variations in some years (see Figure 3.3).

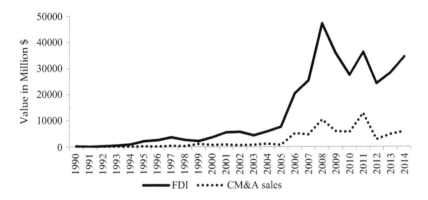

*Figure 3.2* FDI inflows and cross-border flows: India.
Source: Calculated from UNCTAD and FDI/TNC Database.

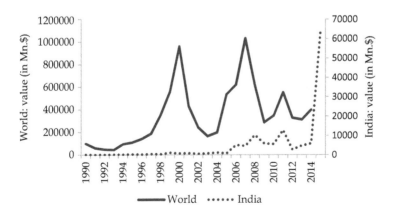

*Figure 3.3* Value of CM&As in India and the world.
Source: Calculated from UNCTAD and FDI/TNC Database.

*Table 3.3* World FDI inflows and cross-border M&As 1990–2014 (in Million $)

| Year | World | | | India | | |
|------|-------|---------|------------------|------|--------|------------------|
|      | FDI   | CM&As   | Share (Percent)  | FDI  | CM&As  | Share (Percent)  |
| 1990 | 204896 | 98050 | 48 | 237 | 5 | 2 |
| 1991 | 154138 | 58885 | 38 | 75 | 0 | 0 |
| 1992 | 163007 | 46939 | 29 | 252 | 26 | 10 |
| 1993 | 220146 | 43496 | 20 | 532 | 81 | 15 |
| 1994 | 254906 | 93877 | 37 | 974 | 90 | 9 |
| 1995 | 341537 | 109938 | 32 | 2151 | 224 | 10 |
| 1996 | 388737 | 141170 | 36 | 2525 | 141 | 6 |
| 1997 | 481230 | 187307 | 39 | 3619 | 399 | 11 |
| 1998 | 692336 | 349728 | 51 | 2633 | 269 | 10 |
| 1999 | 1076313 | 559539 | 52 | 2168 | 1058 | 49 |
| 2000 | 1363215 | 959681 | 70 | 3588 | 708 | 20 |
| 2001 | 684071 | 431757 | 63 | 5478 | 812 | 15 |
| 2002 | 591386 | 243735 | 41 | 5630 | 560 | 10 |
| 2003 | 551993 | 165425 | 30 | 4321 | 729 | 17 |
| 2004 | 682749 | 198597 | 29 | 5778 | 1135 | 20 |
| 2005 | 927402 | 535035 | 58 | 7622 | 698 | 9 |
| 2006 | 1393034 | 619809 | 44 | 20328 | 5114 | 25 |
| 2007 | 1871702 | 1032689 | 55 | 25350 | 4652 | 18 |
| 2008 | 1489732 | 617649 | 41 | 47102 | 10303 | 22 |
| 2009 | 1186513 | 287617 | 24 | 35634 | 5877 | 16 |
| 2010 | 1328215 | 347094 | 26 | 27417 | 5613 | 20 |
| 2011 | 1564935 | 553442 | 35 | 36190 | 12795 | 35 |
| 2012 | 1403115 | 328224 | 23 | 24196 | 2805 | 12 |
| 2013 | 1467149 | 312509 | 21 | 28199 | 4763 | 17 |
| 2014 | 1228283 | 398899 | 32 | 34417 | 5892 | 17 |
| 1990–2014 | 21710740 | 8721091 | 40 | 326415 | 64747 | 20 |

Source: Calculated from UNCTAD Database, 2017.
Cb is for Cross-border.

## 3.2 Industry-wise intensity of cross-border deals

The primary, secondary and tertiary sectors of the world's economy, have undergone a spectacular rise in cross-border deals in terms of absolute value. It was 4-times increase in the case of primary and secondary sectors, whereas the service sector registered a 5-times increase in 2014 compared to 1990. The service sector dominated cross-border sales in all the years except 1994. Interestingly, we see that the overall sales value is associated positively with the M&A movement of the service sector, which peaked in the years 2000, 2007 and 2011 as seen in the case of the overall FDI. Thus, there was a steep decline in M&A activity immediately after the peak years (see Figures 3.4 and 3.5). What explains the steep decline in M&As activity during this period? Regarding the first cycle, the involvement of some components of the service sectors such as Information Technology, finance as well as components of the manufacturing sector such as electrical and

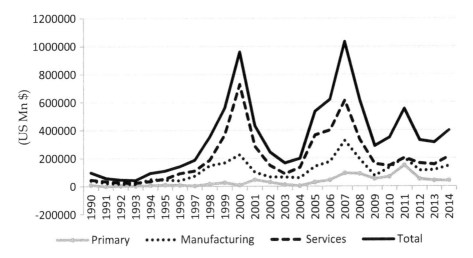

*Figure 3.4* CM&As sales by industry: 1990–2014.
Source: Calculated from UNCTAD.

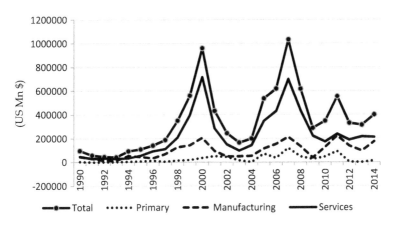

*Figure 3.5* CM&As purchases by industry: 1990–2014.
Source: Calculated from UNCTAD.

electronic equipment, chemical and chemical products etc., declined immediately after a steep rise. It was mainly the service sector M&As activity that
declined, which may be due to the worldwide depression in service sector
economic activity following the terrorist attack on the World Trade Center,
in the USA. There are also other instances to say that M&As follow the
overall macroeconomic conditions. For example, the second merger wave in
the USA ended with the Great Depression of the 1930s. Similarly, the third
merger wave of the mid-1950s ended with the economic downturn caused by

the oil price hike and inflation of 1973. Likewise, this wave followed the economic condition caused by the World Trade Center attack. It can be noticed that another merger wave had been formulated in the year 2004 and onwards, which peaked in 2007 and completed the cycle in 2009. The recession in this cycle was mainly due to the economic crisis. The service sector deals were shaping the overall movement with active involvement from the manufacturing sector compared to the last M&As wave. Within the service sector, it was mainly Information Technology, finance, metals & metal products, chemicals and chemical products etc., that slowed during this time; this is almost the same as the earlier wave. The latest cycle, which peaked in the year 2011, was very small compared to the other two recent cycles.

Except for a few years, the share of the primary sector remained meagre whereas that of the manufacturing sector declined, especially since the mid-1990s, and again started an increasing trend post-2000. The primary sector recently, from 2008 and onwards, shows more than 10 percent shares. As illustrated in Table 3.4, the share of manufacturing sector constituted 42 percent in 1990, which was 37 percent in 2014 and that of the service

*Table 3.4* Sector-wise shares of cross-border sales and purchases

| Year/ Sector | Sales (in Percent) | | | Purchase (in Percent) | | |
|---|---|---|---|---|---|---|
| | Primary | Manufacturing | Services | Primary | Manufacturing | Services |
| 1990 | 10 | 42 | 48 | 5 | 46 | 49 |
| 1991 | −1 | 40 | 61 | 0 | 51 | 49 |
| 1992 | 6 | 39 | 55 | 2 | 28 | 70 |
| 1993 | 6 | 37 | 57 | 4 | 30 | 66 |
| 1994 | 7 | 53 | 39 | 5 | 58 | 36 |
| 1995 | 10 | 42 | 49 | 7 | 41 | 52 |
| 1996 | 6 | 29 | 65 | 9 | 25 | 66 |
| 1997 | 2 | 39 | 59 | 3 | 38 | 60 |
| 1998 | 5 | 42 | 53 | 4 | 36 | 60 |
| 1999 | 5 | 30 | 65 | 3 | 26 | 71 |
| 2000 | 1 | 23 | 76 | 4 | 21 | 75 |
| 2001 | 11 | 23 | 66 | 12 | 22 | 66 |
| 2002 | 12 | 27 | 61 | 18 | 20 | 61 |
| 2003 | 7 | 39 | 54 | 10 | 31 | 59 |
| 2004 | 2 | 30 | 68 | 1 | 27 | 72 |
| 2005 | 5 | 26 | 68 | 14 | 22 | 65 |
| 2006 | 7 | 28 | 65 | 6 | 25 | 69 |
| 2007 | 9 | 31 | 59 | 12 | 21 | 68 |
| 2008 | 14 | 31 | 54 | 8 | 22 | 71 |
| 2009 | 18 | 26 | 56 | 10 | 13 | 77 |
| 2010 | 19 | 38 | 42 | 13 | 37 | 50 |
| 2011 | 27 | 37 | 37 | 17 | 40 | 43 |
| 2012 | 16 | 34 | 50 | 1 | 42 | 57 |
| 2013 | 13 | 37 | 50 | 0 | 31 | 69 |
| 2014 | 10 | 37 | 53 | 4 | 44 | 53 |

Source: Calculated from UNCTAD Database, 2017.

sector was 48 and 53 percent respectively. During the upswing of the two merger waves in 2000 and 2007, the service sector share was also very high levels of 76 and 59 percent. Based on the cumulative value from 1990 to 2014, service sector sales share is 59 percent, and that of manufacturing is 32 percent. Individual sectors in order of importance from the service sector to the primary sector are: finance (18 percent); information technology (14 percent); business services (8 percent); mining, quarrying and petroleum (9 percent). Active sectors within manufacturing are: food, beverages and tobacco; chemicals and chemical products, electrical and electronic equipment with 5 percent shares each (see Table 3.5). The pharmaceutical sector remains one of the top individual sectors with 4.3 percent share. In 2014, it accounted for 11 percent share.

Like the cross-border sales, purchases were also dominated by the service sector. During 1990–2014, the service sector accounted for 59 percent share, and that of manufacturing was only 32. In the year 2014, the share of services was 53 percent, and that of the manufacturing sector was only 44 percent compared to 49 and 46 percent respectively in 1990 (see the Tables 3.4 and 3.5 for a more disaggregated picture). Chemicals, food and beverages, metals and electrical sectors are the dominant purchasers from the manufacturing sector. Among all the sectors the financial services are the big element in driving the cross-border purchases as well as sales from the initial years itself. Next in importance are information technology and business services.

## 3.3 Nature and significance of Indian deals

The foregoing discussion pointed out that the post reform period has been associated with a large amount of cross-border deals all around the world and despite the dominance of developed nations in it; such deals are increasing in the developing countries including India. India adapted its policies to facilitate globalisation since the mid-1980s. Competition became the ground reality and firms were forced to adopt different strategies to face competition in India as well. As said earlier, firms preferred to get into M&As in order to face the challenges posed by globalisation. In this context, the present section tries to understand, to what extent foreign firms are entering the Indian market through this route, the most preferred deal makers in India as well as the preferred sectors in which it is occurring.

### 3.3.1 Data and definitions followed

One of the major problems faced by M&As literature in India was the lack of a proper long term firm level database on mergers, acquisitions and the like consolidation strategies.[6] Without having such a database one cannot get into the ground realities of this phenomenon. In the absence of a proper data, normally what researchers[7] have been doing is to build their own database based on various secondary sources of information such as Centre

Table 3.5 Sector-wise shares of cross-border sales and purchases: at the disaggregated level

| Sector | Sales (Percent) | | | Purchase (Percent) | | |
|---|---|---|---|---|---|---|
| | 1990 | 2014 | 1990–2014 | 1990 | 2014 | 1990–2014 |
| *Primary* | *4.8* | *3.6* | *7.9* | *9.9* | *10.0* | *9.6* |
| Agriculture, forestry and fishing | 0.5 | -0.1 | 0.1 | 2.7 | 0.1 | 0.6 |
| Mining, quarrying and petroleum | 4.3 | 3.6 | 7.8 | 7.2 | 9.9 | 9.1 |
| *Manufacturing* | *46.1* | *43.7* | *28.0* | *42.2* | *36.6* | *31.7* |
| Chemicals and chemical products | 11.6 | 6.8 | 4.3 | 5.0 | 6.3 | 5.1 |
| Coke, petroleum products and nuclear fuel | 0.8 | -4.0 | 0.0 | 0.9 | -2.3 | 0.8 |
| Electrical and electronic equipment | 5.6 | 4.1 | 4.6 | 4.3 | 5.1 | 5.1 |
| Food, beverages and tobacco | 4.3 | 8.5 | 4.1 | 6.1 | 7.8 | 5.3 |
| Machinery and equipment | 1.4 | 1.8 | 1.5 | 1.6 | 3.1 | 0.9 |
| Manufacture of furniture | 0.1 | 0.2 | 0.1 | 0.2 | 0.0 | 0.1 |
| Metals and metal products | 2.9 | 11.6 | 3.0 | 3.9 | 0.8 | 3.0 |
| Motor vehicles and other transport equip. | 7.6 | -0.2 | 1.7 | 7.6 | 0.1 | 2.1 |
| Non-metallic mineral products | 4.4 | 0.6 | 1.6 | 1.6 | 0.4 | 1.6 |
| Other manufacturing | -0.2 | 1.5 | 1.0 | 0.4 | 2.0 | 1.2 |
| Paper and paper products | 2.7 | 0.6 | 0.8 | 1.5 | 0.2 | 0.6 |
| Pharmaceuticals | 1.5 | 11.3 | 4.6 | 6.2 | 12.0 | 4.3 |
| Publishing and printing | 0.1 | 0.0 | 0.1 | 0.2 | 0.0 | 0.1 |
| Rubber and plastic products | 1.3 | 0.6 | 0.2 | 2.2 | 0.2 | 0.5 |
| Textiles, clothing and leather | -0.3 | 0.2 | 0.2 | 0.5 | 0.7 | 0.7 |
| Wood and wood products | 2.3 | 0.2 | 0.2 | -0.4 | 0.1 | 0.2 |
| *Services* | *49.1* | *52.7* | *64.1* | *47.9* | *53.4* | *58.7* |
| Accommodation and food service activities | 3.0 | 4.2 | 0.6 | 4.5 | 4.2 | 1.2 |
| Arts, entertainment and recreation | 0.1 | 1.2 | 0.2 | 0.5 | 1.6 | 0.4 |
| Business services | 3.8 | 8.4 | 5.0 | 7.5 | 12.9 | 8.2 |
| Construction | 0.2 | 0.2 | 0.3 | 0.3 | 0.6 | 1.0 |
| Education | 0.0 | 0.0 | 0.0 | 0.0 | 0.3 | 0.1 |
| Electricity, gas and water | 0.4 | 4.2 | 3.7 | 3.0 | 4.5 | 7.6 |
| Finance | 30.3 | 46.2 | 38.3 | 14.6 | 33.8 | 18.2 |
| Health and social services | 0.1 | 0.7 | 0.2 | 0.3 | 0.5 | 0.6 |
| Information and communication | 6.9 | -19.7 | 11.7 | 11.6 | -15.5 | 14.3 |
| Other service activities | 0.2 | 0.1 | 0.0 | 0.4 | 0.7 | 0.2 |
| Public administration and defense | -0.6 | -1.1 | -0.4 | -0.1 | 1.1 | 0.4 |
| Trade | 2.3 | 7.1 | 2.3 | 3.4 | 6.2 | 3.4 |
| Transportation and storage | 2.4 | 1.2 | 2.0 | 1.9 | 2.6 | 3.2 |
| *Total* | *100* | *100* | *100* | *100* | *100* | *100* |

for Monitoring Indian Economy (CMIE) and newspaper reports. Even though it is a tiresome job, the omissions and repetitions are common errors in this method. Further, correct information on the value of all deals are not always available; this necessitates using the number of deals rather than the magnitude of value. The present study used data compiled from different secondary sources such as Monthly Review of the Indian Economy (MRIE), M&A Database, brought out by CMIE, Newspaper reports and various company reports.[8]

Since we mainly depend on the data given by the different CMIE sources, broadly, we have followed the CMIE definitions. The nationality of the firm is defined on the basis of the 'headquarters'. Cross-border deals are defined as the deals involving foreign firm. The main analysis on the implications of the deals are based on the *deals occurred within India only*. However, in this chapter, we have also portrayed the extent of overseas deals as a background material. We will discuss the nature and structure of M&As scenario in India in the subsequent sections. The data consists of 4035 deals of which 1045 are mergers (26 percent) and 2990 (74 percent) are acquisitions occurred within India during 1978 to November 2007. Out of this, 1415 deals (35 percent of the overall deals) are cross-border deals (see Table 3.6).

As expected, the incidents of acquisitions are higher than that of mergers. Of the total, 44 percent of the acquisitions and 12 percent of the mergers were cross-border deals. There are three distinct phases of M&As activity in India. The majority of the deals were among domestic firms during the 1990s, whereas since the mid-1990s onwards, there is a gradual increase in cross-border deals. Nevertheless, the burgeoning number and value of foreign acquisitions (overseas acquisitions) made by Indian firms is a post-2000 phenomenon. During the pre-liberalisation era, the M&As scenario in India was very small. Owing to the pro-market policies of the government to attract FDI, the mid-1990s onwards cross-border deals began to increase. Following the global trends, Indian cross-border deals were also peaked in the years 1998, 2000 and 2005, whereas those of overall deals were at the top in 2000, 2005 and 2006. Recent trend shows the CM&As further peaked in the years 2008 and 2011 (Saraswathy, B., 2016).

*Table 3.6* Ownership classification of M&As (1978—November 2007)

| Ownership | Acquisitions | | Mergers | | Total | |
|---|---|---|---|---|---|---|
| | *No.* | *Percent* | *No.* | *Percent* | *No.* | *Percent* |
| Cross-border | 1,301 | 44 | 114 | 12 | 1,415 | 36 |
| Domestic | 1,668 | 56 | 853 | 88 | 2,521 | 64 |
| Total | 2,969 | 100 | 967 | 100 | 3,936 | 100 |
| NA | 21 | | 78 | | 99 | |
| Grand total | 2,990 | | 1045 | | 4035 | |

Source: Compiled from various sources explained in the text.

### 3.3.2 Purchases, sales and nationality of deals within India

India had dealings with more than fifty countries through cross-border M&As. Repeating the world trends, USA, UK, Germany were the major partners with India. Out of the merger purchases, 24 percent accounted for by the USA and 11 percent by the UK – USA (336 deals; 26 percent), UK (160; 13 percent), Germany (98; 8 percent) and Mauritius (81; 6 percent) – and dominated the purchase through acquisitions. The presence of Mauritius is interesting since in many cases it is only playing the role of an intermediary between their big headquarters in the USA and the UK and is reaping the advantage of tax concessions such as Double Tax Avoidance treaty between India and Mauritius. Mauritius had the major share in FDI inflows to India during August 1991–September 2005 (Department of Industrial Policy and Promotion [DIPP], 2008) and further during April 2000–January 2012[9] (DIPP, 2012). The majority of the purchases made by the firms from developed countries such as USA, UK, and Japan were pertaining mainly to the emerging sectors like drugs and pharmaceutical, chemicals, telecom, IT, banking and finance, aiming at the vast Indian market and synergy creation through consolidation.

Obviously, Indian firms are the ones, which lose their control to foreign firms in the majority of the cases. 64 (56 percent) Indian firms sold to foreign firms through mergers and 732 Indian firms sold to foreigners (56.3 percent) through acquisitions. Similarly, the USA sold (14 via merger and 117 deals via acquisition), the UK sold (7 via merger and 69 via acquisition), and Germany sold (1 via merger; 44 via acquisition) respectively, through M&As occurred in India. However, when we take the difference between sales and purchases, foreign firms always dominated purchases. In many cases, firms started with a joint venture and subsequently it resulted in merger or acquisition, which may be due to the successful integration. For example, acquisition of Berger Paints by Rajdoot Paints, SAE India from ABB by KEC International, RPG Group, Stiles India by Spartek Ceramics.

Moreover, joint venture firms form a significant share of cross-border deals. The acquisition of Tata Haneywell by Honeywell Inc.; Kirloskar Mahle Filter Systems Pvt by Mahle Filtersystems and Max-GB by Gist Brocades Intl BV among others are examples of such deals. However, their Indian partners have been acquiring the majority of them. 181 such cases were reported, and within them, Indo US (61) and Indo UK (26) joint venture firms constitute a good proportion. Besides this, the joint venture with France, Australia and the Netherlands, was involved in large numbers in this process.

### 3.3.3 Industry-wise intensity of deals

Like the global M&As scenario, Indian firms too preferred to consolidate within the same industry. 66 percent of the mergers and 62 percent (69 percent in terms of value) of the acquisitions were horizontal,[10] i.e. it occurred within the same industry. It is also notable that this tendency increases in the case of cross-border deals since the risk of consolidation[11] is higher in this case. Within cross-border deals, 70 percent of mergers and 69 percent (69.1 percent in terms of value) of acquisitions were horizontal integration. It further raises the issue of the creation of a foreign monopoly and the consequent rise in price level. A clearer picture can be arrived at when we disaggregate[12] the incidence of the entire deals into different industries.

Like the global trends, the primary sector has only a meagre share; this is applicable to the sales and purchases of cross-border M&As too. The manufacturing sector was the largest seller, but the majority of the purchases were committed by the service sector in terms of the number of deals. Within manufacturing, drugs and pharmaceutical sector registered the highest number of *purchases*[13] (266, 7.3 percent) followed by other chemicals (264, 7.2 percent), domestic appliances (143, 3.9 percent), automobiles (131, 3.6 percent), metals and metal products (126, 3.4 percent), cement and glass (101, 2.8 percent). In the case of *sales,* the drugs and pharmaceutical sector is also in the top list (307, 8.5 percent). Other major sellers are other chemicals (289, 8 percent), metals and metal products (171, 4.7 percent), automobiles (166, 4.6 percent), domestic appliances (130, 3.6 percent), cement and glass (129, 3.6 percent), machinery (119, 3.3 percent). Even though the extent and significance of consolidation depend upon the intra-industry shares of M&As rather than inter-industry shares, it clearly brings out a pattern in favour of chemicals including pharmaceuticals. Also, in the case of *cross-border deals*, more or less, the same trend is visible. Here the highest number of purchases is made by the chemicals sector (110, 8.3 percent), drugs and pharmaceutical (88, 6.6 percent), domestic appliances (73, 5.5 percent), automobiles and shipyard (72, 5.4 percent) and that of sales are also done by the same sectors.

The service sector is the major purchaser of deals but not the highest seller as mentioned earlier, which may be due to the recent surge in the service sector growth. The sector has made 2008 (55 percent) purchases and 1713 sales (47.5 percent). Within the services, it was the banking and finance sector firms which dominated purchases as well as sales (1113, 30.4 percent; 603, 5.8 percent respectively). Information technology (291; 7.9 percent), Telecom (124; 3.4 percent), follows the next purchases. In the case of sales, the next in importance was information technology (435; 12 percent), Telecom (158; 4.4 percent), trading (106; 2.9 percent). The same pattern is observed in the case of cross-border purchases as well as sales.

If we are considering the value of deals as the criteria,[14] 57 percent of the overall purchases and 63 percent of the cross-border purchases were done by the service sector, and that of manufacturing was 43 and 37 percent respectively. Within services, it was banking and finance,[15] which contributed most of the overall as well as cross-border deals (27 and 32 percent respectively). The Telecom sectors, irrespective of being less important in terms of the number of purchases, constituted 11 percent of all deals and 11 percent of cross-border deals. Even though the importance of the IT sector in acquisitions is a recent phenomenon, it has occupied a very large portion of the overall deals (9 percent) and that of cross-border deals (12 percent) too. Manufacturing, petroleum and natural gas (9 and 56 percent) were in the top sub-sector for overall deals, whereas cement and glass dominated the cross-border deals with a share of 7 percent (9 percent for all acquisitions). Next in importance were power generation, drugs and pharmaceutical industry. In the case of sales of deals, the share of manufacturing, as well as services, was more or less equal (50.1 and 49.8 percent). Within this, Telecom were the major seller with 18 percent of overall sales and 19 percent of cross-border sales. The rest of the pattern is same as the purchases as mentioned above. Thus, when we take the value of deals, the dominant sectors in terms of number, seldom come to the top, which clearly shows the incidence of mega deals in the emerging sectors such as Telecom and IT.

Cross-border intensity appears high among some of the non-dominant sectors defined in terms of the number of the overall acquisitions. Though the number of cross-border *purchases* was relatively low in the machinery sector, in terms of value, it accounts for the highest (95 percent). The next in importance were Domestic appliances (86 percent in terms of value; 51 percent in terms of number), Drugs and Pharmaceutical (68 percent value; 33 percent number), Chemicals (68 percent value, 42 percent number), Electrical Appliances and allied (64 percent value; 51 percent number). The same for service sector were, Information technology (72; 41), Banking and Finance (63 percent value; 41 percent number), Telecom (54 percent value; 43 percent number). Almost all the sub-sectors had been showing high cross-border intensity in terms of the value of purchases more than that in terms of number. The only exception was small-scale dominated sectors such as textiles, footwear & leather products; metals & metal products and automobiles, which clearly shows that even though the cross-border deals in these sectors were less in number, they were high-valued deals.

In the case of cross-border *sales* within the sectors, it was electrical appliances and allied dominated in terms of value (96 percent in terms of value, 47 percent in terms of number), whereas machinery sector dominated in terms of the number of cross-border sales (85 percent value, 58 percent numbers.). The next in importance in the manufacturing sector were construction (90 percent value; 39 percent number) and chemicals (79 percent value; 40 percent sales). Information technology (65 percent value, 37 percent number) banking and finance (62 percent value, 28 percent number) and Telecom (58 percent value, 51 percent number) had the higher cross-border intensity within the services. These are also the top FDI recipient sectors in India.[16] Some industries are having a very high intensity of horizontal deals. More than 75 percent of deals in drugs and pharmaceutical industry, petroleum and natural gas, cement, Telecom, machinery were the horizontal type, which raises different issues about the future performance of these sectors.

### 3.3.4 *Value involvement in the deals*

It is very difficult to capture the exact value involved in transactions particularly in the case of mergers since most of them are announced in terms of swap ratios.[17] From the available information on 68 percent of acquisitions,[18] it is evident that almost 77 percent of the acquisitions occurred after 2000, which amounts to around 92 percent of the overall value involved in acquisitions. Among the cross-border deals, 73 percent of the deals occurred after 2000, which constituted around 93 percent of the value involved in cross-border acquisitions. Out of the 2020 deals for which information is available, 420 (21 percent) are mega deals,[19] and 1600 (79 percent) are small deals. Interestingly, this 79 percent of the small deals make only 13 percent of the overall value involved in the transaction and the rest 87 percent are accounted for by 420 mega deals. Most of the mega deals had been occurring in the banking and finance sector, Telecom, information technology, petroleum and natural gas, cement and glass, advertisement and consultancy, automobiles, chemicals and pharmaceutical sectors.

Strikingly, 55 percent of the 420-mega deals are cross-border acquisitions. Within the cross-border cases, 229 (28 percent) are mega deals, and 583 (72 percent) are small deals. The five largest deals accounted for Rs. 20962 crores, which is 16 percent of the total amount involved in cross-border deals and the same for top ten and twenty deals is around 26 and 38 percent respectively. Here also a large number of small deals make only 12 percent of the overall value, and the rest is accounted for by the mega deals. The cross-border mega acquisitions occurring sectors are the same as the overall acquisitions discussed above. USA, UK and German firms are mostly involving in cross-border mega deals in India.

## 3.4 Foreign acquisition of Indian firms abroad (overseas acquisitions)

Apart from the sales and purchases of the firms within India, another salient feature of the current phase of M&As is the active participation of Indian firms in the international market as a purchaser of firms from many countries. The number and value of such deals are increasing over the years, which is surely an indication of the new type of consolidation strategy of the Indian firms. In many cases, this has helped the Indian firms to become world leaders in the respective field of operation. There were 563 overseas acquisitions made by Indian firms during the year 1994 to November 2007. Out of this, most of the deals occurred after 2000 and the year 2007 marked the highest number of deals (121). In recent years, the number of outward acquisitions is even higher than that of the overall inbound acquisitions. This clearly points to the fact that Indian firms prefer to expand their market outside India alongside the domestic market. Out of the 563 cases, many of the acquisitions were partial in the form of plant and other assets aiming at expanding the capacity abroad. There were 35 such acquisitions and within this 15 (43 percent) were for getting brand names. Brand acquisitions are mainly occurring in the drugs and pharmaceutical industry, where consumers (indirectly the prescribing doctors) are accustomed with the brand names rather than chemical names. Besides, brand acquisitions are also occurring in information technology and chemical industry, which may be since the brand acquisition is an easy way to enter the foreign market and expand consumer base.

Out of the 528 acquisitions,[20] we have information on the amount of consideration for 55 percent of the deals. The cumulative value of acquisitions abroad from 1994 to November 2007 amounts to Rs. 200257 crores and around 97 percent of it is accounted for by the 115 (40 percent of the total number) mega deals, whereas the small deals make 61 percent of the total attributed to only 3 percent of the value of transactions. The largest ten purchases constituted around 68 percent (Rs. 136652 crores) of the total. Interestingly, the conventional top purchaser industries that were seen in the case of inbound deals were not the top valued purchasers here. The industries, which were top purchasers, include steel, aluminium, petrochemicals, and electricity. Some of the top valued purchases were, the acquisition of Corus Group Plc (UK based) by Tata Steel Ltd in October 2006 for $7.6 billion, the acquisition of Novels, a US based firm by Hindalco Industries in 2007, Basel (US based firm) by Purnendu Chatterjee, a petrochemical firm in 2005 and Algoma Steel Inc., a Canadian steel producer by Essar Steel Ltd. in April 2007. The first three deals accounted for more than Rs. 20000 crores per deal. The largest purchase in the IT sector was undertaken by Computer Sciences Corporation India Pvt. Ltd. by purchasing Covansys (India) spending Rs. 5350 crores in April 2007 followed by Wipro Ltd.'s Rs. 2430 crores acquisition of Infocrossing Inc., a US based IT enabled service provider in August 2007. The drugs and pharmaceutical industry's top purchase was Rs. 2760 crore acquisition of Eurocor GmbH, a German medical equipment producer by Opto Circuits (India) Ltd. in December 2005 preceded by Sun Pharma acquisition of Taro Pharma, Israel for Rs. 1837 crores in May 2007.

Indian firms have made purchases in more than 85 countries, of which industrialized countries such as USA and UK remained as the major sources similar to the inbound deals.[21] Two earlier studies on Indian overseas deals done by Pradhan (2007) and Nayyar (2007) also underlined this fact. Around 215 US based firms (40 percent), were purchased by the Indian firms, whereas that of UK firms are 59 (11 percent). Besides, Indian firms have also purchased a good number of German (20, 4 percent), Singapore (20, 4 percent) and Australian (16, 3 percent) based firms. Like the cross-border sales and purchases inside the country, overseas acquisitions showed a more or less similar picture of the service sector (52 percent) domination over the manufacturing sector (47 percent), and that of the primary sector was again very meagre. An emerging trend in the overseas acquisition scenario is the purchase of a large number of IT sector firms and these firms are not only pure IT sector *per se*, but also IT enabled services, IT consulting, BPO along with a wide range of computer software firms. They are mainly headquartered in the USA. This amounts to around 37 percent (191 deals) of the overall overseas purchases made by the Indian firms, which was followed by the Drugs and Pharmaceutical industry with the acquisition of 61 (12 percent) foreign firms abroad, despite the active involvement in other forms of consolidation such as brand acquisition and inbound deals. One major difference between IT and Pharmaceutical sector acquisition abroad is that the majority of IT sector deals were concentrated on the USA, while that of pharmaceuticals were from several countries ranging from USA (24 percent) to South African countries such as Botswana, Uganda. Further, the majority of the deals in these two sectors were the horizontal type of consolidation. More than 90 percent of deals in the drugs and pharmaceutical industry and 65 percentage in the information technology were such deals. Chemicals, metals and metal products, automobiles are the other sectors, which could make a substantial number of acquisitions in the overseas market. Thus, it is clear from the above discussion that the IT sector along with Drugs and Pharmaceutical industry has been the leading industries in the overseas acquisitions. The banking sector, which constituted a substantial portion of the inbound deals, constitutes only a very small proportion of the overseas deals.

Horizontal integration constitutes around 73 percent of the acquisitions. The vertical type constitutes 26 percent, and that of conglomerate cases were only very few. It is equally important that many of the foreign acquisitions are made by the same firms repeatedly, especially firms from Drugs and Pharmaceutical industry, IT sector, Steel, Aluminium sectors. For example, Ranbaxy Laboratories[22] has made 11 overseas acquisitions despite a large number of inbound acquisitions, for Reliance it is seven deals, Wipro has made nine deals, whereas Tata, with its diverse product portfolio ranging from tea to software, acquired 22 foreign firms abroad.

There is enough evidence to suggest that the international acquisition strategy followed by the Indian firms helped them become top players in the international market. For example, based on various media reports, Tata Steel was the 56th largest producer of steel in the world in 2005, but the world saw the emergence of Tata as the fifth-largest steel producer group in the world in October 2006 with the acquisition of Corus, which resulted in a production capacity of 24-million tonnes per annum. Likewise, the acquisition of Novelis has turned Hindalco into the world's largest aluminium rolling company and one among the biggest producers of primary aluminium in Asia. It is also India's leading copper producer. The acquisition of Whyte & Mackay, a Scottish fourth largest scotch whiskey producer by United Spirits, a Vijay Mallya owned UB group firm resulted in making the second largest liquor producer in the world, which outweighed Pernod-Ricard SA of France. A similar type of evidence is common in many industries, which is changing the ranks and market power of the firms substantially.

## 3.5  Issues for research

The foregoing discussion pointed out a number of issues that require in depth research in studying the burgeoning phenomenon of cross-border M&As. These *interalia*, include technology spillovers, productivity and efficiency, market concentration and corporate governance aspects, which have their implications on the growth process of developing countries like India.

The study observed that there is a gradual shift in organic ways of foreign investment to inorganic means of brownfield investment. This must have led to the so-called technology spillovers. The industrialized countries such as UK, USA and Germany are the most common dealmakers in India. Adding to this, most of the top valued M&As are occurring in technology intensive sectors such as drugs and pharmaceutical, telecom, petroleum, power generation etc. and there are high instances of horizontal and vertical deals. It follows that the growing cross-border M&As are expected to generate high spillovers since they are in a similar line of business activity. However, the intensity of spillovers depends on the absorption capacity of the domestic firms too, which is considered to be less than that of the foreign firms. But it can vary from industry to industry, firm to firm and time to time. Within cross-border and domestic deals, the intensity of it can vary according to the type of integration such as horizontal, vertical or conglomerate deals; it is expected to be higher with the first two types.

If consolidation helps generate technology spillovers, it will automatically lead to more productivity and efficiency. Efficiency can be increased not only through spillovers but also through deriving synergies, cutting down of the many expenses and increased capacity utilisation (that is, through deriving economies of scale and scope). Besides, a number of studies suggest that M&As in general changes inefficient managers and exert pressure on the existing non-merging firms to restructure their operations in order to strengthen themselves. In other words, it is expected to accompany good corporate governance, which will lead to higher productivity and efficiency of the firms unless the 'Agency Problems' arise, which can operate here. Similar to the technological performance, there will be a significant difference in the productivity performance of cross-border and domestic firms and also according to the type of the deal.

The high occurrence of horizontal deals, especially in cross-border deals raises another issue namely the foreign control. Moreover, as it is evident from data, a good proportion of the deals are mega deals, and many of them are repeatedly engaging in consolidation strategies in order to grow faster than that of organic means. Here also it is important to examine whether the horizontal and vertical deals will make more competition or concentration compared to the conglomerate deals. It will also help us to find out the trade-off between efficiency and concentration creation through M&As.

In short, the gradual shift in organic ways of foreign investment to inorganic means of brownfield investment should ideally result in more innovation efforts, and thereby higher productivity and efficiency. The occurrence of these deals in more technology intensive sectors by firms from more industrialised countries adds more flavour to this. The occurrence of a large number of horizontal deals especially the cross-border deals raises another issue namely the foreign control. Moreover, as it is evident from the data, a good proportion of deals are mega deals, and many of them are repeatedly engaging in consolidation strategies in order to grow faster than that of organic means. Thus, the current surge in cross-border deals should be viewed in a multi-factor dimension, which involves the push factors from home country such as market constraint, need for low priced factors of production, increasing global competition as well as the pull factors from foreign countries such as the wider market, technology, efficient operation. M&As can be rightly considered as the response of the firms to the aftermath of globalisation in the form of less time and more action. Given this backdrop, the study will examine some of these issues in the forthcoming chapters. The next chapter analyses the technological performance of firms after getting into consolidation.

## Notes

1 In order to bring out the global trends, we have used United Nations Conference on Trade and Development (UNCTAD) Database on Cross-border M&As and FDI (UNCTAD, 2017. This data starts from the year 1990. Thus, the initial year taken for the study is also 1990. However, it should be noted that earlier version of the data changed very much later (extracted in the year 2008, see Saraswathy, 2010, 2013 for the results based on that). This is occurring since the reporting countries revise the data from time to time.
2 From 1990 onwards many of the erstwhile closed economies opened for either free trade or less market intervention by the Governments.
3 Healy and Palepu (1993) also support this point (as cited in Jones, 2005).
4 World Investment Report (2000) says Brownfield investment actually occurs only if the acquiring firm makes a new investment in the existing firm and almost completely replaces the existing firm. But such data is seldom available. So, for practical purposes, everybody uses this term to denote the investment through M&As. We are also following this.
5 World Investment Report (2000) cautions the direct comparison of FDI and foreign investment through M&As because the former is a balance of payment concept and measured on a net basis whereas the latter is a gross concept. However, the report itself makes a comparison between these two in the absence of other reliable data sources. Saraswathy (2016a) discussed on the limitations of this comparison.
6 Recently some databases like Venture Intelligence, Emerging Markets Information Service (EMIS) started to collect data on M&As. However, this data covers recent data only.
7 See for instance Beena (2000, 2004, 2008), Beena, S. (2008) Agarwal (2002), Kumar (2000), Basant (2000), Pradhan (2007).
8 MRIE covers data up to the period May 2001, and M&A Database starts from the month of November 2001. These two data sources are explanatory nature. However, both of these suffers from the fact that they are based on announcement basis rather than the effective date of deals. Securities and Exchange Board of India (SEBI) covers data for acquisitions from 1997 onwards.

9 During April 2000 to January 2012, 40 percent of the FDI inflows to India has been from Mauritius.

10 Horizontal M&As is defined as the M&As between firms in the similar line of business activity whereas those of vertical M&As occur between firms in buyer seller relationship. Conglomerate M&As occur between firms, which are totally unrelated.

11 The success of a cross-border deal depends on the successful integration of the firms belonging to two different nations, which involves different risks other than domestic consolidation such as language and culture.

12 The industry classification we are following is National Industrial Classification, 2004. We have followed a four-digit industrial classification at the base level. However, in the case of many industries such a classification is irrelevant due to the relatively less number of deals. Such cases, we again aggregated into sectors to a broader category.

13 Include M&As; Finance sector is defined broadly in the study since our major focus is on industry.

14 Here we are restricting the analysis to the acquisitions alone due to the non-availability of data for all cases.

15 Defined broadly. The sales and purchases made by individuals also included in this category.

16 During April 2000 to January 2012, the top FDI recipient sectors were telecommunications, computer software and hardware, housing and real estate, construction activities, drugs and pharmaceutical, power, automobile, metallurgical, petroleum, chemicals etc. (DIPP, 2012).

17 Swap ratio is the ratio in which one firms' shares are transferred to the other firm.

18 Here we are excluding merger due to the above-mentioned reason.

19 Mega deals are defined as the deals for which value is more than Rs. 100 crores and others are the small deals.

20 Here we are excluding 35 partial acquisitions as mentioned above.

21 For the rest of the analysis, we will be dealing with 528 deals, excluding the 35 partial acquisitions as we mentioned above.

22 In June 2008, Ranbaxy entered an alliance with Daiichi Sankyo Company Ltd., one of the largest Japanese innovator companies to create an innovator and generic pharmaceutical powerhouse. In March 2015, Ranbaxy was acquired by Sun Pharma.

## References

Agarwal, M. (2002). *Analysis of Mergers in India*. M. Phil. Delhi School of Economics.

Basanth, R., (2000). Corporate Response to Economic Reforms. Economic and Political Weekly. 35(10): 813–22

Beena, P.L. (2004). *Towards Understanding the Merger Wave in the Indian Corporate Sector: A Comparative Perspective*. Working Paper No. 355. Thiruvananthapuram: Centre for Development Studies.

Beena, P.L. (2008). Trends and Perspectives on Corporate Mergers in Contemporary India. *Economic and Political Weekly,* 43(39), pp. 48–56.

Beena, P.L. (2011). *Financing Pattern of Indian Corporate Sector under Liberalisation: With Focus on Acquiring Firms Abroad*. Working Paper No. 440. Thiruvananthapuram: Centre for Development Studies.

Beena, S., (2008). Concentration via Consolidation in the Indian Pharmaceutical Industry: An Inquiry. The ICFAI Journal of Mergers and Acquisitions. 5(4).

Centre for Monitoring Indian Economy (CMIE). Size and Market Shares. Various Issues.

Centre for Monitoring Indian Economy (CMIE). Monthly Review of the Indian Economy. Various Issues.

Centre for Monitoring Indian Economy (CMIE). M&A Database. Various Issues.

Department of Industrial Policy and Promotion (2008). *Fact Sheet on Foreign Direct Investment*. New Delhi, Ministry of Commerce and Industry: Government of India.

Department of Industrial Policy and Promotion (2012). *Fact Sheet on Foreign Direct Investment*. New Delhi: Ministry of Commerce and Industry, Government of India.

Gaughan, Patrick. A. (1999). Mergers and Acquisitions and Corporate Restructuring. New York: John Wiley & Sons.

Healy, P. and Palepu, K.G. (1993). International Corporate Equity Acquisitions: Who, Where and Why. In: K. Froot, ed., *Foreign Direct Investment*. Chicago: University of Chicago Press.

Jones, G. (2005). Multinational and Global Capitalism from 19th to the 20th Century. UK: Oxford University Press.

Kumar, N. (2000). Mergers and Acquisitions by MNEs: Patterns and Implications. *Economic and Political Weekly,* 35(32), pp. 2851–2858.

Nayyar, D. (2007). *The Internationalisation of Firms from India: Investment, Mergers and Acquisitions*. SLPTMD Working Paper Series No. 004. University of Oxford: Department of International Development.

Pradhan, J.P. (2007). *Trends and Patterns of Overseas Acquisitions by Indian Multinationals*. Working Paper No. 10. New Delhi: Institute for Studies in Industrial Development.

Saraswathy, B. (2010). Cross-Border Mergers and Acquisitions in India: Extent, Nature and Structure. Working Paper No. 434. Thiruvananthapuram, India: Centre for Development Studies.

Saraswathy, B. (2013). "Global Trends in Cross-Border Mergers and Acquisitions". In: K.R. Chittedi, ed., *The Economic and Social Issues of Financial Liberalisation: Evidence from Emerging Countries*. New Delhi: Bookwell Publishing, pp. 26–40.

Saraswathy, B., (2016), An Assessment of Foreign Acquisitions in India. Working Paper No. 193. Institute for Studies in Industrial Development, New Delhi.

UNCTAD (2017). Database on Cross-Border Mergers and Acquisitions. Available at: www.unctad.org/fdistatistics [Accessed on 7th January 2017].

UNCTAD, FDI/TNC Database (2017). Available at: www.unctad.org/fdistatistics [Accessed on 7th January 2017].

World Investment Report (2000). *Cross Border Mergers and Acquisitions and Development*. New York and Geneva: UNCTAD.

# 4 M&As and technological performance

The nexus between consolidation and innovation has been a relatively new issue in the antitrust literature compared to the efficiency-concentration trade off. The merger enforcement statistics of US Department of Justice and Federal Trade Commission indicates the increasing importance of innovation in antitrust regulations overtime. From 1990 to 1994, only in 3 percent of merger cases, the reason for merger challenge was related to the adverse impact on innovation, which increased to 38 percent during 2000–2003 (Gilbert, 2007). Based on the analysis in the previous chapter it is clear that in India, an unprecedented surge in the value and volume of mergers and acquisitions (M&As) in technology intensive sectors is visible too. The presence of cross-border M&As and the consequent disappearance of competent domestic firms further raised questions on nationality and technology spillovers to the domestic firms. This chapter is an attempt to bring out whether the firms could effectively operationalise their desired objective of enhancing innovation efforts through M&As. The chapter is organised into five sections. First section deals with the role of M&As in innovation creation, followed by the innovation concerns in the Competition Act in the second section, Data and methodology in the third section, observations based on the analysis of the nexus between M&As and technological performance in the fourth section and the fifth section concludes with policy implications.

## 4.1 M&As and innovation creation

### 4.1.1 On the direction of relationship

Acquisitions can affect acquirer's subsequent innovation through two channels. One is through the absorption of the acquired firm's knowledge base into the knowledge base of the acquiring firm. This combination is expected to enhance the knowledge base of the combined firm. However, the acquisition also involves a substantial amount of attention towards integration of acquired assets, which may disrupt the established routines of the acquired and acquiring firms and thereby reduced productivity (Ahuja, G and Katila, 2001). In the first case, the combined firm can reduce the cost of production through deriving economies of scale and scope in research output. Moreover, the time needed for innovation comes down substantially through combining the knowledge base of surviving and target firms. Another advantage is the sharing of uncertainties related to innovation. Sharing of uncertainties becomes most important for firms which are engaged in a substitutable or similar line of research activities; this will help firms to reduce the competition for innovation and thereby the huge capital requirement for innovation can be treated rationally.

The monopolisation of innovation and the consequent increase in firm size has been one of the major challenges arising out of consolidation. The link between firm size and innovation has been well discussed in the literature. According to the neo-Schumpeterian literature, firm size favours innovation activity. It is argued that big firms can invest more in technology since they can mobilize resources from the capital market (Kumar and Siddharthan, 1997). M&As are a major tool through which size can be expanded.

Similarly, the effect of market structure on innovation is widely debated in the literature on the economics of innovation. The Competition Policy Brief of European Commission (2016) identifies the existence of two major strands of literature on the relationship between market structure and innovation. First is the Schumpeterian perspective of continuous innovation and creative destruction, which suggests that less competition fosters more innovation at least in hi-tech and dynamic industries for which competition is mainly for developing new products and services rather than price and output; this occurs since the post innovation rewards are higher in less competitive markets compared to the competitive market structure. High rewards incentivise firms to invest more on Research and Development (R&D) activities. The second stream of literature is related to the views of Kenneth Arrow and other scholars in his stream. According to them, product market competition spurs innovation. The need for innovation will be higher when the firms face high competitive pressure, which necessitates them to introduce better quality cost effective products to outperform the other firms in the market. Innovation incentives depend on the difference between pre- and post-innovation rents. Hence less competition reduces innovation incentives. Shapiro's is the unified framework. Shapiro (2012) argues that both Schumpeterian and Arrowian schools of thought are compatible and converge on three principles. Both frameworks accept: (1) need of contestable markets[1] for promoting innovation (2) increased appropriability will increase innovation incentive (3) synergies[2] will increase the ability to innovate. While Arrowians stresses the *ex-ante* perspective on how to foster innovation, the Schumpeterian views mainly focus on the *ex post* perspective that the incentive to invest in innovation will be higher if they are able to appropriate the fruits of innovation. Hence if the competition policies promote contestable market without altering the appropriability of firms, both Arrow's and Schumpeter's views are compatible. In this regard,

Aghion et al., argue that too much or too little competition would negatively affect innovation (European Commission, 2016).

### 4.1.2  Cross-border M&As and technological performance

The entry of foreign firms through the route of M&As brings in the horizon of opportunities as well as challenges. Similar to the positive elements of foreign investment, it is expected that the cross-border mergers and acquisitions (CM&As) increase technological spillovers to the domestic counterparts through combining the better skill and human resource capabilities of the foreign firms. Meeting the huge capital requirement for innovation is another commonly mentioned advantage. Often, the foreign acquisitions are criticized for not generating fresh investment while transferring the domestically build capabilities to the foreign owners. From the M&As scenario in India, it is evident that the many times the competent domestic firms are taken over by the foreign firms, which raised concerns from the nationality point of view. It is possible that the foreign counterpart import the required technology from their foreign headquarters. There are arguments that foreign purchase of technology is a substitute for in-house R&D creation. Hence, the import of technology can be inimical to the development of local technological capabilities (Pillai, M. 1979). Import of technology can be complementary to the in-house R&D creation, which requires a certain level of in-house R&D investment (Kumar and Siddharthan, 1997). Firms depend on import of technology under when free market conditions exist, however under protection, import of technology is only complementary in nature (Subrahmanian, K.K., 1991; Kumar and Siddharthan, 1997). Thus, if import of technology is a substitute to own innovation creation, it will adversely affect the prospects of spillovers to the domestic firms. Another major challenge is the absorption capacity of firms in developing countries (Narulla, 2003). The extent of spillovers from the foreign firms depends on the existing level of knowledge of the domestic firms. In this background, our attempt in this chapter is to understand whether the technological performance of firms increased after getting into M&As.

It is important to mention that there were only a few attempts to study the relationship between M&As and innovation globally. Some of them are Hagedoorn and Duysters (2000), Guellec and Potterie (2001), Dessyllas and Alan Hughes (2005), Ravenscraft and Scherer (1987), Kleer (2006) and so on (see Saraswathy, B (2017) for a detailed discussion). In the Indian context, there are studies which passively mentions technological performance through M&As (Beena, P.L., 2004, 2008). There have been scant analytical studies on the relationship between M&As and technological performance. Saraswathy, B (2017) applied regression framework to understand the impact of M&As on technological performance and found that M&As influenced R&D intensity, while cross-border firms were found to be more technology import intensive. In similar lines, this study applied a statistical framework to assess the implication of

M&As on technological performance. In Chapter 3, we have seen that most of the top valued M&As are occurring in technology intensive sectors such as drugs and pharmaceutical, telecom, IT, power generation etc., and there is a high occurrence of horizontal and vertical deals. Horizontal and vertical deals are expected to generate more synergies and involves higher cost cutting. It follows that the growing value and volume of cross-border M&As are expected to improve the technological performance of firms since they are in a similar line of business activity.

## 4.2　Innovation concerns in the competition act

As mentioned earlier, during the initial years of merger activity, the major concern was the trade off between efficiency generation and market concentration. Innovation concerns are increasingly becoming important in the enforcement of antitrust regulations in developed countries. The competition authorities intend to protect the innovation effort of firms without harming the consumers. When two or more R&D intensive firms in the same market go for M&As, it can adversely affect the new product and process development, especially when no other substitutable firm exists in the market, which will further reduce the future competition in the said market. In India, as per section 3(5) of the Competition Act, reasonable conditions necessary for protecting any Intellectual Property Rights (IPR) will not attract competition regulations. Rather, unreasonable conditions attach to the IPR attract competition provisions. This essentially meant adverse effect on prices, quantity, quality etc., arising out of this will fall within the purview of the Competition Act as long as they are not in reasonable juxtaposition with the bundle of rights that go with IPRs (GoI, 2007). Evergreening of a patent is such an example. Here it may be noted that IPRs provide temporary monopoly power to the right holder whereas Competition Act intends to sustain competition. Hence both are having contrasting objectives from the first instance. However, competition concern arises only in the case of abuse of the right, which results in competition concerns for the public.

## 4.3　Data and methodology

The study applied the data discussed in Chapter 3 to the PROWESS database of CMIE, to get data on the financial performance of the firms. The data covers 1631 M&As[3] in the *manufacturing sector,* of which PROWESS database provides data on 1060 deals (i.e. in the case of 65 percent of the M&As, the corresponding surviving firms can be identified from PROWESS database). Regarding CM&As, the data is available on 61 percent of the deals (383 deals out of 631). The study analysed pre- and post-four and six-year performance of M&As from 1988–1989[4] to 2009–10.[5] The analysis is restricted to the M&As occurred between 1993 and 2004 for the pre- and post-four-year analysis and 1993–2002 for the six-year analysis. Post six-years performance was calculated mainly to allow more years for post-M&As integration. The study examined each industry separately to account for sector-wise variations in performance.[6] With this methodology, the present study tried to overcome the problems associated with some of the previous studies on M&As in the Indian context.[7] The study is not capturing the effect of each event separately; instead, it will be focusing on each surviving firm. The year of first merger or acquisition is taken as the cutoff point to treat a firm as 'surviving' firm. In this context, it is very important to note that many of the firms went for multiple M&As, which reduced the number of surviving firms further. The number of firms in the sample got reduced considerably when all these criteria are considered. The total number of surviving firms available is 484; out of this, 278 firms involved only in domestic deals and 206 are involved in cross-border deals. The intensity of multiple deals (that is the average frequency of a surviving firm to undertake M&As) is two for overall deals and in some sectors, such as pharmaceutical industry it is high at 4 deals per firm.

Acquisitions affect innovative input such as R&D expenditure as well as innovative output such as patenting frequency (Hitt et al., 1991 as in Ahuja and Katila, 2001). However, patents as a measure of innovative output has a limitation that economic value of each patent differ considerably. Technological performance in the study is defined in terms of two major input measures of technology, such as R&D intensity and payments made for royalties and technical know-how.[8] Here, the major question emerges would be, what is the appropriate indicator of an improvement in technological performance after getting into M&As?

## 4.4  Major observations based on pre- and post-M&As performance

### 4.4.1  R&D intensity

In the case of R&D intensity, most of the firms either increased their spending towards R&D after getting into M&As or remained the same without change in their spending (see Table 4.1). For manufacturing sector as a whole, 39 percent of the firms increased their spending after getting into merger and another 36 percent remained the same after merger. A good proportion of firms from pharmaceutical industry (64 percent), food and beverages (50 percent) and machinery (45 percent) increased their R&D intensity. Overall, post-six-years performance also shows a trend in favour of increased spending on R&D (44 percent of firms; decreased 25 percent and no change 36 percent;). One striking point to be mentioned here is that there has been a rise in the percentage of firms whose R&D intensity increased during the post-six-year period. This increase was mainly contributed by the shift in the spending of 'No change' category firms during post four year, towards 'increased' spending category in the post six years. This may

Table 4.1 R&D intensity: domestic vs. cross-border firms (post four years)

| Sector | Category | Increased | | Decreased | | No Change | | Total Available | |
|---|---|---|---|---|---|---|---|---|---|
| | | No. | Percent | No. | Percent | No. | Percent | No. | Percent |
| Chemicals | Domestic | 21 | 43 | 11 | 22 | 17 | 35 | 49 | 100 |
| | Cross-border | 12 | 40 | 11 | 37 | 7 | 23 | 30 | 100 |
| | All | 33 | 42 | 22 | 28 | 24 | 30 | 79 | 100 |
| Drugs and pharmaceutical | Domestic | 15 | 75 | 5 | 25 | 0 | 0 | 20 | 100 |
| | Cross-border | 8 | 50 | 7 | 44 | 1 | 6 | 16 | 100 |
| | All | 23 | 64 | 12 | 33 | 1 | 3 | 36 | 100 |
| Machinery | Domestic | 25 | 49 | 13 | 25 | 13 | 25 | 51 | 100 |
| | Cross-border | 18 | 40 | 15 | 33 | 12 | 27 | 45 | 100 |
| | All | 43 | 45 | 28 | 29 | 25 | 26 | 96 | 100 |
| Metals & minerals | Domestic | 1 | 5 | 8 | 36 | 13 | 59 | 22 | 100 |
| | Cross-border | 2 | 18 | 2 | 18 | 7 | 64 | 11 | 100 |
| | All | 3 | 9 | 10 | 30 | 20 | 61 | 33 | 100 |
| Non-metallic minerals | Domestic | 4 | 25 | 2 | 13 | 10 | 63 | 16 | 100 |
| | Cross-border | 2 | 29 | 3 | 43 | 2 | 29 | 7 | 100 |
| | All | 6 | 26 | 5 | 22 | 12 | 52 | 23 | 100 |
| Transport | Domestic | 4 | 36 | 4 | 36 | 3 | 27 | 11 | 100 |
| | Cross-border | 4 | 50 | 3 | 38 | 1 | 13 | 8 | 100 |
| | All | 8 | 42 | 7 | 37 | 4 | 21 | 19 | 100 |
| Textiles | Domestic | 9 | 28 | 5 | 16 | 18 | 56 | 32 | 100 |
| | Cross-border | 4 | 57 | 0 | 0 | 3 | 43 | 7 | 100 |
| | All | 13 | 33 | 5 | 13 | 21 | 54 | 39 | 100 |
| Food and beverages | Domestic | 9 | 56 | 1 | 6 | 6 | 38 | 16 | 100 |
| | Cross-border | 4 | 40 | 0 | 0 | 6 | 60 | 10 | 100 |
| | All | 13 | 50 | 1 | 4 | 12 | 46 | 26 | 100 |
| Manufacturing | Domestic | 90 | 39 | 51 | 22 | 88 | 38 | 229 | 100 |
| | Cross-border | 54 | 36 | 45 | 30 | 50 | 34 | 149 | 100 |
| | All | 148 | 39 | 96 | 25 | 138 | 36 | 382 | 100 |

Source: Calculated from PROWESS, CMIE.

indicate the fact that immediately after M&As, firms may try to integrate and utilize their existing resources properly and therefore the R&D intensity may remain more or less constant. But when the time needed for proper integration exceeds, they start to spend more on R&D as the firm is now in a better position to undertake innovation. How much time each firm requires to reach this stage will be subjected to different aspects relating to each merger. In our sample, all the sectors except transport equipment show this trend.[9]

Further, the domestic and cross-border classification of firms shows almost similar results, that is either increase or no change. A notable rise in R&D intensity occurred among the domestic deals in pharmaceutical (75 percent), food and beverages (56 percent), machinery (49 percent) and the cross-border deals in the textiles sector (57 percent). Earlier, it is seen that the above mentioned first three are the major sectors that experienced increase in the overall R&D spending; now it becomes clear that this increase was mainly contributed by the domestic deals in these sectors than cross-border deals (see Table 4.1). When the R&D spending of the domestic and cross-border deals are compared, it is interesting to note that, in majority of the M&As and technology intensive sectors, the domestic firms' increase was above than that of cross-border firms. A comparison of post four years results with that of post six years also found that there has been a clear increase in the percentage of firms 'increased R&D' after six years, which confirms the earlier findings.

### 4.4.2 *Payments made for royalties and technical know-how*

Next, the study analysed the payments made for royalties and technical know-how. Here, majority of the firms were not showing any change in their spending during the post-merger period compared to the pre-merger period. Almost all the sectors were showing the same trends with machinery and transport equipment showing some smaller variations in this trend (see Table 4.2). Domestic and cross-border behaviour is in line with the overall result. However, another interesting trend can be observed is in the magnitude of increase in the number of firms. When the domestic and cross-border deals are compared, the latter's spending remained higher than that of the former in all the sectors, which is essentially showing that the cross-border firms are depending more on the import of technology after getting into M&As. However, when the study allowed a long period (six-years post-merger), there is slight change in the behaviour of firms in two sectors-textiles and transport equipment. Here it may be remembered that in these sectors, cross-border deals increased their R&D spending compared to the domestic firms during the post M&As period. These firms may be investing more in their in-house R&D creation, which help them to reduce their dependence on foreign technology purchase in the long run. This may be to face the domestic competition powerfully.

Table 4.2 Royalties and technical know-how fees paid: domestic vs. cross-border M&As (post four years)

| Sector | Type | Increased | | Decreased | | No Change | | Total Available | |
|---|---|---|---|---|---|---|---|---|---|
| | | No. | Percent | No. | Percent | No. | Percent | No. | Percent |
| Chemicals | Domestic | 7 | 15 | 5 | 11 | 34 | 74 | 46 | 100 |
| | Cross-border | 13 | 46 | 5 | 18 | 10 | 36 | 28 | 100 |
| | All | 20 | 27 | 10 | 14 | 44 | 59 | 74 | 100 |
| Drugs and pharmaceutical | Domestic | 1 | 4 | 2 | 9 | 20 | 87 | 23 | 100 |
| | Cross-border | 5 | 31 | 1 | 6 | 10 | 63 | 16 | 100 |
| | All | 6 | 15 | 3 | 8 | 30 | 77 | 39 | 100 |
| Machinery | Domestic | 19 | 37 | 14 | 27 | 18 | 35 | 51 | 100 |
| | Cross-border | 21 | 47 | 9 | 20 | 15 | 33 | 45 | 100 |
| | All | 42 | 44 | 21 | 22 | 33 | 34 | 96 | 100 |
| Metals and metal products | Domestic | 4 | 15 | 4 | 15 | 18 | 69 | 26 | 100 |
| | Cross-border | 3 | 27 | 2 | 18 | 6 | 55 | 11 | 100 |
| | All | 7 | 19 | 6 | 16 | 24 | 65 | 37 | 100 |
| Non-metallic mineral products | Domestic | 4 | 27 | 4 | 27 | 7 | 47 | 15 | 100 |
| | Cross-border | 4 | 57 | 1 | 14 | 2 | 29 | 7 | 100 |
| | All | 8 | 36 | 5 | 23 | 9 | 41 | 22 | 100 |
| Transport equipment | Domestic | 4 | 36 | 2 | 18 | 5 | 45 | 11 | 100 |
| | Cross-border | 6 | 60 | 1 | 10 | 3 | 30 | 10 | 100 |
| | All | 10 | 48 | 3 | 14 | 8 | 38 | 21 | 100 |
| Textiles and leather | Domestic | 2 | 6 | 5 | 16 | 25 | 78 | 32 | 100 |
| | Cross-border | 1 | 13 | 2 | 25 | 5 | 63 | 8 | 100 |
| | All | 3 | 8 | 7 | 18 | 30 | 75 | 40 | 100 |
| Food and beverages | Domestic | 3 | 18 | 3 | 18 | 11 | 65 | 17 | 100 |
| | Cross-border | 4 | 40 | 2 | 20 | 4 | 40 | 10 | 100 |
| | All | 7 | 26 | 5 | 19 | 15 | 56 | 27 | 100 |
| Manufacturing* | Domestic | 44 | 19 | 39 | 16 | 154 | 65 | 237 | 100 |
| | Cross-border | 61 | 40 | 23 | 15 | 69 | 46 | 151 | 100 |
| | All | 107 | 27 | 62 | 16 | 222 | 57 | 392 | 100 |

Source: Calculated from PROWESS, CMIE.

Note: * Including misc. manufacturing.

Next the study examined whether the effect of M&As on technological performance changes according to the nature and structure of deals (see Table 4.3). For 39 percent of the horizontal deals, there was no change in the R&D intensity after getting into M&As; 35 percent of the firms increased and for the rest of the firms it decreased during the post-four-year period. A slightly reverse trend is noticed for the post-six-year period. Here majority of the firms increased (38 percent) while 36 percent of firms did not show any change in it. Notably, Drugs and Pharmaceutical sector is the only sector where more than 60 percent of the firms increased their R&D intensity after getting into M&As and this trend again increased when allowed more time period. Similarly, 'no change' was noticed in Metals and Minerals (69 percent) and Non-metallic minerals (63 percent). Thus, it seems that one major reason why the pharmaceutical firms are going for M&As may be to ensure technological advantage. As discussed earlier, this is one of the major sectors in which policy changes drastically occurred, which necessitated the fast restructuring and re-strengthening of the previously dominant firms to face the challenges of the changed global environment, which necessitated the unavoidable investment on innovation.

Horizontal deals within the CM&As were showing more decreasing trend, while the same for domestic deals were remaining constant. Cross-border firms were shifting towards increased R&D intensity during the six-year period compared to the four year (see Tables 4.4 and 4.5). For payments for royalties and technical know-how, the post M&As period for the horizontal and vertical deals are associated with increased spending for majority of the firms. However, for the conglomerate deals (only less number of deals), it shows a mixed result of increase and decrease.

*Table 4.3* R&D intensity after M&As: horizontal deals

| | Four Years | | | | | | | Six Years | | | | | | |
| | Number | | | Percent | | | TA | Number | | | Percent | | | |
| Sector | I | D | N | I | D | N | No | I | D | N | I | D | N | N |
|---|---|---|---|---|---|---|---|---|---|---|---|---|---|---|
| Chemicals | 17 | 16 | 10 | 40 | 37 | 23 | 43 | 15 | 14 | 7 | 42 | 39 | 19 | |
| Drugs and pharmaceutical | 18 | 10 | 1 | 62 | 34 | 3 | 29 | 17 | 9 | 0 | 65 | 35 | 0 | 2 |
| Machinery | 23 | 15 | 17 | 42 | 27 | 31 | 55 | 19 | 13 | 16 | 40 | 27 | 33 | 4 |
| Metals and minerals | 2 | 3 | 11 | 13 | 19 | 69 | 16 | 1 | 3 | 10 | 7 | 21 | 71 | |
| Non-metallic minerals | 1 | 5 | 10 | 6 | 31 | 63 | 16 | 1 | 5 | 10 | 6 | 31 | 63 | |
| Transport | 4 | 5 | 4 | 31 | 38 | 31 | 13 | 4 | 5 | 2 | 36 | 45 | 18 | |
| Textiles | 8 | 4 | 13 | 32 | 16 | 52 | 25 | 10 | 2 | 11 | 43 | 9 | 48 | 2 |
| Food and beverages | 5 | 1 | 8 | 36 | 7 | 57 | 14 | 6 | 1 | 5 | 50 | 8 | 42 | |
| Manufacturing | 81 | 61 | 91 | 35 | 26 | 39 | 233 | 76 | 53 | 71 | 38 | 27 | 36 | 20 |

Source: Calculated from PROWESS, CMIE.

Note: I denotes Increased; D for Decreased; N is for No change; TA is total available.

Table 4.4 R&D intensity and structure of M&As

| Deal | Type | Four Years Post (No. of Firms) | | | | | | Six Years Post (No. of Firms) | | | | | |
| | | Increase | | Decrease | | No Change | | Increase | | Decrease | | No Change | |
| | | No. | Percent | No. | Percent | No. | Percent | No. | Percent | No. | Percent | No. | Percent |
| Cross-border | Horizontal | 38 | 33 | 41 | 36 | 35 | 31 | 35 | 41 | 26 | 31 | 24 | 28 |
| | Vertical | 3 | 20 | 7 | 47 | 5 | 33 | 3 | 20 | 7 | 47 | 5 | 33 |
| | Conglomerate | 1 | 50 | 0 | 0 | 1 | 50 | 1 | 50 | 0 | 0 | 1 | 50 |
| Domestic | Horizontal | 43 | 33 | 30 | 23 | 56 | 43 | 41 | 36 | 27 | 23 | 47 | 41 |
| | Vertical | 21 | 43 | 9 | 18 | 19 | 39 | 21 | 49 | 7 | 16 | 15 | 35 |
| | Conglomerate | 3 | 33 | 1 | 11 | 5 | 56 | 3 | 33 | 1 | 11 | 5 | 56 |

Source: Calculated from PROWESS, CMIE.

*Table 4.5* Payments for royalties and technical know-how and the type of deal

| Deal | Type | Four years post (No. of Firms) | | | Six years post (No. of firms) | | |
|------|------|----------|----------|-----------|----------|----------|-----------|
| | | Increase | Decrease | No change | Increase | Decrease | No change |
| Cross-border | Horizontal | 20 | 15 | 56 | 25 | 11 | 60 |
| | Vertical | 2 | 3 | 8 | 1 | 3 | 5 |
| | Conglomerate | 1 | 0 | 2 | 1 | 0 | 2 |
| Domestic | Horizontal | 23 | 26 | 108 | 28 | 21 | 98 |
| | Vertical | 7 | 6 | 21 | 10 | 5 | 14 |
| | Conglomerate | 2 | 0 | 2 | 2 | 0 | 1 |

Source: Calculated from PROWESS, CMIE.

## 4.5 Concluding observations and policy implications

In the context of increasing number and value of cross-border consolidation strategies, the present study analysed whether this has actually led to the expected increase in technological performance during the post M&As period and whether it changes according to the nature and structure of deals. Using two major input measures of technology, the inter-firm variations in performance is analysed for each firm separately and found that R&D intensity of majority of the firms increased or remained the same during the post M&As period. Payments for royalties remained constant for majority of the firms. Major observation from the cross-border and domestic classification is that R&D intensity of domestic firms is higher than the cross-border cases in more technology and M&As intensive sectors. Whereas, cross-border firms are more technology import intensive than engaging in in-house R&D. The investigation on the impact of structure of M&As is not showing much impact on the technological performance excluding the cross-border deals, in which case R&D intensity declined for a good proportion of firms during the post-four-years, which again increased during the post six years. It may be showing that firms use the existing resources immediately after getting into M&As and when they become properly integrated, they try to invest more as they are in a relatively better position to do so in the long run. The following table summarises the results (Table 4.6).

However, one should also realize the fact that in India, consolidation strategies are of recent origin unlike the US or UK experience. Consolidation was a market expansion strategy rather than a technology driver until recently. However, the results show that the cross-border firms are more technology import intensive than investing in domestic R&D, which is similar to the findings of studies on FDI in India, which found that the foreign firms in India are paying royalties than strengthening the inbound R&D locations. There is no provision in the current Competition Act to examine,

*Table 4.6* Trends in R&D behaviour

| Indicator | Domestic > Cross-border | Cross-border > Domestic |
|---|---|---|
| R&D intensity | Chemicals<br>Drugs and pharmaceutical<br>Machinery<br>Food and beverages | Metals and minerals<br>Non-metallic minerals<br>Transport equipment<br>Textiles |
| Payments on<br>  royalties and<br>  technical<br>  know-how | | Chemicals<br>Drugs and pharmaceutical<br>Machinery<br>Metals and minerals<br>Non-metallic minerals<br>Transport equipment<br>Textiles<br>Food and beverages |

Source: Calculated from PROWESS, CMIE.

Note: Domestic > cross-border refers to the percentage number of increase is higher for domestic deals compared to cross-border deals.

whether the proposed deal is actually bringing the desired outcomes such as efficiencies, technical know-how and ultimately the consumer satisfaction, given the merger control laws are *ex ante* in nature. In this context, the study demands the competition authorities in developing countries to undertake periodic review of the outcome of transactions and make necessary changes while approving deals.

## Notes

1 The extent to which a firm can capture the value created from innovation and protect the competitive advantage associated with it.
2 Such as arising from the combination of complementary capabilities necessary to engage in R&D.
3 Excluding primary and service sector.
4 Now PROWESS gives information from 1987–1988, but the coverage for the firms is very low for the initial period.
5 Restricted this analysis till this period since from 2011 onwards CCI regime started, which makes a difference in policy regime.
6 However, we will be concentrating on major industrial categories due to the data limitation and less occurrence of deals in certain sectors.
7 These studies were mainly concentrating on the financial performance of surviving firms. Beena, P.L. (2004) studies are based on an assumed pre- and post-merger period. It is not taking into account the year of the merger of each firm separately. Even though Manthravadi and Vidyadhar Reddy (2007) make such a distinction, it is a very short period (3 years) to realise the effect of M&As. One of the major limitations of this study is that the analysis is not based on the M&As triggered aimed at increasing technological performance. Such kind of information is not available from the existing databases on M&As.
8 Patents would have been another good indicator, however in the Indian context; only a few firms are able to make such innovation. Moreover, the number of patents is not an appropriate indicator of the qualitative value of a particular

innovation. Linking the patent to a particular merger or acquisition is also a difficult task.

9 Non-metallic minerals remained the same.

## References

Ahuja and Katila., (2001). Technological Acquisitions and the Innovation Performance of Acquiring Firms: A Longitudinal Study. Strategic Management Journal. 22(3):197–220.

Beena, P.L. (2004). *Towards Understanding the Merger Wave in the Indian Corporate Sector: A Comparative Perspective*. Working Paper No. 355. Thiruvananthapuram: Centre for Development Studies.

Beena, P.L. (2008). Trends and Perspectives on Corporate Mergers in Contemporary India. *Economic and Political Weekly,* 43(39), pp. 48–56.

Centre for Monitoring Indian Economy (CMIE), Various Publications.

Dessyllas and Hughes (2005). R&D and Patenting Activity and the Propensity to Acquire in High Technology Industries. Working Paper No. 298. ESRC Centre for Business Research, University of Cambridge.

European Commission (2016). *Competition Policy Brief: EU Merger Control and Innovation*. Brussels: Competition Directorate General of the European Commission. Available at: http://ec.europa.eu/competition/publications/cpb/2016/2016_001_en.pdf [Accessed on 23rd May 2017].

Guellec, D. and Bruno. Van. Pottlesbeghe. de la Potterie., (2001). The Internationalisation of Technology Analysed with Patent Data. Research Policy. 30(8).

Galleco, B.C. (2010). Intellectual Property Rights and Competition Policy. In: M. C. Correa, ed., *Research Handbook on the Protection of IPR under WTO Rules*, vol. 1. USA: Edward Elgar.

Gilbert, R.J. (2007). *Competition and Innovation*. Working Paper Series qt9xh5p5p9. UC Berkeley: Institute for Business and Economic Research.

Government of India (2007). *The Competition (Amendment) Act*. New Delhi: Competition Commission of India.

Hagedoorn, J. and Duysters, G. (2000). *The Effects of Mergers and Acquisitions on the Technological Performance of Companies in a High-Tech Environment*. MERIT, Netherlands: University of Maastricht.

Kleer, R. (2006). *The Effect of Mergers on the Incentive to Invest in Cost Reducing Innovation*. BGPE Discussion Paper No. 11, Wuerzburg.

Kumar, N and Siddharthan., (1997). Technology, Market Structure and Internationalisation: Issues and Policies for Developing Countries. New York: Routledge.

Manthravadi, P. and Vidyadhar, A.R. (2007). Relative Size in Mergers and Operating Performance: Indian Experience. *Economic and Political Weekly,* 42(39), pp. 3936–3942.

Pillai, P. Mohanan., 1979., Technology Transfer, Adaptation and Assimilation", *Economic and Political Weekly,* 14(47): M121–M126.

Narula, R. (2003). *Globalisation and Technology: Interdependence, Innovation Systems and industrial Policy*. UK: Cambridge Polity Press.

Ravenscraft, D.J. and Scherer, F.M. (1987). *Mergers, Sell-offs and Economic Efficiency*. Washington, DC: The Brooking Institution.

Saraswathy, B (2017). Innovation Consolidation Nexus: Evidence from India's Manufacturing Sector. In Siddharthan and Narayanan, K. *Globalisation of Technology*. Springer (forthcoming).

Shapiro, C. (2012). Competition and Innovation: Did Arrow Hit the Bull's Eye? In: J. Lerner and S. Stern, eds., *The Rate and Director of Inventive Activity Revisited*. USA: NBER, University of Chicago Press. pp. 361–410. NBER. University of Chicago Press, USA.

Subrahmanian, K.K., (1991). Technological Capability under Economic Liberalism: Experience of Indian Industry in Eighties. Economic and Political Weekly. XXVI (35): M87–M89.

# 5 Production efficiency of firms with mergers and acquisitions

## 5.1 Efficiency generation via consolidation

The relationship between mergers and acquisitions (M&As) and efficiency has been one of the most discussed issues in merger literature, and the debate is continuing. Most of the early studies on M&As were concerned with the developed countries, especially the USA and the UK mergers as part of their state policy formulation during the initial merger waves. During this time, the emphasis was on the welfare trade-off between the generation of market power and market efficiency through consolidation. According to Meeks (1977), the advocates of *laissez-faire* economists faced a dilemma over the state policy on mergers. Two groups of conflicting views can be observed. One has argued that merger undermines the competitive conditions which are required if *laissez-faire* has to achieve allocative efficiency.[1] So they have supported the outright ban on M&As. The other group has argued against the state interference in the merger process, not only on political grounds but also on economic grounds emphasising that merger will be in the public interest.[2] Thus those who supported M&As based their argument on the efficiency defence, whereas the others raised competition concerns arising out of market power creation. However, separating the efficiency effects of M&As is not an easy task.

Consolidation is expected to reduce the overall cost of production through economies of scale and scope. M&As are expected to generate more efficiency on three grounds. First is through the re-organization of production, second, more efficient allocation of inputs, especially in the case of vertical mergers it enables to get the inputs at lower prices, and third by providing expanded sales and distribution network. A single network may function efficiently as compared to the previously operated two separate networks (Pesendorfer, 2003). Synergy creation is considered to be more in the case of horizontal and vertical deals since the firms are linked in similar or vertical products. Hindley (1973) also pointed out that a transaction occurs if only the buyer of the firm expects higher returns and if it is satisfied, and so higher private profitability will be associated with social gains such as reduction in the cost of production per unit of output. Hindley based his argument on the expected gains in economic efficiency and cost reduction through M&As. Consolidation is further expected to make management more efficient through hostile merger/takeover threat[3] (Meeks, 1977).

As discussed in Chapter 1, Williamson (1968) raised the question of 'trade-off' while framing the merger policies for the US and favoured the net efficiency gains and says that "even then the cost differential is too low; the net benefits will offset the losses". If the cost reduction effect exceeds the dead-weight loss, then the net welfare effect is positive and vice versa. Even though the economists are not in consensus regarding the net outcome, the study assumes that the M&As may lead to increased efficiency via the reduced cost of production, which may increase the market power of the firms, and a consequent rise in prices can be expected after the deal. Further, when the firms face inefficiency, undertaking a merger or acquisition is expected to enhance efficiency. However, the implications of consolidation may be different from deal to deal. The present study attempt to understand whether the surviving firms[4] could generate the expected efficiency effects from M&As in India. The study has also focused on the cross-border and domestic deals separately in the study. It is to be noted in this context that, there has not been any previous attempt to study the efficiency effects of M&As in India. However, there are studies, which concentrated on the profitability aspect and found a declining trend in profitability after getting into M&As.[5] We shall discuss the measurement of efficiency with M&As in the next section.

## 5.2 Data and methodology for measuring efficiency

According to Farrell (1957), economic efficiency is classified into technical[6] and allocative[7] (see Coelli, Donnel and Battese, 2005). From the foregoing discussion, it is clear that M&As effects both technical efficiency and allocative efficiency. With the limited data on the price of various inputs used for production, the measurement of allocative efficiency is difficult. Hence, most of the studies in the Indian context concentrated on the measurement of Technical Efficiency (TE) alone. The present study is also following the same. TE gains are the movement towards "best practices" or elimination of technical and organisational inefficiencies (OECD, 2002). The basic assumption underlying the measurement of technical efficiency is that normally there exists a gap between actual and potential levels of technical performance. For measuring TE, we do not have information on the potential level of output, and hence, the studies used various alternative methodologies for estimating it. Various statistical packages estimate it via linear programming method (Kalirajan and Shand, 1994). It is needless to say that there are conceptual differences depending on the estimation technique used. The present study used the stochastic production function approach (SFP) for estimation. SFP is discussed in detail by various studies including Greene (2011); Kalirajan and Shand (1994). The study followed Battese and

Coelli (1995) model for measuring technical inefficiency effects. Translog production function is applied, which is well-known for its less restrictive assumptions,[8] which enables us to get more robust results. Variables construction and the sources of data are discussed next.

### 5.2.1 Variables construction

*Output:* Deflated value of output for each sector is used.[9]

*Labour*: After reviewing various studies, it is observed that the feasible best measure is average wages paid per labour hour. The study followed Srivastava (1996), methodology to arrive at the actual labour hours employed for measuring labour content. For this, Annual Survey of Industries (ASI) is used for calculating the average wages paid per labour hour at two-digit level.[10] This rate is applied to the corresponding industrial classification of PROWESS, Centre for Monitoring Indian Economy (CMIE) to get the firm level value.[11] It is to be noted that, though PROWESS gives information on the number of employees, here a separation between part-time and full-time employees has not been made, which inflates the labour counts.

*Capital Stock*: Hashim and Dadi (1973) cautions that there are several problems associated with the definition and measurement of capital stock. Firstly, capital stock is a "composite commodity", which consists of different types of goods and this will change over time. The changing composition of capital over time makes the measurement of capital stock a difficult task. Also, the capital stock existing at any time has no linkage with current market valuations. The available data on capital stock is expressed in terms of historical prices. Each firm has to undergo several restructuring and replacement of its capital assets due to depreciation and other unexpected damages. If the study uses the value expressed in historical prices, we may be underestimating these expenses incurred over the years. Here arises the need for calculating the replacement value of capital in order to give importance to the replacement value incurred in the production process. Moreover, the productivity of the capital stock is not constant during its lifespan, which makes the measurement of capital in relation to its original cost difficult which raises the controversy over the methods of depreciation and the concept of replacement cost etc. The majority of the studies on manufacturing sector productivity depended on the Perpetual Inventory Method (PIM) to construct the capital stock (see Srivastava, 1996; Parameswaran, 2002; Balakrishnan, Pushpangadan and Suresh Babu, 2002, etc.). The present study also followed the methodology used by Srivastava (1996) to measure capital stock (see Appendix 1 for details).

*Intermediary Inputs*: Following Goldar (2004) and Balakrishnan and Pushpangadan, K. (1994), the sum of the deflated values of raw material cost, power and fuel, and other intermediate inputs is calculated for measuring it. In order to deflate into the real value of inputs, we have calculated the weighted average price indices. For this, the study used Input Output

Transaction Table 2003–2004 published by Central Statistical Organisation (CSO), Government of India (GOI) (2008) and the respective sector's Wholesale Price Indices published by the Office of the Economic Advisor, Ministry of Commerce & Industry, GOI.[12] Weights were assigned considering the respective share of each input in the total inputs used. Further, added the purchase of materials done by 68 sectors in the manufacturing sector from various other sectors, which includes the supplies made by one industry to another as well as the intra-industry transactions. This data is used to construct the weight of each sector. Then the corresponding Wholesale Price Index (WPI) is used to prepare Weighted Price Index. Similarly, we have created Energy input series separately. The study used fuel, power, light and lubricants price index for deflation[13] based on 1993–1994 prices. Next is the services purchased by the industrial units such as outsourced professional jobs, insurance premiums paid etc., which makes a good proportion of the other input costs (Goldar, 2004). So, we have calculated another deflated series by taking the service cost incurred by each sector from the Input Output Transaction Table and implicit deflator calculated from the Gross Domestic Product (GDP) at current and constant prices using National Accounts Statistics.[14]

### 5.2.2 Variables in the inefficiency model

As mentioned earlier, one major advantage of using SFP is that we can capture the inefficiencies associated with production. We have included Research & Development Intensity (RD), Payments made for Royalties and Technical Know-how (royal), Export Intensity (export), Raw Materials Import Intensity (rawimp), Age of firm (firmage), Year Dummy of Merger (yeardum), Domestic M&As (domestic), Cross-border M&As (cbdeals) and Time Variables ($t$ and $t^2$) to assess this. Here, R&D Intensity is defined as the ratio of R&D to sales. Increased R&D intensity is expected to reduce the inefficiency by strengthening the already available technology. Payments made for royalties and technical know-how is also taken as a percentage of sales of the firm. It indicates the import of technology, which is considered to enhance the efficiency of the firms since, under normal conditions, technology is imported if only it leads to improvements in production in future. Export intensity (export) will capture the competitiveness of the firms because the firms trading with other countries necessitate the firm to become more competitive, which may pressurise the firm to operate more efficiently. Higher quality of the imported raw materials, enhance the production efficiency. Moreover, the need for importing raw materials arises when the domestic market is facing supply shortage for perfect substitutes or if the prevailing price in the domestic market is higher than that of the international prices. Age of firm indicates the extent of experience a firm owns, which is expected to reduce the inefficiency. However, it can become the other way if the firm is operating with the outdated machinery for production. In order to understand whether the inefficiencies declined after getting into M&As, a dummy variable is added, which will take the value '0' up to the year of the deal and '1' after that. In order to understand the influence of domestic and cross-border deals[15] on inefficiencies, the number of domestic deals and cross-border deals is used. The logic being that when more M&As occur, the inefficiency might tend to reduce, since M&As are expected to make the firms more efficient by using the resources more efficiently. Consolidation is expected to generate more labour productivity because when two firms integrate their operation, it will get an opportunity to re-arrange their existing labour force, which results in better productivity of the labour. Similarly, capital and intermediaries' utility also increases due to the expanded scale of operation and synergy creation. When a cross-border merger (or acquisition) occurs, it is argued that normally they acquire those firms, which are already efficient comparing the other firms in the same sector (Griffith et al., 2004 as in Schiffbauer, Iulia and Frances, 2009). In addition to that, foreign firms assumed better performance would bring more efficient operation of the firm. *Time Variables (t and $t^2$):* This is in order to allow the inefficiency effects to change with respect to time. However, this is different from the time variable included in the stochastic frontier, which accounts for the Hicks neutral technological change.[16]

Specified the model as follows:

$$\ln Y_{it} = \beta_k k_{it} + \beta_l l_{it} + \beta_m m_{it} + \beta_t t_{it} + 1/2\beta_{kk} k_{it} k_{it} + 1/2\beta_{ll} l_{it} l_{it} +$$
$$1/2\beta m_{it} m_{it} + 1/2\beta_{tt} t_{it} t_{it} + \beta_{kl} k_{it} l_{it} + \beta_{km} k_{it} m_{it} + \beta_{kt} k_{it} t_{it} + \beta_{lm} l_{it} m_{it} +$$
$$\beta_{lt} l_{it} t_{it} + \beta_{mt} m_{it} t_{it} + V_{it} \quad U_{it}. \tag{5.1}$$

The model for technical inefficiency effects is assumed to be:

$$U_{it} = \delta_0 + \delta_1 RD + \delta_2 royal + \delta_3 \exp ort + \delta_4 rawimp + \delta_5 t +$$
$$\delta_6 t^2 + \delta_7 firmage + \delta_8 yeardum + \delta_9 domestic + \delta_{10} cbdeals + W_{it}. \tag{5.2}$$

Where $i$ denotes the $i$th firm, $t$ is $t$th year, $k$ is the log of capital stock, $l$ is the log of labour unit, $m$ is the log of material inputs used in the production process, $t$ is time trend included in the model to allow the frontier to shift over time. $V_{it}$ is assumed to be independently and identically distributed $N$ (0, $\sigma_v^2$) random errors independently distributed of the $U_{it}s$. $U_{it}$ is the nonnegative random variable associated with the technical inefficiency of production, which is assumed to be independently distributed, such that it is obtained by truncation (at zero) of the normal distribution with mean $z_{it}\delta$ and variance $\sigma^2$. $z_{it}$ is a (1 × m) vector of explanatory variables associated with the technical inefficiency of production of firms over time and $\delta$ is (m × 1) vector of unknown coefficients. $W_{it}$ is defined by the truncation of the normal distribution with zero mean and variance $\sigma^2$ such that the point of truncation is $-z_{it}\delta$ that is, $W_{it} \geq -z_{it}\delta$ (see Battese and Coelli, 1995 for details). The technical efficiency of production for the $i$th firm at the $t$th year is defined as,

$$TE_{it} = \exp(-U_{it}) = \exp(-z_{it}\delta - W_{it}).$$ (5.3)

For the analysis, we have taken M&As that occurred in the years 1994, 1997, 2002 and 2004[17] and then prepared an unbalanced panel data consisting of 20 years from 1988–1989 to 2007–2008. Many of the surviving firms go for multiple deals, which reduces the number of firms in the analysis considerably.[18] Hence, restricted the estimation of inefficiency effects to the aggregate level only, though we understand that sector-wise analysis would be more comprehensive.[19] We have estimated the mean technical efficiency across sectors also. Mean Technical efficiency we have calculated for pre- and post-M&As. Pre-M&A values are the average values for the years prior to the deal, and post-M&A values are defined as the average values post-M&As. The analysis is restricted to the M&As occurred from 1994 and up to 2004 to allow a reasonably good pre- and post-M&As time period. The highest number of deals is present in the 1997 sample (63 deals) followed by 1994 (38 deals), 2002 (37 deals) and 2004 (18 deals).

## 5.3  Empirical estimation results

Before getting into the results, we have tested the usual assumptions behind the frontier and inefficiency model in order to understand the adequacy of the model specified (see Appendix 2). Next, we shall move to the estimation results of the inefficiency model (see Table 5.1). As we expected, the spending on R&D induces a negative pressure on inefficiency. However, it is statistically significant only for 1997 deals; this is important since chapter 4 shows that M&As induce more spending on R&D. Here our result indicates that not only the spending on technology increases but also it helps to reduce the hindrances to achieve efficient utilization. Regarding the payments made for royalties and technical know-how, it is positive and significant only for firms which went for M&As in 1994. Import of raw materials was also expected to reduce the inefficiencies related to production. It is positive and significant in the case of M&As occurred in 2002 and 2004. Thus, the import of technology and raw materials are not reducing inefficiencies associated with production. Interestingly, the export performance of the firms is not helping them to reduce inefficiencies. Similarly, the age of the firms is also an inefficiency enhancing factor for the 1997 deals indicating the lack of modernization. All three M&A variables show negative pressure on inefficiency related to production. However, it is significant only in the case of 1994 deals. Here the cross-border deals have a strong negative pressure, whereas domestic ones are not significant anywhere. Thus, we can infer that even though both cross-border and domestic deals exert negative pressure, like the R&D

Table 5.1 Maximum likelihood estimation results of the stochastic frontier and inefficiency model

| | 1994 | | 1997 | | 2002 | | 2004 | |
|---|---|---|---|---|---|---|---|---|
| | coefficient | t-ratio | coefficient | t-ratio | coefficient | t-ratio | coefficient | t-ratio |
| Constant | 9.14 | 8.24 | 9.08 | 13.61 | 6.97 | 7.46 | 5.55 | 5.62 |
| $\beta_k$ | -0.04 | -0.83 | 0.06 | 1.79 | 0.03 | 0.71 | -0.01 | -0.15 |
| $\beta_l$ | -0.46 | -2.40 | -0.59 | -5.10 | -0.10 | -0.61 | 0.14 | 0.72 |
| $\beta_m$ | 2.03 | 8.37 | 1.76 | 16.13 | 1.10 | 5.12 | 0.97 | 4.52 |
| $\beta_t$ | -0.11 | -1.99 | -0.05 | -1.17 | -0.22 | -2.81 | 0.00 | 0.05 |
| $0.5\beta_{kk}$ | 0.00 | -1.06 | 0.00 | 4.79 | 0.01 | 4.93 | 0.01 | 6.46 |
| $0.5\beta_{ll}$ | 0.04 | 2.45 | 0.08 | 7.12 | 0.02 | 1.10 | -0.02 | -0.73 |
| $0.5\beta_{mm}$ | 0.15 | 4.09 | 0.16 | 17.81 | 0.00 | 0.17 | 0.10 | 4.24 |
| $0.5\beta_{tt}$ | 0.01 | 2.97 | 0.00 | 1.26 | 0.04 | 2.63 | 0.00 | -1.36 |
| $\beta_{kl}$ | 0.01 | 2.59 | -0.01 | -3.41 | 0.00 | 0.08 | 0.00 | -0.18 |
| $\beta_{km}$ | 0.01 | 2.09 | -0.01 | -1.96 | -0.01 | -1.27 | -0.03 | -6.38 |
| $\beta_{kt}$ | 0.00 | -2.93 | 0.00 | 1.06 | 0.00 | 0.90 | 0.00 | -0.51 |
| $\beta_{lm}$ | -0.12 | -6.41 | -0.07 | -7.16 | -0.04 | -2.16 | -0.01 | -0.39 |
| $\beta_{lt}$ | 0.01 | 1.81 | 0.00 | 1.14 | 0.00 | 1.53 | 0.01 | 1.55 |
| $\beta_{mt}$ | -0.01 | -1.74 | -0.01 | -3.01 | 0.00 | -0.92 | 0.00 | 0.08 |
| Constant | -2.58 | -2.64 | -3.14 | -3.90 | -1.74 | -2.69 | -0.07 | -0.55 |
| R&D | -0.01 | -0.66 | -0.33 | -3.50 | -0.01 | -0.55 | -0.05 | -4.76 |
| Royalties | 9.66 | 2.48 | -2.83 | -1.66 | 2.59 | 0.99 | 0.74 | 0.75 |
| Export | 0.37 | 2.18 | 0.04 | 1.02 | 0.19 | 1.93 | 0.54 | 4.97 |
| Import Rawm. | -0.80 | -1.91 | 0.00 | -0.90 | 0.87 | 3.95 | 0.21 | 3.31 |
| Time (t) | 0.40 | 2.93 | 0.16 | 1.75 | 0.12 | 1.01 | 0.06 | 3.27 |
| $t^2$ | -0.01 | -2.44 | 0.00 | -0.97 | 0.01 | 0.99 | 0.00 | -4.15 |
| Firm age | 0.15 | 1.70 | 0.36 | 3.14 | 0.00 | -0.02 | -0.03 | -1.38 |
| Merger dummy | -0.71 | -2.28 | 0.06 | 0.33 | -0.04 | -0.51 | 0.00 | 0.00 |
| Domestic deals | 0.00 | -0.10 | -0.01 | -0.34 | -0.01 | -0.29 | -0.07 | -1.90 |
| Cross-border | -0.22 | -3.29 | -0.05 | -0.95 | -0.03 | -0.96 | 0.01 | 0.15 |
| $\sigma^2 = \sigma_u^2 + \sigma_v^2$ | 0.19 | 5.81 | 0.36 | 9.41 | 0.12 | 11.69 | 0.07 | 10.78 |
| $\gamma = \sigma_u^2/\sigma_v^2 + \sigma_u^2$ | 0.68 | 9.21 | 0.80 | 25.63 | 0.57 | 7.39 | 0.00 | 6.57 |
| LR test of one sided error | 114.78 | | 89.39 | | 60.73 | | 26.88 | |
| LLF1 | -202.80 | | -313.98 | | -116.82 | | -19.67 | |
| Mean TE | 0.69 | | 0.78 | | 0.43 | | 0.89 | |
| Total No. of observations in the unbalanced panel | 587 | | 773 | | 468 | | 229 | |
| No. of firms | 38 | | 63 | | 37 | | 18 | |

effects, as discussed above, it is not enough to overcome production inefficiencies, which will be clear from the subsequent analysis. The mean technical efficiency of firms, which went for M&As, is shown in Table 5.2. It is
evident that during the post deal period,[20] the technical efficiency of domestic
as well as cross-border firms declined except for 2004 deals. The sector-wise
analysis also shows similar results that the technical efficiency declined for
the majority of the cases during the post M&As period. However, the technical efficiency of the cross-border firms remained higher than that of domestic
firms for the majority of the cases (see Figure 5.1).

*Table 5.2* Pre and post deal mean technical efficiency of firms

| Deal year | Domestic | | Cross-border | | All | |
|---|---|---|---|---|---|---|
| | *Pre* | *Post* | *Pre* | *Post* | *Pre* | *Post* |
| 1994 | 0.84 | 0.62 | 0.87 | 0.71 | 0.85 | 0.64 |
| 1997 | 0.82 | 0.73 | 0.85 | 0.77 | 0.83 | 0.75 |
| 2002 | 0.74 | 0.09 | 0.75 | 0.11 | 0.74 | 0.1 |
| 2004 | 0.87 | 0.96 | 0.88 | 0.97 | 0.87 | 0.96 |

Source: Calculated from the estimated model.

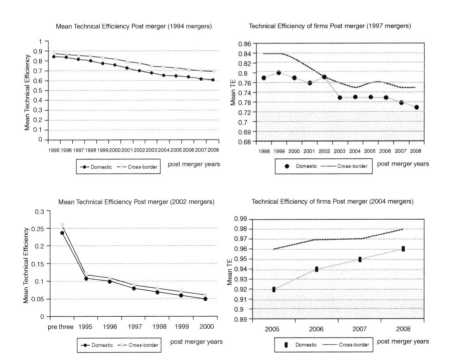

*Figure 5.1* Technical efficiency: time trend.
Source: Calculated from the estimated model and PROWESS, CMIE.

In the case of drugs and pharmaceutical industry, the technical efficiency of domestic firms increased during the post-M&As period for 1997 deals. In the case of 2004 deals, it improved in all cases. As mentioned earlier, our earlier study found that in the majority of the cases, there has been an increase in the spending on technology—both in-house and import of technology. Here the result shows that there has been a decline in the technical efficiency after getting into M&As. In order to understand it better, the mean technical efficiency of firms is decomposed, for which spending on technology increased during the post deal period.[21] Here also the same trend of declining efficiency is observed except for 2004 M&As during the post deal period (see Table 5.3).

The study has also examined the pre- and post-M&As technical efficiency of horizontal and vertical deals to understand the process closely. The pre- and post-M&As average technical efficiency is calculated. The results show that (see Table 5.4) except for the 2004 M&As, the technical efficiency declined for horizontal and vertical deals for both cross-border and domestic deals. This result is interesting because the theoretical prediction is that horizontal and vertical deals are expected to create more synergies, which enhance efficiencies after getting into M&As. However, the results did not validate this prediction, which may be indicating the absence of adequate synergies after getting into M&As. Further, for the majority of the years, the technical efficiency of the cross-border firms (both horizontal and vertical deals) remained above than that of domestic deals.

*Table 5.3* Average TE of firms for which technology spending increased post merger

| Merger year | Category | Merger | R&D Intensity | Royalties* |
|---|---|---|---|---|
| 1994 | Domestic | Pre | 0.86 | 0.84 |
| | | Post | 0.61 | 0.62 |
| | Cross-border | Pre | 0.88 | 0.87 |
| | | Post | 0.75 | 0.71 |
| 1997 | Domestic | Pre | 0.83 | 0.82 |
| | | Post | 0.74 | 0.73 |
| | Cross-border | Pre | 0.86 | 0.85 |
| | | Post | 0.75 | 0.77 |
| 2002 | Domestic | Pre | 0.78 | 0.74 |
| | | Post | 0.09 | 0.09 |
| | Cross-border | Pre | 0.76 | 0.75 |
| | | Post | 0.09 | 0.11 |
| 2004 | Domestic | Pre | 0.86 | 0.87 |
| | | Post | 0.92 | 0.96 |
| | Cross-border | Pre | 0.87 | 0.88 |
| | | Post | 0.98 | 0.97 |

Source: Calculated from the estimated model.

Note: *Spending on royalties and technical know-how.

*Table 5.4* Pre and post merger technical efficiency of horizontal/vertical deals

| Merger Year | Category | Merger | Horizontal | Vertical |
|---|---|---|---|---|
| 1994 | Domestic | Pre | 0.84 | 0.84 |
| | | Post | 0.62 | 0.6 |
| | Cross-border | Pre | 0.88 | 0.86 |
| | | Post | 0.66 | 0.8 |
| 1997 | Domestic | Pre | 0.8 | 0.85 |
| | | Post | 0.72 | 0.76 |
| | Cross-border | Pre | 0.85 | 0.85 |
| | | Post | 0.78 | 0.75 |
| 2002 | Domestic | Pre | 0.74 | 0.24 |
| | | Post | 0.09 | 0.09 |
| | Cross-border | Pre | 0.6 | 0.75 |
| | | Post | 0.1 | 0.11 |
| 2004 | Domestic | Pre | 0.86 | 0.97 |
| | | Post | 0.95 | 0.9 |
| | Cross-border | Pre | 0.87 | 0.88 |
| | | Post | 0.99 | 0.96 |

Source: Calculated from the estimated model.

*Table 5.5* Average input elasticity

| Year of Merger | Capital | Labour | Material |
|---|---|---|---|
| 1994 | 0.12 | 0.46 | 0.52 |
| 1997 | 0.00 | 1.83 | 1.20 |
| 2002 | 0.02 | 0.16 | 0.64 |
| 2004 | 0.01 | 1.60 | 0.98 |

Source: Calculated from the estimated model.

The estimated elasticity[22] of output with respect to different inputs are of considerable analytical interest. The elasticity reflects on the production technology. We have seen that in 50 percent of the cases labour is contributing more to the changes in production and capital is contributing less (see Table 5.5). It may be reflecting that in many cases firms may not be able to utilize the capital to the maximum capacity owing to two reasons. One is, through the operation of synergies the amount of capital required for the existing level of production reduces. Secondly, it leads to the excess capacity, if production is undertaken at the same production possibility frontier that is no expansion in production after M&As.[23]

## 5.4 Profitability and cost as efficiency indicators

We have calculated the cost and profitability per unit of output since most of the merger studies in India concentrated on these measures. In order to understand the profit rate, the profit to sales ratio has been used, which indicates the amount of profit per unit of sales. The average for 4 years pre- and post-M&As as well as all years post M&As is calculated. Interestingly, this ratio declined for the majority of years for both cross-border as well as domestic firms (see Table 5.6) except for a few sector-wise variations[24] (see Table 5.7). In order to calculate the cost per unit of output, we have used the ratio Total Cost/Value of Output in the absence of a comparable input quantity across the firms and products.[25] It shows a general trend of increasing cost after getting into M&As (see Table 5.6), which is same across the sectors also (see Table 5.8). It validates the findings regarding profitability too.

This result is in accordance with most of the merger studies in India as well as the international context (see Meeks, 1977; Singh, 1971; Ravenscraft and Scherer, 1989). One major question that arises here is why post-M&As profit declined regardless of the theoretical prediction that consolidation increases profitability through the reduction of various costs. Though this question is beyond the scope of the present paper, it seems, the decline in profitability may be due to the acquisition of loss making or less efficient firm(s); decline in capacity utilization during the post-M&As period due to the lack of proper post-M&As integration of the firms; overall macro-economic determinants and the problems associated with the financing of the deal etc. If the firm borrowed money to finance the acquisition and the interest payments exceed the expected earnings, then, this phenomenon can occur.

*Table 5.6* Pre and post merger mean profit and cost of firms

| Merger Year | Category | Merger | PAT/Sales | Expenses/Value of Output |
| --- | --- | --- | --- | --- |
| 1994 | Domestic | Pre | 0.06 | 0.96 |
| | | Post four | 0.06 | 1.17 |
| | | Post merger | −0.22 | 1.37 |
| | Cross-border | Pre | 0.04 | 0.99 |
| | | Post four | 0.05 | 0.98 |
| | | Post merger | 0.02 | 1.05 |
| 1997 | Domestic | Pre | 2.35 | 16.45 |
| | | Post four | −0.36 | 2.44 |
| | | Post merger | −0.75 | 2.27 |
| | Cross-border | Pre | 0.6 | 13.81 |
| | | Post four | 0.56 | 17.44 |
| | | Post merger | 0.17 | 10.15 |
| 2002 | Domestic | Pre | 0.03 | 1.21 |
| | | Post four | 0.05 | 0.99 |
| | | Post merger | 0.06 | 1.11 |
| | Cross-border | Pre | 0.05 | 0.98 |
| | | Post four | 0.07 | 1.24 |
| | | Post merger | 0.06 | 0.97 |
| 2004 | Domestic | Pre | 0.06 | 0.9 |
| | | Post four | 0.01 | 0.99 |
| | Cross-border | Pre | 0.00 | 1.31 |
| | | Post four | 0.03 | 7.87 |

Source: Calculated from the estimated model.

Table 5.7 Sectoral pre and post merger (four years) profit to sales

| Year of Merger | Category | Merger | Drugs | Chemicals | Machinery | Metals | Non-metallic | Textiles | Food | Transport |
|---|---|---|---|---|---|---|---|---|---|---|
| 1994 | D | Pre | 0.09 | 0.08 | 0.05 | 0.02 | 0.07 | 0.07 | 0.05 | 0.02 |
| | | Post | 0.07 | 0.03 | -0.04 | 0.01 | 0.06 | 0.06 | 0.01 | 0.03 |
| | C | Pre | 0.05 | 0.01 | 0.02 | 0.09 | | 0.05 | | |
| | | Post | 0.05 | 0.07 | 0.00 | 0.04 | | 0.02 | | |
| 1997 | D | Pre | 0.13 | 8.97 | 0.14 | 0.10 | 0.06 | 0.08 | 0.05 | 0.09 |
| | | Post | 0.13 | -0.11 | 0.42 | 0.05 | -0.19 | -3.08 | 0.02 | 0.05 |
| | C | Pre | 0.11 | 0.08 | 0.07 | 3.48 | 0.06 | 0.07 | 0.05 | 0.04 |
| | | Post | 0.00 | -0.02 | 0.08 | 3.54 | 0.02 | 0.01 | 0.04 | 0.03 |
| 2002 | D | Pre | 0.09 | 0.04 | -0.04 | 0.04 | | 0.06 | 0.01 | 0.07 |
| | | Post | -0.02 | 0.06 | 0.10 | 0.05 | | 0.06 | -0.03 | 0.09 |
| | C | Pre | | 0.06 | 0.05 | 0.11 | 0.03 | | 0.00 | -0.05 |
| | | Post | -0.02 | 0.07 | 0.08 | 0.08 | 0.11 | | 0.07 | |
| 2004 | D | Pre | 0.05 | 0.05 | 0.07 | 0.07 | | | | |
| | | Post | | | 0.04 | | | -0.06 | | 0.03 |
| | C | Pre | 0.01 | -0.01 | 0.07 | -0.02 | | | | |
| | | Post | | | 0.05 | | | 0.00 | | 0.03 |

Source: Calculated from the estimated model.

Note: 'D' denotes Domestic and 'C' denotes cross-border deals.

Table 5.8 Sectoral pre and post merger (four years) expenditure per unit of output

| Year of Merger | Category | Merger | Drugs | Chemicals | Machinery | Metals | Non-metallic | Textiles | Food | Transport |
|---|---|---|---|---|---|---|---|---|---|---|
| 1994 | D | Pre | 0.93 | 0.95 | 0.97 | 6.32 | 0.94 | 0.96 | 0.98 | 1.01 |
|  |  | Post | 1.01 | 1.01 | 1.11 | 1.00 | 0.95 | 0.98 | 1.05 | 0.99 |
|  | C | Pre | 0.96 | 1.02 | 1.01 | 0.94 |  | 0.97 |  |  |
|  |  | Post | 0.98 | 0.96 | 1.03 | 0.99 |  | 0.99 |  |  |
| 1997 | D | Pre | 0.94 | 61.65 | 1.61 | 0.81 | 0.66 | 1.13 | 0.96 | 0.92 |
|  |  | Post | 0.91 | 1.13 | 3.27 | 0.82 | 1.07 | 8.48 | 0.99 | 0.95 |
|  | C | Pre | 0.93 | 0.93 | 0.94 | 84.67 | 1.01 | 0.94 | 0.96 | 0.72 |
|  |  | Post | 1.04 | 1.04 | 0.94 | 108.08 | 1.03 | 1.08 | 0.97 | 0.67 |
| 2002 | D | Pre | 1.18 | 0.99 | 2.70 | 0.98 |  | 0.98 | 1.02 | 0.95 |
|  |  | Post | 1.03 | 0.97 | 1.19 | 1.00 |  | 1.49 | 1.05 | 0.93 |
|  | C | Pre |  | 0.96 | 0.99 | 0.90 | 0.98 |  | 1.00 | 1.06 |
|  |  | Post | 1.04 | 0.95 | 1.04 | 0.94 | 0.92 |  | 0.96 |  |
| 2004 | D | Pre | 0.93 | 0.87 | 0.79 | 0.97 |  |  |  | 0.92 |
|  |  | Post |  |  | 0.92 |  |  | 1.19 |  |  |
|  | C | Pre | 0.83 | 1.18 | 3.15 | 1.77 |  |  |  |  |
|  |  | Post |  |  | 12.60 |  |  | 11.11 |  | 1.19 |

Source: Calculated from the estimated model.

Note: 'D' denotes Domestic and 'C' denotes cross-border deals.

## 5.5 Concluding observations and policy implication

One important consideration while approving M&As by the competition authorities across the world is efficiency defense that is the possible generation of efficiencies. However, there has been a dearth of literature empirically verifying the actual generation of efficiencies through consolidation strategies. The study addressed the question, whether M&As were actually generating efficiency as debated by the economists. The logic being that M&As leads to cost reduction due to the operation of synergies. The study used stochastic frontier production function along with inefficiency effects introduced by Battese and Coelli (1995). The major observation from this analysis has been that the post-merger technical efficiency of the firms involved in M&As declined for the majority of the firms and M&As has not significantly contributed to reducing the inefficiencies except for 1994 deals. The sector-wise analysis also supports the aggregate level findings. Further, in general, there is a clear decline in profitability during the post-merger period, which is also applicable to both cross-border and domestic deals. This result is in line with the earlier studies on the post-merger profitability of the firms both in the Indian and international context, which may be due to the increasing cost of M&As or due to the acquisition of loss making counterpart, lack of proper integration of the firms during post-merger period or it may be reflecting the increased interest payments after undertaking huge investment for M&As.

In short, the study argues for rethinking the efficiency defence argument put forward by the competition authorities while approving the combinations. Presently, there is no provision in the Indian Competition Act to examine, whether the approved deal is actually bringing efficiencies, technical know-how and ultimately the consumer satisfaction, since the merger control provisions are *ex ante* in nature. This is especially important for the deals, which are sanctioned based on efficiency criteria. It is to be noted that so far, almost all deals sanctioned by the Competition Commission of India (CCI) are based on the likely impact of the deal on market competition only. The efficiency criteria have not been given much importance while assessing the effect of the deal. However, in future, the Commission may have to look into the efficiency effects as well. Though the deals examined in the study pertains to the old regime, i.e., Monopolies and Restrictive Trade Practices Act,[26] it is an indication of the impact of efficiency effects in general. The merger regulations in India as per Competition Act, 2002, became effective since June 2011 only, which makes the number of post-M&A years too less to carry out any meaningful efficiency analysis. However, it seems there should be periodic review of the approved deals that, it is generating efficiency, or not or raising a threat to competition, as the case may be, at least for the past 3 to 5 years from the approval of the deal. Otherwise, the 'competition enhancement' strategy adopted by the Government will, in turn, lead to enhance market power of the firms.

## Notes

1  For instance, Rowley and Peacock (1975) emphasised, mergers are certainly against the conditions of perfect competition in which the *laissez-faire* ideals would be best fulfilled (as in Meeks, 1977).
2  Lord Robbins says that "...my feeling about policy relating to mergers and takeovers is that there is a certain presumption against preventing people from buying or selling such property as seems them to be desirable" (as in Meeks, 1977).
3  Agency issues arising out of consolidation has been raised in the literature, which we are not taking up here since it is beyond the scope of the present study.
4  Surviving firms are the firms exist in the market after consolidation.
5  For e.g. Beena, 2004, 2008, 2014 etc. Overall productivity and efficiency of the Indian manufacturing sector have been widely debated. See for example, Brahmananda (1982), Goldar (1986), Ahluwalia (1991), Balakrishnan (2004), Balakrishnan and K Pushpangadan (1995, 1996, 1998), Balakrishnan, K. Pushpangadan and Suresh Babu (2002), Rao, J.M. (1996), Pradhan and Barik (1998), Trivedi, Prakash and Sinate (2000), Unel, B. (2003) etc., for related debates.
6  Technical efficiency (TE) is defined as the ability of the firms to get the maximum or potential level of output, given the inputs.
7  Whereas, allocative efficiency (AE) is the ability of the firm to equate its marginal value product to its marginal cost.
8  Unlike some other specifications, it is not based on the assumptions of constant elasticity of substitution, Hicks-neutral technical progress and constant returns to scale (Parameswaran, 2002).
9  Output includes the firm level sales and changes in the stock of finished and unfinished goods. Sectorwise Wholesale Price Index (WPI) is used for deflation.
10  ASI provides man-days worked, and total emoluments paid. Following the Srivastava (1996) methodology, we have calculated emoluments paid per labour hour (man-hours are man-days multiplied by 8 hours).
11  We have taken the above mentioned average wages from ASI to apply with the amount of compensation paid as in PROWESS and calculated the labour hours worked.
12  We have used 1993–1994 base year.
13  This is based on coal mining, mineral oils and electricity (GOI, Various years).
14  Implicit deflator is calculated using the ratio of GDP at current and constant prices. The weights are based on the flows from service to the manufacturing sector. Base year of GDP used is 1999–2000.
15  The term 'deal' is used to denote M&As in this paper.
16  The distributional assumptions on the inefficiency effects permit the effect of technological change and time varying behaviour of the inefficiency effects to be identified, in addition to the intercept parameters $\beta_0$ and $\delta_0$ (Battese and Coelli, 1995).
17  Logic being the number of mergers, data availability and the distance between the years selected.
18  This, in turn, means that if we are taking the deal number instead of the surviving firms' number, the coverage of the sample is more.
19  This is mainly due to the data availability across various sectors also.
20  Pre- and post-merger is defined in terms of the year of the first merger. Pre-merger constitute 1988–1989 to the year of merger and post-merger period constitutes the year thereafter.
21  Pre- and post-four-year average have been taken (see Saraswathy, B., 2009).

22 The elasticity in translog production function is defined below.

$$\frac{\delta \mathrm{Ln}Q}{\delta \mathrm{Ln}K} = \beta_k + \beta_{kk}\mathrm{Ln}K + \beta_{kl}\mathrm{Ln}L + \beta_{km}\mathrm{Ln}M + \beta_{kt}\mathrm{Ln}T$$

$$\frac{\delta \mathrm{Ln}Q}{\delta \mathrm{Ln}L} = \beta_L + \beta_{lk}\mathrm{Ln}K + \beta_{ll}\mathrm{Ln}L + \beta_{lm}\mathrm{Ln}M + \beta_{lt}\mathrm{Ln}T$$

$$\frac{\delta \mathrm{Ln}Q}{\delta \mathrm{Ln}M} = \beta_m + \beta_{mk}\mathrm{Ln}K + \beta_{ml}\mathrm{Ln}L + \beta_{mm}\mathrm{Ln}M + \beta_{mt}\mathrm{Ln}T$$

23 A disaggregation across the industries would have provided more insights especially in the context of the technological intensity of the sectors. However, since here the co-efficient is the same for the entire group of firms, it is not possible to do it sector wise.

24 For example, in the case of machinery, the profitability increased for mergers occurred in some years. Similarly, the profitability of pharmaceutical industry either remained the same or declined.

25 The majority of the firms are multi-product firms, difficult to capture the unit cost of production.

26 We have not analysed the CCI sanctioned deals since it is too early to assess it since the number of post-merger years are too few to carry out meaningful efficiency analysis.

# References

Ahluwalia, I.J. (1991). *Productivity and Growth in Indian Manufacturing.* New Delhi: Oxford University Press.

Balakrishnan, P. (2004). Measuring Productivity in Manufacturing Sector. *Economic and Political Weekly,* 39(14–15), pp. 1465–1471.

Balakrishnan, P. and Pushpangadan, K. (1994). Total Factor Productivity Growth in Indian Industry: A Fresh Look. *Economic and Political Weekly,* 29(31), pp. 2028–2035.

Balakrishnan, P. and Pushpangadan, K. (1995). Total Factor Productivity Growth in Manufacturing Industry. *Economic and Political Weekly,* 30(9), pp. 462–464.

Balakrishnan, P. and Pushpangadan, K. (1996). TFPG in Manufacturing Industry. *Economic and Political Weekly,* 31(7), pp. 425–428.

Balakrishnan, P. and Pushpangadan, K. (1998). What Do We Know about Productivity Growth in Indian Industry? *Economic and Political Weekly,* 33(33–34), pp. 2241–2246.

Balakrishnan, P., Pushpangadan, K. and Suresh, B. (2002). *Trade Liberalization, Market Power and Scale Efficiency in Indian Industry.* Working Paper No. 336. Thiruvananthapuram: Centre for Development Studies.

Battese, G.E. and Coelli, T.J. (1995). A Model for Technical Inefficiency Effects in a Stochastic Frontier Production Function for Panel Data. *Empirical Economics,* 20, pp. 325–332.

Beena, P.L. (2004). *Towards Understanding the Merger Wave in the Indian Corporate Sector: A Comparative Perspective.* Working Paper No. 355. Thiruvananthapuram: Centre for Development Studies.

Beena, P.L. (2008). Trends and Perspectives on Corporate Mergers in Contemporary India. *Economic and Political Weekly,* 43(39), pp. 48–56.

Beena, P.L. (2014). *Mergers and Acquisitions: India under Globalisation*. New Delhi: Routledge.

Brahmananda, P R., (1982). Productivity in the Indian Economy: Rising Inputs for Falling Outputs, Mumbai: Himalaya Publishing House.

Coelli, P.R., Donnel, C.J. and Battese, G.E. (2005). *An Introduction to Efficiency and Productivity Analysis*. USA: Springer.

Farrell, M.J., (1957). The Measurement of Productive Efficiency. Journal of the Royal Statistical Society, 120, pp. 253–281.

Goldar, B. (1986). *Productivity Growth in Indian Industry*. New Delhi: Allied Publishers.

Goldar, B. (2004). Indian Manufacturing: Productivity Trends in the Pre and Post Reform Periods. *Economic and Political Weekly*, 35(42), pp. 5033–5043.

Greene (2011). *Econometric Analysis*. New Jersey: Prentice Hall International.

Government of India (1989). *National Accounts Statistics: Sources and Methods*. New Delhi: Central Statistical Organisation.

Government of India (2008). *Input-Output Transaction Table (Ministry of Statistics and Programme Implementation)*. New Delhi: Central Statistical Organisation.

Government of India, National Accounts Statistics. New Delhi: Central Statistical Organisation. Ministry of Statistics and Programme Implementation, Various Years.

Government of India, Office of the Economic Advisor. New Delhi: Ministry of Commerce and Industry, Various Years.

Hashim, S.R. and Dadi, M.M. (1973). *Capital-Output Relations in Indian Manufacturing (1946–1964)*. The Maharaja Sayajirao University Economics, Series No. 2, Baroda, India.

Hindley, B., 1970. Industrial Merger and Public Policy.: Institute of Economic Affairs Hobart Papers. 50. London.

Kalirajan, K.P. and Shand, R.T. (1994). *Economics in Disequilibrium: An Approach from the Frontier*. New Delhi: Macmillan.

Meeks, G. (1977). *Disappointing Marriage: A Study of the Gains from Merger*. Cambridge: Cambridge University Press.

muenchen.de/7816/1/MPRA_paper_7816.pdf [Accessed on 8th October 2008].

Parameswaran, M. (2002). *Economic Reforms and Technical Efficiency: Firm Level Evidence from Selected Industries in India*. Working Paper No. 339. Thiruvananthapuram: Centre for Development Studies.

Pesendorfer, M. (2003). Horizontal Mergers in the Paper Industry. *The RAND Journal of Economics*, 34(3), pp. 495–515.

Pillai, P.M. and Sreenivasan, J. (1987). Age and Productivity of Machine Tools in India. *Economic and Political Weekly*, 22(35), pp. M95–M100Pradhan, G. and Barik, K. (1998). Fluctuating Total Factor Productivity in India: Evidence from Selected Polluting Industries. *Economic and Political Weekly*, 33(9), pp. M25–M30.

Ravenscraft, D.J. and Scherer, F.M. (1989). The Profitability of Mergers. *International Journal of Industrial Organisation*, 7(1), pp. 101–116.

Rao, J.M., (1996). Manufacturing Productivity Growth: Method and Measurement. Economic and Political Weekly, 31(44), pp. 2927–2936.

Rowley, C. K. and Peacock, A. T., (1975). Welfare Economics. A liberal Restatement. Oxford: Martin Robertson.

Schiffbauer, M., Iulia, S. and Frances, R. (2009). *Do Foreign Mergers and Acquisitions Boost Productivity*. Working Paper No. 305. Dublin: Economic and Social Research Institute.

Singh, A. (1971). *Takeovers: Their Relevance to the Stock Market and the Theory of the Firm*. Cambridge: Cambridge University Press.

Srivastava, V. (1996). *Liberalization, Productivity and Competition: A Panel Study on Indian Manufacturing.* New Delhi: Oxford University Press.

Trivedi, P., A. Prakash and D. Sinate (2000), Productivity in Major Manufacturing Industries in India: 1973–74 to 1997–98, Study No. 20, DRG, RBI, August.

Unel, B. (2003). *Productivity Trends in India's Manufacturing Sectors in the Last Two Decades.* Working Paper No. 22. Asia and Pacific Department, Washington, DC: IMF.

Williamson, O.E. (1968). Economies as an Antitrust Defense: The Welfare Tradeoffs. *The American Economic Review,* 58(1), pp. 18–36.

# Appendix 1

# Measurement of capital stock

Finding out the Replacement Cost of Capital is one of the major steps involved in efficiency estimation (see Parameswaran, 2002 for a detailed discussion). Replacement Cost of Capital is defined as the Revaluation factor ($R^G$) multiplied with the Value of Capital Stock at Historical Cost. Replacement Cost of Capital measurement is discussed here. It is important to note that this method is an approximation. Since no other better measure is available, we are also using it for the other studies in this context. $R^G$ is defined as,[1]

$$R^G = \frac{\left[(1+g)(1+\Pi) - 1\right]}{g(1+\Pi)} \tag{5.4}$$

Where 'g' is the growth rate of investment and $\Pi$ is the change in the price of capital. Growth rate of Investment can be obtained by using the formula, $g = I_t/I_{t-1} - 1$. Here our assumption is that Investment (I) has increased for all the firms. Change in the price is measured through, $\Pi = P_t/P_{t-1} - 1$. Here $P_t$ is obtained by constructing capital formation price indices[2] from the series for Gross Fixed Capital Formation in Manufacturing using various issues of National Accounts Statistics of India. Here more realistically, our assumption is that capital stock does not date back infinitely, but its earliest vintage is '$t$' period, then the above equation becomes,

$$R^G = \frac{\left[(1+g)^{t+1} - 1\right](1+\Pi)^t \left[(1+g)(1+\Pi) - 1\right]}{g\left\{\left[(1+g)(1+\Pi)\right]^{t+1} - 1\right\}}. \tag{5.5}$$

We have assumed that the lifespan of capital stock is 20 years following the Report of Machine Tools-1986 (Government of India, 1989; Pillai, M. and Srinivasan, 1987). We have selected 1999–2000 as the base year.[3] So following Srivastava, no firm has any capital stock in the year 1999–2000 of a vintage earlier than 1979–1980. In the case of firms incorporated before 1979–1980, it is assumed that the earliest vintage capital in their capital mix dates back to the year of incorporation. As Srivastava notes, for some firms the vintage of the oldest capital in the firm's asset mix and incorporation year may not coincide. Since no other better alternative is available, we are also following this methodology. After getting the Revaluation factor ($R^G$). As we mentioned earlier, we calculated the Replacement Cost of Capital from the Revaluation factor ($R^G$) and the Value of Capital Stock at historical cost. We have used Gross Fixed Assets[4] of the firms for the estimation. This enabled us to apply the Perpetual Inventory Method to construct the capital stock. This is defined as,

$$k_{t+1} = k_t + I_{t+1}$$
$$k_t = k_{t-1} + I_t$$
$$k_{t-2} = k_t - I_t - I_{t-1} \text{ and so on.}$$

## Notes

1 See Srivastava (2001), Balakrishnan, Pushpangadan and Suresh Babu, (2002) Parameswaran (2002) for details.
2 Price is equal to Gross Fixed Capital Formation at Current prices divided with the same at constant prices.
3 Based on the data available from the PROWESS database, this year is having the largest number of M&As.
4 Deflated by the Wholesale Price Index for machinery and machine tools (Source: Office of the Economic Advisor, Ministry of Commerce & Industry, GOI, Various Years) with the base year 1999–2000.

# Appendix 2

Testing of hypothesis in the Battese and Coelli model of Stochastic Frontier

| Hypothesis (H₀) | 1994 | 1997 | 2002 | 2004 | Critical value* |
|---|---|---|---|---|---|
| Cobb-Douglass production function $\delta_1 = \delta_2 = ... = \delta_{10} = 0$ | 888.29 109.72 | 1460 65.79 | 698.9 60.73 | 470.5 26.88 | 21.03 16.274 |
| $\delta_5 = \delta_6 = 0$ | 24.94 | 14.16 | 41.32 | 11.35 | 5.99 |
| $\gamma = \delta_1 = \delta_2 = ... = \delta_{10} = 0$ | 53.96 | 121.13 | 99.94 | 60.53 | 17.67** |
| LLF1 | −202.80 | −313.98 | −116.82 | −19.67 | |
| No of firms | 38 | 63 | 37 | 18 | |
| Total no of observations in the unbalanced panel | 587 | 773 | 468 | 229 | |

Source: Calculated from PROWESS, CMIE

Notes: *Critical value corresponds to the 95th percentile for the corresponding chi-square distribution. **Critical value is taken from Kodde, David A and Franz C. Palm (1986).

The first assumption is regarding the production function. Our hypothesis is that the production function is of Cobb-Douglass form, given the translog production function. As it can be seen from the table, the generalized likelihood ratio-tests (LR statistic)[1] reject this hypothesis, which indicates that the input elasticity and substitution relationships are not constant across the firms. Thus, the translog form better suits the data. The next hypothesis that the inefficiency effects are not a linear function of the explanatory variables specified in the model is also rejected, which implies that the joint effect of these variables on the inefficiency of production is significant even if the individual effect of one or more of variables may not be statistically not significant. From the table, it can be further seen that the assumption of no time effect is also rejected. The next hypothesis that inefficiency effects are absent from the model is also strongly rejected, which indicates that the production function is not same as the traditional average response function which can be estimated efficiently by ordinary least square method. The value of variance parameter, $\gamma$ is close to one in all the years except 2004, which indicates that inefficiency effects are likely to be highly significant in the analysis of production except for 2004 deals.

## Note

1  LR statistic $\lambda = -2\{\log[\text{Likelihood}(H_0)] - \log[\text{Likehihood}(H_1)]\}$. It has a chi-square distribution (or a mixed chi-square distribution) with degrees of freedom equal to the difference between the parameters in the alternative and null hypothesis.

# 6 Mergers, competition and concentration

In this chapter, our attempt is to understand the role of mergers in changing the market competition of different industries since mergers are expected to reduce the actual number of firms in the industry, which, in turn, is likely to allow the merged entity to strengthen and derive benefits from increased market power. This study consists of four sections. After introducing the relationship between mergers and competition, the second section deals with important studies undertaken and the methodological issues, while the third section summarises the major findings from the analysis. This is followed by concluding observations in the final section.

## 6.1 The relationship between mergers and competition

The adverse effect of mergers on consumer welfare arises on two grounds. First is due to the *unilateral effects* and the second is through the *coordinated* or *pro-collusion effects*. In the first case, the merger will allow the firms to unilaterally increase their prices, which reduces consumer surplus and increases producer surplus. Here, there is a divergence of views among economists. Those who consider "price" as the decision-making variable argue that it will increase the price of insiders as well as outsiders. And those who favour "quantity" as the decision-making variable argue that the insiders' production will decline while that of the outsiders will increase. However, both will reduce consumer welfare since the net increase in outsiders' output will be lower than the reduction in insiders' output. The coordinated effects imply that mergers create favourable conditions for collusion. Collusive outcomes, which might not have been possible during the pre-merger period, become possible during the post-merger period mainly due to a reduction in the number of firms (Motta, 2004). In this context, Stigler's (1950) diagrammatic explanation brings out the impact of mergers on competition.

### 6.1.1 Monopoly and oligopoly formation and merger

Stigler (1950) discussed the existence, of monopoly and oligopoly, when a merger occurs. Stigler's model is based on four assumptions: (1) the long-run average and marginal cost of production are equal for all firms; (2) entry of new firms is free, though not necessarily inexpensive; (3) demand for output of the industry is stable, and (4) the specialised resources employed in the industry are indestructible (fixed factors). Under these conditions, is it possible for mergers to create monopoly power; this is the central question that Stigler attempted to answer. Let us consider his major argument.

Consider an industry which satisfies all the assumptions mentioned above and consists of numerous identical firms which are in the long-run competitive equilibrium. Each firm will have a short run cost curve. Initially, the firm is in equilibrium, where MC equals MR. At this level, the firm is not making any economic profit.[1] If all firms are merged into a monopoly at this point, the AR and MR curves will become "downward sloping".[2] Each firm will have a pro rata share of AR, with corresponding marginal revenue, MR. Accordingly, the total amount of output supplied will decline compared to the initial condition. However, attracted by the lucrative profits earned by the industry, new firms will enter the market, prices will fall, and profit will decline. Eventually, the number of firms will grow until the merger is reduced to the long-run equilibrium since neither the merger nor the new rivals can withdraw from the industry. If the entry is not too rapid, then the merger may make monopoly profit for a considerable period, and even though the losses are permanent after that, their discounted value need not be so large as to wipe out the initial gains. Therefore, the time required for long-run equilibrium is important. Moreover, if we relax the assumption, it is also possible that the merged firms can create entry barriers, which reduces the entry and keep the monopoly profits to the long run. Thus, Stigler says, in the long run, the monopoly profits may be positive since it outweighs the losses.

From the foregoing discussion, the following effects are likely to be generated: (1) increased prices and profitability, and (2) reduced output. Further, mergers may reduce the number of firms in the long run, which, in turn, is likely to increase the market share of the surviving firms. However, this is an empirical issue, which needs to be examined. Thus, on the basis of the above predictions, our study intends to examine the disappearance of firms through mergers and its consequent influence on the market power of firms. Before discussing the empirical estimation, we shall review the major contributions made to the merger-concentration studies and the measures used by them.

## 6.2  A review of relevant studies

### 6.2.1  Studies on the direction of relationship

It is important to note that different schools of thought emerged on the possible effect of competition on market structure; this has a bearing on the discussion on the relationship between merger and competition. First is the Structure, Conduct and Performance (SCP) paradigm developed by the traditional Harvard School in the 1950s (Structuralistic view). It says that structural remedies are of great importance as their central message is that *structure influences conduct and conduct, in turn, affects performance.* They emphasised that Competition Law (CL) has an important 'interventionist' role in curbing the market power and believed less in the market mechanism. In contrast, in the 1970s and 1980s, the Chicago school revolutionised the anti-trust thinking—that there is no need to worry much about market concentration since the market is a remedy for curbing market power. They pointed out that government intervention is usually *inefficient.* Accordingly, CL should not be too "interventionist" as emphasised by the Harvard school (Dhall, 2007). The second relates to the Chicago school, which argued that mergers should be allowed—even if it reduces consumer surplus in the short run—as the overall welfare will be higher. Defenders of this view argued that many consumers are also shareholders of the firm and therefore are anxious about the profitability of the firms in which they are investing. Demsetz (1973) pointed out that large firms with their superior efficiency may own more market share and earn higher profits. Hence, a high correlation between profit and market concentration may not be a true indicator as increased market power may be the outcome of higher efficiency generation. Thus, concentration should not be treated as bad, and mergers should be allowed. The post-Chicago school argued that consumer benefits and efficiency should be the criteria. Farrel and Shapiro (1990) argued that instead of calculating the overall effects, it is better to measure the net external welfare, that is, the joint welfare of consumers and non-participating firms (Glais, 2000). The studies dealing with mergers and concentration were positioned mainly in the context of the initial merger waves that occurred in the USA and the UK. There have been five such waves in the USA and four in the UK.[3] Most of the early literature on mergers focused on the first three and two waves that occurred in the USA and the UK respectively. It is estimated that around 1800 firms disappeared and approximately 71 formerly competitive industries converted into virtual monopolies during the first merger wave of USA. Around 12000 firms disappeared during the second wave. In this context, there is a vast literature which has studied the implication of mergers on market concentration. This includes Weston (1953), Federal Trade Commission Report (1948), Cook (1954), Nutter (1954), Stigler (1956) and so on. We shall discuss some of these in the following paragraphs.

Weiss (1965), in his case study of 6 industries for the period 1920–1958, found that a merger is an important tool in determining market concentration when more majors[4] are considered. At 4 or 20 firm level, mergers are more likely to represent "rationalisation" and less likely to create a monopoly. It seems certain that beginning from the 1920s, most mergers in these industries can at the least be defended as harmless and socially desirable as only sub-optimal plants were subjected to mergers. Taking a sample of 1956–1957 mergers, Ijiri and Simon (1971) observed that M&As do not greatly affect the Pareto curve slope.[5] According to their study, the overall growth of a firm encompasses both internal growth (that is due to M&As[6]) and external growth (due to growth outside the firm). At the sectoral level, Desvousges and Piette (1979) studied the impact of mergers in the context of the changing concentration levels of petroleum sector during 1955–1975. It found that concentration is more likely to increase at eight-or twenty-firm levels and the role of mergers increases as more leaders are included. For example, out of the total change of concentration 2.2, the contribution of the merger was 1 for the period 1955–1960 for four major firms. Similarly, for the period 1960–1965, the contribution of the merger was 0.3 out of the total change of 3.5. When we consider 20 major firms, the contribution of merger becomes 2.5 and 4.9[7] of the total change of 3.1 and 4.8 percent respectively for the two time periods. This result is almost similar to that of Weiss's (1965) study.

The UK merger waves lack a long history like the US. There were four merger waves in the UK; most of the studies concentrated on the first and second waves. Hart and Prais (1956) pointed out that there was an increase in concentration in the quoted segment of manufacturing and mining sectors during 1885–1939, which declined during war time but again increased between 1950 and 1955 (Hart, 1957, 1960). However, the classic article by Hart and Prais (1956) reached the conclusion that the impact of mergers on concentration is not significant. This generated a debate with Hannah and Kay (1977). They found that mergers play an important role in changing the levels of concentration. The findings of this study are similar to that of Aaronovitch and Sawyer (1975), which pointed out that about one-fourth to one-third of the growth is acquisitions. Large firms recorded better survival prospects compared to small firms, and M&As have a substantial role in increasing concentration. The growth of firms is not systematically related to the initial size distribution. Thus, this study is in line with the argument made by Ijiri and Simon (1971). However, another study by Utton (1971) says that concentration has increased in industries, largely due to the tendency of the large firms to grow at a faster pace than the small firms.[8] An important part of the change in the concentration is due to mergers.

In the case of Germany, the first systematic analysis of the relationship between mergers and concentration is credited to Müeller (1976) for the period 1858–1971. This study decomposed the changes in concentration into five elements—internal growth, displacement, mergers, exit, and entry. This framework has been used by Weiss (1965), Desvousges and Piette (1979), and others. The study found that merger is a dominant factor in changing the 4 firm concentration ratio while at the eight-firm level, both internal growth and mergers are important. However, sector wise there are small variations. A summary of the other studies is given in Table 6.1.

From the studies cited above, we can infer that there is wide variation in the findings of different studies owing to differences in the samples, techniques used, time period and the underlying motives of the merger. It points

*Table 6.1* Selected studies on mergers and concentration

| Study | Period | Country | Findings |
|---|---|---|---|
| *Case study approach* | | | |
| Moody (1904) | 1887–1904 | USA | Substantial increase in market control. |
| Livermore (1935) | 1887–1904 | USA | Used Moody's list of deals. Found that half of the deals formed during the first merger movement were failures and many of them obtained no significant increase in market power. |
| Evely and Little (1960) | 1951 | UK | In most of the cases, mergers have been responsible for high market concentration in different sectors. |
| Hart, Utton, Walshe (1973) | 1958–1963 | UK | Impact varies; internal and external effects have equal impact on concentration. |
| Hart and Clark (1980) | 1958–1968 | UK | Half the increase in average product concentration is due to mergers. |
| Walshe (1974) | 1958 | UK | Only in 11 out of the 32-products concentration increased due to mergers. It is an important weapon to prevent subsequent erosion of market power. |
| *Correlation based analysis between Merger and Concentration* | | | |
| George (1972, 1975) | 1958–1968 | UK | Those sectors which experienced the sharpest increase in concentration also tended to display a big reduction in the number of firms which is mainly due to mergers. The second article found that merger predominant sectors experienced a larger degree of concentration. |
| *Size distribution, internal growth etc.* | | | |
| Hart and Clark (1980) | 1935–1975 | UK | Even though the merger variable is significant, its contribution in changing overall concentration is low. |
| Hart and Prais (1956) | 1896–1950 | UK | Used variance of log size. Only a small proportion of the increase in concentration is due to mergers. |
| Utton (1971) | 1954–1975 | UK | Used variance of log size. Merger is a dominant factor leading to concentration in several industrial groups. |
| Hannah and Kay (1977) | 1919–1973 | UK | Separated into four time periods and found that merger is mainly responsible for increasing concentration. |

Source: Compiled from Curry and George (1983) and other studies.

to the need for studying the events not only at the aggregate level but also separately in the context of industry specific deals. However, from these studies, it is clear that merger is an important factor in determining the structure of different sectors of the manufacturing industry in different countries at different time periods. Moreover, in the Indian case, we have seen that the occurrence of the merger to a notable extent is only a recent phenomenon, more specifically of the 1990s (see Beena, S., 2010). Thus, our initial phase of the merger is comparable to the fourth and fifth merger waves of UK and USA. Consequently, the literature on mergers is also a recent one. Existing studies have not dealt with this issue in detail. Here, our attempt is to understand the impact of mergers on the structure of the Indian manufacturing sector since the 1990s in light of the available information. Next, we shall discuss the standard measures of market competition, which are important in the context of increasing mergers.

### 6.2.2 Measurement of competition

When we talk about merger analysis, a relevant question is how to measure the possible effects of mergers on competition. Measurement of competition itself has been one of the seriously contested topics in the industrial organization literature. The competition can be viewed as either static or dynamic. Static competition is a traditional way of looking at the competition, whereas dynamic competition refers it as a process. According to Bladwin, J. and Gorecki (1998), at the conceptual level, these two approaches may not disagree as to what constitutes highly competitive markets; rather they differ on practical measurement. Baldwin, J. and Gorecki (1998) and Curry and George (1983) clearly bring out the debate centred on measurement issues.[9] The notable measures of competition have been the K-firm Concentration Ratio, Hirschman-Herfindahl Index, Variance of Logarithms of Firm Size, Price-Cost Margin (PCM) and Relative Profit Difference (RPD). The first four are the most popular, while the last one is of recent origin. However, there is still a lack of consensus among scholars on the best measure of concentration. Realizing the fact that all concentration measures suffer from some inadequacy, attempts were made to set forth the necessary properties of a concentration measure (see Hall and Tideman, 1967; Hannah and Kay, 1977). The fourth axiom of Hannah and Kay argues that *mergers should increase concentration*. However, there is disagreement among economists regarding this axiom, which is discussed in the literature section in detail. Hart (1979) and Ijiri and Simon (1971) argued that it may not be necessary under all circumstances. According to Stigler (1950) and Hart (1954), a merger between an intermediate size firm may lead to increased competition for the larger existing firm because it will lead to the formation of more cohesive oligopoly group and thus more effective collusive behaviour. Thus, the outcome may be determined by a number of other factors such as actual number of firms in the industry and the size distribution of firms following mergers (Curry and George, 1983). In addition, the implication of cross-border deals on market structure is also missing in the literature. Curry and George, rightly pointed out that "[n]o concentration measure will succeed in capturing every conceivable aspect of business behaviour. The best that can be done is to devise sensible measures of concentration and exercise caution in using them… Given that no concentration measure can be expected to reflect every aspect of firm's behaviour, some exceptions and anomalies have to be tolerated."

## 6.3 Data and methodology

From the preceding discussion, it is clear that measurement issues are complex. We have two sets of firms—the *targets* or *disappeared firms*, which lose their identity after mergers as well as the *bidders* or *surviving firms*, which continue to exist after mergers. Both sets of firms are important in the merger analysis. The disappeared firms are important in determining the market structure since the "disappearance" from a particular sector may lead to changes in the existing structure of that particular industry. The surviving firms, being the receivers of the disappeared firms, are expected to contribute to the increase in market shares owing to the absorption of disappeared firms into them (invisibility). In our analysis, we have focused on the disappearance rate, survival probability and the effect of invisibility on the dominance of leaders. Being aware of all limitations, we have used the largest four (C-4) and ten firms' (C-10) market shares[10] to understand the market power of the *disappeared* firms. We have selected these ratios considering the data availability as well as the applicability of these indicators in the context of mergers. For *surviving* firms, we have used two static statistical measures: market shares and ranking. We have followed the two-digit level of Standard Industrial Classification (SIC) 2004 since the number of mergers turns out to be quite low if the analysis is undertaken at the product level. However, this is feasible in some industries even at the four-digit level due to the high intensity of deals. We have taken drugs and pharmaceuticals sector separately (at four-digit level) since a relatively large number of deals have been struck in this sector.[11] Nevertheless, understanding the fact that the two-digit level analysis is not good for market concentration analysis, we have also carried out product level analysis for important sectors at a later stage. Market shares are calculated based on sales figures. The major problem with using this method is that it is not adjusted for direct imports. Data on imports given by PROWESS, CMIE relates to raw materials and other such goods and services purchased by firms, which is different from the final goods import. Hence, even if we aggregate the imports at the sectoral level, this data will not serve our purpose. Since we do not have information on this, it remains as a limitation imposed by lack of data. Therefore, we have limited the analysis to mergers alone. The data will also capture the effect of the entry of new firms.

*The Data:* The period of analysis for our study is 1988–1989 to 2008–2009. This is in accordance with the firm level data available from PROWESS, CMIE for a longer time period.[12] We understand that the PROWESS database is not a completely reliable source for understanding the true market structure. However, like other studies, we, too, depend on this source owing to the non-availability of superior firm level data sources. We have not used the Size and Market Shares (published by CMIE) since we are dealing with additional firm level aspects for a longer time period, for which it is not a reliable source. Further, it covers only a selected number of top firms from each sector. The data is unbalanced panel as the disappearance through consolidation is against the balanced panel form of data.

## 6.4 The results: disappearance, survival and invisibility

### 6.4.1 Old and new leading firms

To start the analysis, we provide a general picture of the overall behaviour in the concentration ratios for the manufacturing sector. This is only the beginning. A detailed analysis of disappearance and survival will follow in the subsequent sections. We have examined the four-and ten-firm concentration ratios for various sectors in 1988–1989 and 2008–2009. While there was not much consolidation activity during 1988–1989, 2008–2009 witnessed a large number of deals. It can be seen in Figure 6.1 that, broadly, there has been a decline in the concentration ratios (C4 and C10) in the recent years compared to 1988–1989, except for chemicals. A slightly increasing trend in four-firm concentration ratio is also visible in the case of food products (see Figure 6.1). This context raises confusion about what is happening to the shares of the old leading firms. Will the older tigers be able to continue

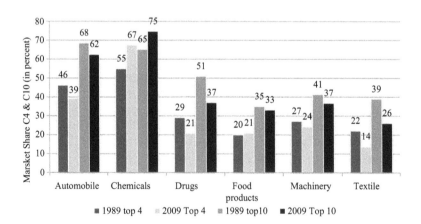

*Figure 6.1* Market share: 1989 and 2009.
Source: Calculated from PROWESS, CMIE.

Table 6.2 Disappearance rate of merged firms (1988–1989 to 2008–2009)

| Year | Automobiles | Chemicals | Drugs & Pharmaceutical | Food | Footwear | Machinery | Metals | Non-metallic | Paper | Petroleum | Rubber Plastic | Textiles | Wood & Products | Total |
|---|---|---|---|---|---|---|---|---|---|---|---|---|---|---|
| 1989 | 3.1 | 5.0 | 8.1 | 5.1 | 0.0 | 3.8 | 3.0 | 5.9 | 8.3 | 5.9 | 6.6 | 1.2 | 6.3 | 4.3 |
| 1990 | 1.9 | 0.8 | 0.0 | 1.1 | 0.0 | 1.7 | 0.5 | 2.2 | 0.0 | 0.0 | 0.0 | 0.0 | 0.0 | 0.9 |
| 1991 | 0.0 | 0.6 | 0.0 | 0.0 | 0.0 | 0.3 | 0.4 | 0.0 | 1.3 | 0.0 | 1.0 | 0.0 | 0.0 | 0.3 |
| 1992 | 0.0 | 0.6 | 1.6 | 1.1 | 0.0 | 2.0 | 0.0 | 0.0 | 0.0 | 0.0 | 1.9 | 1.0 | 0.0 | 0.9 |
| 1993 | 0.6 | 0.5 | 0.6 | 2.6 | 0.0 | 0.2 | 0.0 | 0.0 | 0.0 | 0.0 | 0.0 | 0.3 | 0.0 | 0.5 |
| 1994 | 0.5 | 1.1 | 0.5 | 1.5 | 2.3 | 1.5 | 0.7 | 1.1 | 0.0 | 0.0 | 1.0 | 0.4 | 0.0 | 1.0 |
| 1995 | 0.0 | 0.8 | 1.4 | 0.0 | 0.0 | 1.2 | 1.0 | 0.5 | 0.0 | 0.0 | 0.0 | 0.5 | 0.0 | 0.6 |
| 1996 | 1.4 | 0.2 | 1.4 | 0.9 | 0.0 | 0.9 | 1.2 | 0.5 | 0.0 | 2.0 | 0.0 | 0.2 | 0.0 | 0.7 |
| 1997 | 0.9 | 0.5 | 1.2 | 1.0 | 0.0 | 0.7 | 1.3 | 1.1 | 0.0 | 0.0 | 0.0 | 0.8 | 0.0 | 0.7 |
| 1998 | 0.4 | 0.9 | 0.7 | 1.3 | 0.0 | 0.3 | 0.4 | 0.6 | 0.0 | 0.0 | 0.4 | 0.8 | 0.0 | 0.6 |
| 1999 | 0.0 | 0.8 | 0.7 | 1.4 | 1.9 | 0.8 | 1.0 | 0.5 | 0.0 | 2.0 | 1.1 | 0.4 | 0.0 | 0.8 |
| 2000 | 0.9 | 0.9 | 2.7 | 2.0 | 0.0 | 0.7 | 0.3 | 0.5 | 0.5 | 0.0 | 0.4 | 0.5 | 0.0 | 0.9 |
| 2001 | 0.6 | 0.9 | 2.0 | 2.2 | 0.0 | 0.7 | 0.5 | 1.0 | 2.1 | 7.3 | 1.8 | 0.2 | 0.0 | 1.1 |
| 2002 | 0.7 | 0.7 | 2.6 | 0.9 | 0.0 | 0.8 | 0.8 | 1.0 | 0.0 | 0.0 | 0.7 | 0.5 | 0.0 | 0.8 |
| 2003 | 0.6 | 0.6 | 0.3 | 0.3 | 0.0 | 0.6 | 0.4 | 0.0 | 0.4 | 0.0 | 0.6 | 0.5 | 0.0 | 0.4 |
| 2004 | 0.6 | 1.2 | 1.0 | 0.5 | 0.0 | 0.4 | 0.8 | 0.8 | 0.7 | 1.4 | 0.3 | 0.8 | 0.0 | 0.7 |
| 2005 | 0.8 | 2.0 | 0.3 | 1.0 | 0.0 | 1.2 | 0.3 | 1.2 | 0.3 | 1.4 | 0.5 | 0.8 | 1.9 | 0.9 |
| 2006 | 1.7 | 0.3 | 0.8 | 0.0 | 0.0 | 0.9 | 0.3 | 1.2 | 0.7 | 0.0 | 0.0 | 0.4 | 0.6 | 0.5 |
| 2007 | 1.9 | 0.7 | 0.5 | 0.5 | 0.0 | 0.3 | 0.6 | 0.8 | 0.3 | 1.4 | 0.6 | 0.3 | 0.0 | 0.6 |
| 2008 | 0.3 | 0.4 | 0.3 | 0.3 | 0.0 | 0.6 | 0.3 | 0.9 | 0.4 | 1.4 | 0.0 | 0.1 | 0.0 | 0.3 |
| 2009 | 0.0 | 1.0 | 0.7 | 0.5 | 0.0 | 0.6 | 0.6 | 1.0 | 0.0 | 1.6 | 0.0 | 0.3 | 0.0 | 0.5 |
| Merged (No.) | 41 | 109 | 60 | 112 | 2 | 117 | 69 | 34 | 18 | 12 | 28 | 53 | 5 | 660 |
| Total (No.) | 545 | 1278 | 653 | 1354 | 137 | 1500 | 1342 | 422 | 452 | 114 | 555 | 1267 | 237 | 9856 |
| Share (percent) | 7.5 | 8.5 | 9.2 | 8.3 | 1.5 | 7.8 | 5.1 | 8.1 | 4.0 | 10.5 | 5.0 | 4.2 | 2.1 | 6.7 |

Source: Calculated using PROWESS, CMIE.

Note: Values in percentage share to the total number of firms reported data unless specified.

their dominance or will the new entrants overtake them? After considering these questions, we will analyse mergers. In order to understand the market shares of the new and old leaders, we have examined the market shares of the 1989 and 2009 leaders, which led us to the following observations.[13] The 1989 leaders stagnated or lost their market share substantially whereas those of 2009 gained market power. In all industries, except chemicals, a similar pattern can be noticed. In some industries, the firm structure itself undergoes a remarkable change. In some other cases, even though the 1989 leaders still function at their previous pace, they are unable to catch up with the present leaders due to the comparatively faster rate of growth of the new leaders. The details can be seen from Figure 6.2 and Table 6.2.

Both the 1989 and 2009 leaders increased their shares in the chemicals sector. However, the growth rates of new leaders outweighed that of the old leaders. In fact, the new leaders were not driven by new entrants, but by the repositioning of the existing low-ranked firms. Out of the five new leaders, four were already in existence. In the automobile sector, the 1989 leaders lost their shares considerably and were replaced by three new entrants—Hyundai Motor India Ltd (1996), Bajaj Auto Ltd (2007), and Honda Siel Cars India Ltd (1995). However, it is to be noted that the shares of the leading four firms in this sector are less affected because three of them—Tata Motors, Maruti Suzuki, and Mahindra & Mahindra—are still in the top-four list. Shares were lost to the subsequent leaders, that is, from the top five firms onward. The specialty of firms in the drugs and pharmaceuticals sector is their high mobility. Seven out of the ten leaders are new in the 2009 leaders list. Like in the chemicals sector, here, too, it was not new entries; only a repositioning of firms occupying the lower ranks. In the food and food products sector as well as the textiles sector, eight out of ten leaders were new on the list. Here, the replacement is not caused by repositioning of the existing low-ranked firms; rather, it is because of the entry of new firms in the 1990s. In the food sector, four leaders were new entrants, while it was five in the textiles sector. This is the reason for the "X" shaped graphs for new and old leaders in both the sectors, which clearly indicates "loss" for old and "gain" for new leaders (see Figure 6.2). Even though the machinery sector experienced restructuring, it was a repositioning of the existing firms rather than the entry of new firms. Six firms were new on the list, out of which only one was a new entrant. Among the sectors mentioned above with new entrants, the entry of foreign firms replaced domestic leadership only in the automobiles sector. New entrants in sectors such as food, textiles and machinery were the domestic firms.

Now the question is: What happened to the old leaders? Did have they completely disappeared from the market at all or do they still exist? It is evident that many of the 1989 leaders have disappeared because of mergers. In the pharmaceutical sector, three such instances are noticeable. They are Parke-Davis (India) Ltd. (7th ranked); Burroughs-Wellcome (India) Ltd. (8th rank); and SmithKline Beecham Pharmaceuticals

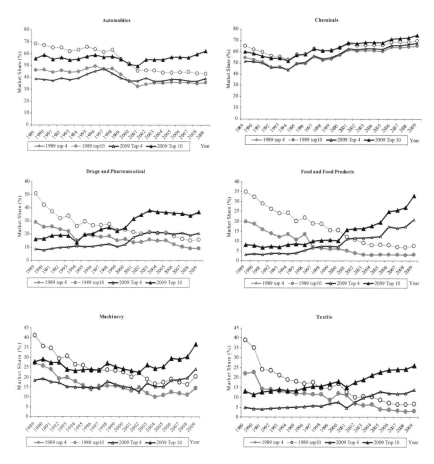

*Figure 6.2* Market power of 1989 and 2009 "Majors".
Source: Calculated from PROWESS, CMIE.

(India) Ltd. (10th rank). All of these are foreign firms. In the food and food products sector also, three such deals also occurred in the food and food products sector, and even with the first-ranked number one firm disappeared in this the process. Brooke Bond Lipton India Ltd. (1st rank); Shaw Wallace & Co. Ltd. (3rd rank); and McDowell & Co. Ltd. (9th rank) were the targets in this sector. In the chemicals sector, the case of Indian Petrochemical Corporation Ltd. (1st rank) is another example. A closer examination of this process leads us to the fact that it is not disappearance, but invisibility for the survival of the best, in the process of acute competition in the era of the market regime. These firms are absorbed by the surviving firms (mostly the leaders), which leads to increased market concentration. As discussed earlier, mergers are expected to reduce the number of firms in the industry, which may result in increased market concentration unless it has been overtaken by a proportionate entry of new firms in the industry. Thus, the number of firms in the industry is an important determinant of the prevailing market structure. In order to understand the effect of mergers on the number of firms, we have calculated the disappearance rate and survival probability for different sectors. This technique has been used by Ijiri and Simon (1971). Disappearance Rate is defined as the total number of firms that disappeared because of mergers divided by the total number of firms in the industry. It is to be noted that the exit of firms may be attributed to a number of reasons other than mergers. Here, we are considering exit through merger alone. Survival Probability is the total number of firms in the industry minus number of firms that disappeared due to mergers divided by the total number of firms in the industry. Thus, if the value of survival probability is near to one, it means that survival probability is high, whereas, if the value of disappearance rate is near to one, it indicates that the survival rate of firms in that industry is very low.[14]

From Table 6.2, it can be seen that a large number of firms from the manufacturing sector have disappeared due to mergers. It amounts to 660 firms for manufacturing as a whole, which make up 7 percent of the firms reported. Sector-wise, in certain sectors such as petroleum and petroleum products, it is as high as 10.5 percent. In this sector, the ratio is high because of the fewer number of firms in the sector as a whole. For drugs and pharmaceuticals sector, it is 9.2 percent, chemicals 8.5 percent, food and food products 8.3 percent, and non-metallic minerals 8.1 percent. It is to be mentioned that the disappearance rate will be even higher if we take into account only those firms that are currently in operation in the respective sectors. We have taken all firms—irrespective of their disappearance due to other reasons—for calculating the total number of firms in the industry. In addition, there have been a substantial number of acquisitions, which are not covered in the CMIE list. Even without these, the disappearance rate was substantial.

However, if the disappearance is adversely affecting the market depends on whether the absence of these firms from the market increases the market power of the existing leaders. In order to understand this, we have examined two factors. One is whether the disappeared firms are strong enough to influence the market during the pre-merger period, which will also give an indication of future performance; this is very important because we will not get post-merger data on firms that have disappeared since they are now part of the surviving firms, which requires us to infer the future impact based on the available information. The second factor is to see where these disappeared firms are visible. Are they absorbed into the leaders or the low-ranked firms? This will determine the market power of the leaders. If they are absorbed into the low-ranked firms, then it may increase competition rather than concentration. The following section will deal with this aspect.

*Table 6.3* Disappearance, survival probability and firm size at the time of merger

| Size Rs. Crores | Automobile | Chemicals | Drugs & Pharmac. | Food and Products | Footwear | Machinery | Metals | Non-metal Minerals | Paper and Printing | Petroleum Products | Rubber & Plastic | Textiles | Wood and Furniture | Total |
|---|---|---|---|---|---|---|---|---|---|---|---|---|---|---|
| **Disappearance Rate** | | | | | | | | | | | | | | |
| >3000 | 0.00 | 0.08 | 0.00 | 0.00 | | 0.00 | 0.06 | 0.00 | 0.00 | 0.30 | 0.00 | | 0.00 | 0.06 |
| 2000–3000 | 0.00 | 0.25 | 0.00 | 0.33 | | 0.00 | 0.14 | 0.00 | 0.00 | 0.00 | 0.00 | | 0.00 | 0.10 |
| 1000–2000 | 0.10 | 0.03 | 0.00 | 0.16 | | 0.00 | 0.05 | 0.00 | | | 0.00 | 0.00 | 0.00 | 0.04 |
| 500–1000 | 0.00 | 0.09 | 0.04 | 0.19 | 0.00 | 0.05 | 0.11 | 0.00 | 0.17 | 0.20 | 0.14 | 0.00 | 0.00 | 0.07 |
| 100–500 | 0.08 | 0.11 | 0.14 | 0.09 | 0.00 | 0.13 | 0.07 | 0.12 | 0.09 | 0.27 | 0.04 | 0.06 | 0.04 | 0.09 |
| <100 | 0.09 | 0.10 | 0.11 | 0.11 | 0.03 | 0.11 | 0.06 | 0.08 | 0.03 | 0.04 | 0.06 | 0.06 | 0.03 | 0.08 |
| Total | 0.08 | 0.10 | 0.11 | 0.11 | 0.02 | 0.10 | 0.06 | 0.08 | 0.04 | 0.12 | 0.06 | 0.05 | 0.03 | 0.08 |
| **Survival Probability** | | | | | | | | | | | | | | |
| >3000 crores | 1.00 | 0.92 | 1.00 | 1.00 | | 1.00 | 0.94 | 1.00 | | 0.70 | 1.00 | | 1.00 | 0.94 |
| 2000–3000 | 1.00 | 0.75 | 1.00 | 0.67 | | 1.00 | 0.86 | 1.00 | 1.00 | 1.00 | 1.00 | 1.00 | 1.00 | 0.90 |
| 1000–2000 | 0.90 | 0.97 | 1.00 | 0.84 | | 1.00 | 0.95 | 1.00 | 1.00 | | 1.00 | 1.00 | 1.00 | 0.96 |
| 500–1000 | 1.00 | 0.91 | 0.96 | 0.81 | 1.00 | 0.95 | 0.89 | 1.00 | 0.83 | 0.80 | 0.86 | 1.00 | 1.00 | 0.93 |
| 100–500 | 0.92 | 0.89 | 0.86 | 0.91 | 1.00 | 0.87 | 0.93 | 0.88 | 0.91 | 0.73 | 0.96 | 0.94 | 0.96 | 0.91 |
| <100 | 0.91 | 0.90 | 0.89 | 0.89 | 0.97 | 0.89 | 0.94 | 0.92 | 0.97 | 0.96 | 0.94 | 0.94 | 0.97 | 0.92 |
| Total | 0.92 | 0.90 | 0.89 | 0.89 | 0.98 | 0.90 | 0.94 | 0.92 | 0.96 | 0.88 | 0.94 | 0.95 | 0.97 | 0.92 |

Source: Calculated using PROWESS, CMIE.

### 6.4.2  On disappeared firms in the sample

The size of a disappeared firm is very important in determining the market share. In order to examine this, we have, firstly, examined the disappearance rate and survival probability across different sizes of firms. Disappearance rate is defined as the number of firms that have disappeared in size category because of a merger divided by the total number of firms in that size category; this is different from the earlier analysis since here we are defining disappearance according to the size category of firms. Size classification for merged firms is done according to their value of sales at the time of the merger. The corresponding figures for all firms are calculated using the average sales value for the period, 2004–05 to 2008–09, which will help avoid fluctuations that occurred because of specific events such as economic crisis. Similarly, survival probability is defined as the total number of firms in a size class minus the disappeared firms in that class as a proportion of the total number of firms in that size class.

From Table 6.3, it can be seen that, in general, the survival probability is higher for mega-sized firms, especially if the sales turnover is beyond Rs 1000 crore. Aaronovitch and Sawyer (1975) also found that large firms have a better survival record than small ones. However, in our analysis, there are variations across sectors. In certain industries such as petroleum, chemicals, metals and food, a good proportion of the big firms disappeared through mergers. Overall, 6 percent of the firms fall in the size category "greater than Rs 3000 crore disappeared through mergers". The disappearance rate in the other categories are: 10 percent (Rs. 2000–3000 crore), 4 percent (Rs. 1000–2000 crores), 7 percent (Rs. 500–1000 crores), 9 percent (Rs. 100–500 crores) and 8 percent (Rs. 100 crores) respectively.[15] It is interesting to note that none of the disappeared firms in the drugs and pharmaceuticals sector and the machinery sector belonged to the size category "beyond Rs. 1000 crores at the time of merger". In the non-metallic and textiles case, this limit is Rs. 500 crores and in the automobiles, it is Rs. 2000 crores.

In order to understand the strength of the disappeared firms, we have to see what happened to the market structure in the absence of these firms. As mentioned earlier, we normally do not get data for firms that disappear after a merger. The shares of the disappeared firms are added to those of the merging firms. Therefore, in order to understand the market power of the disappeared firms, the pre-merger scenario has to be taken into consideration. It will enable us to understand the significance of the disappeared firm in a particular industry. If the market shares of the leaders increased in the absence of merged firms, it indicates that the disappeared firms had played an important role in that particular sector in determining the market structure during the pre-merger period. The degree of importance of the disappeared firms depends on the increase in the shares of the leaders when we remove these firms from the list of the overall manufacturing firms. A somewhat similar technique has been used by Aaronovitch and

Sawyer (1975). We have calculated the market share of the four and ten leaders from 1988–1989 to 2008–2009 and the share of leaders with and without
merged or disappeared firms. This analysis is also done for different sectors.
The following are the major observations from this analysis (see Table 6.4;
Tables 6.5A–D and Figure 6.3).

While analysing the changes in four- and ten-firm concentration ratios,
overall, we get three types of influences. The impact varies from no effect
(nil) to high degree. In some sectors, its impact is nil or low moderate, and in
some other sectors, it is very high. Automobiles, footwear, wood and furni-
ture are sectors in which there is no change in concentration levels registered.
This result is not surprising since these are sectors in which the disappearance rate is very low, except for the automobile sector. Paper and printing,
textiles, rubber and plastic show low levels of change, while for machinery
and non-metallic it is at moderate levels. This observation is applicable to
both the leading four and the leading ten ratios. In the case of the top ten
firms, the disappearance rate is higher than that of the top four firms.

On the other side, chemicals, drugs and pharmaceuticals, food and food
products, metals and petroleum products responded well to mergers. It seems
the effect of a change in concentration levels and disappearance rate are moving in tandem, which clearly indicates the direction of change because of
mergers (see Table 6.6). The degree of change in concentration ratio is higher
for the leading ten firms compared to the leading four firms; this means that
when we add more leaders, the impact of merger also increases. This finding
is similar to the observation made by Weiss in 1965 for UK mergers. From

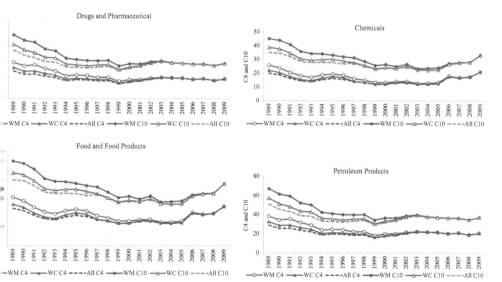

*ure 6.3* With and without merged firms.
*rce:* Calculated from PROWESS, CMIE.

Table 6.4 Market share of 1989 and 2009 leaders (in percent)

| | Year | | 1989 | 1990 | 1991 | 1992 | 1993 | 1994 | 1995 | 1996 | 1997 | 1998 | 1999 | 2000 | 2001 | 2002 | 2003 | 2004 | 2005 | 2006 | 2007 | 2008 | 2009 |
|---|---|---|---|---|---|---|---|---|---|---|---|---|---|---|---|---|---|---|---|---|---|---|---|
| Automobile | 1989 | T4 | 46.2 | 46.4 | 44.3 | 45.7 | 44.1 | 44.9 | 47.7 | 49.3 | 47.1 | 47.4 | 42.5 | 37 | 32.2 | 34.1 | 35.5 | 35.1 | 36.1 | 35.7 | 35.7 | 34.9 | 35.7 |
| | | T10 | 68.5 | 67.1 | 65.1 | 65.1 | 62 | 63.1 | 65.7 | 63.9 | 61.4 | 63.2 | 55.6 | 51.6 | 45.5 | 45.7 | 45.9 | 44 | 44 | 44.4 | 44.6 | 43.4 | 43 |
| | 2009 | T4 | 38.7 | 38.1 | 37.3 | 39.3 | 37.7 | 39.5 | 42.6 | 45.1 | 47.1 | 43.3 | 39.4 | 36.9 | 36.8 | 39.4 | 36.6 | 37.1 | 38.6 | 38.1 | 37.1 | 36.6 | 39.1 |
| | | T10 | 55.8 | 58.8 | 55.3 | 56.8 | 54.6 | 55.4 | 57.7 | 59 | 57.1 | 57.7 | 55.2 | 51.2 | 49.6 | 54.8 | 55.1 | 55 | 57 | 57 | 56.7 | 59.7 | 62.4 |
| Chemicals | 1989 | T4 | 54.9 | 52.9 | 51.1 | 46.3 | 46.7 | 43.4 | 49.2 | 49.4 | 55.2 | 52.4 | 53.7 | 56.9 | 61.4 | 60.5 | 61.1 | 60.9 | 60.3 | 63.8 | 63.6 | 64.3 | 65.2 |
| | | T10 | 65.1 | 62.2 | 59.5 | 56.4 | 55.8 | 52.9 | 57.6 | 57.8 | 62.7 | 60.6 | 61.2 | 63.2 | 67 | 65.5 | 65.8 | 66 | 65.6 | 68.1 | 68.7 | 68.5 | 69.6 |
| | 2009 | T4 | 51.4 | 51.1 | 49.9 | 45.6 | 46 | 43.5 | 49.7 | 50.5 | 56.4 | 53.6 | 54.6 | 57.9 | 62.7 | 61.9 | 62.5 | 62.6 | 62.1 | 65.4 | 65.4 | 66.2 | 67.4 |
| | | T10 | 59.9 | 58.3 | 55.9 | 54.3 | 54.1 | 51.7 | 57 | 57.5 | 62.5 | 60.9 | 61.3 | 63.8 | 67.9 | 67.2 | 68 | 68.3 | 67.8 | 71.2 | 71.9 | 72.4 | 74.7 |
| Drugs and pharmaceutical | 1989 | T4 | 29 | 25.5 | 25.8 | 23.7 | 22.1 | 15.4 | 19.1 | 19 | 18 | 18.7 | 15.2 | 16.2 | 13.8 | 14 | 16 | 15.1 | 15.2 | 12.4 | 10.6 | 9.3 | 9.2 |
| | | T10 | 50.9 | 42.2 | 37.3 | 32 | 33.8 | 26.1 | 29.7 | 26.8 | 26.9 | 27.6 | 22.7 | 23.4 | 21.5 | 20.5 | 21.6 | 20.8 | 21.1 | 18.7 | 16.5 | 15.2 | 15.8 |
| | 2009 | T4 | 8.7 | 7.7 | 9 | 9.8 | 10.3 | 11.2 | 10.5 | 10.9 | 11.7 | 12.6 | 10.5 | 12.3 | 17.8 | 19.8 | 21.5 | 21.2 | 20.9 | 20.2 | 21 | 19.1 | 20.7 |
| | | T10 | 16.3 | 16.4 | 18.8 | 19.2 | 19 | 13.7 | 19.9 | 20.4 | 23.6 | 25.1 | 22.5 | 25 | 31.8 | 34.9 | 38.2 | 36.9 | 36.6 | 36 | 35.8 | 34.3 | 37 |
| Foodproducts | 1989 | T4 | 19.9 | 18.7 | 15.9 | 14 | 12.1 | 13.6 | 10.7 | 13.6 | 6.9 | 6.4 | 5.9 | 6.1 | 5.1 | 3.9 | 3.2 | 3.1 | 3.3 | 3.2 | 3.2 | 3 | 3.2 |
| | | T10 | 35 | 32.4 | 29 | 26.4 | 24.1 | 24.2 | 20.1 | 21.9 | 18.9 | 18.7 | 15.6 | 15.4 | 12.2 | 10.7 | 9.2 | 7.9 | 8.2 | 8 | 6.9 | 6.7 | 7.5 |
| | 2009 | T4 | 3.2 | 3.6 | 3.3 | 3.7 | 3.9 | 3.6 | 4 | 5.4 | 6.6 | 7.4 | 7.3 | 7.2 | 15.7 | 11.6 | 11.5 | 11.9 | 12.4 | 17.4 | 16.6 | 17.3 | 21 |
| | | T10 | 8.2 | 7.7 | 6.7 | 7.3 | 6.9 | 8.2 | 8.5 | 8.2 | 9.9 | 10.3 | 10.5 | 10.2 | 15.7 | 16.2 | 16.4 | 17.7 | 19.5 | 24.8 | 25.7 | 27.1 | 33.1 |
| Machinery | 1989 | T4 | 27.1 | 25.8 | 24 | 19.3 | 19.9 | 18 | 16 | 13.9 | 15.4 | 15.8 | 15.7 | 14.6 | 13.2 | 14.8 | 11.9 | 10.2 | 10.9 | 12.5 | 11.9 | 11.1 | 14.4 |
| | | T10 | 41.3 | 35.6 | 34.7 | 29.4 | 30.6 | 26.5 | 25.9 | 23.4 | 23.5 | 23.7 | 23.4 | 22.6 | 20.2 | 22.2 | 19.1 | 16.7 | 17.4 | 19.1 | 17.5 | 16.3 | 20.4 |
| | 2009 | T4 | 18.4 | 19.3 | 17.6 | 17.3 | 15.2 | 14.9 | 14.8 | 14.9 | 14.3 | 17.9 | 16.3 | 15.3 | 14.7 | 12.6 | 17.1 | 15.3 | 15.3 | 18.3 | 18.7 | 19.7 | 24.3 |
| | | T10 | 27.8 | 29.1 | 27.3 | 27.4 | 24 | 23.2 | 23.7 | 24 | 23.6 | 27.2 | 25.2 | 24.3 | 23.2 | 22.3 | 26.2 | 24.5 | 25.4 | 29.6 | 29.2 | 30.5 | 36.7 |
| Textile | 1989 | T4 | 22.1 | 22.8 | 14.2 | 14 | 13 | 12.7 | 11.9 | 12 | 11.6 | 11.5 | 8.7 | 12.1 | 11.1 | 6.9 | 6 | 6.4 | 4.1 | 3.7 | 3.3 | 3 | 3.1 |
| | | T10 | 38.9 | 34.9 | 24.2 | 23.5 | 21.2 | 19 | 18 | 17 | 17.7 | 14.7 | 14.8 | 16.9 | 12.8 | 10.1 | 10.6 | 10.3 | 8.7 | 7.2 | 6.5 | 6.4 | 6.6 |
| | 2009 | T4 | 4.9 | 4.2 | 4 | 4.4 | 4.6 | 4.8 | 5 | 5.3 | 5.8 | 5.5 | 7 | 7.5 | 4.7 | 7.5 | 9.7 | 11.2 | 12.8 | 12 | 11.9 | 12.1 | 13.8 |
| | | T10 | 13.2 | 11.3 | 12.6 | 13.2 | 14 | 13.5 | 13.4 | 14.7 | 15.6 | 15.6 | 17 | 18.1 | 15.2 | 17.5 | 18.9 | 21.2 | 22.7 | 23.8 | 24 | 24.2 | 26.2 |

Source: Calculated using PROWESS, CMIE.

Note: T4 and T10 show the top 4 and 10 firms of 1989 and 2009.

Table 6.5A  Concentration levels for leading four with and without merged (and cross-border merged) firms (in percent)

| Top 4 | Chemicals | | | Drugs & Pharmaceutical | | | Food & Food Products | | | Machinery | | | Metals | | | Petroleum Products | | |
|---|---|---|---|---|---|---|---|---|---|---|---|---|---|---|---|---|---|---|
| | WM | WC | All | WM | WC | All | WM | WC | All | WM | WC | All | WM | WC | All | WM | WC | All |
| 1989 | 25.7 | 23.1 | 22.3 | 38.1 | 32.5 | 29.0 | 25.7 | 22.0 | 19.9 | 29.5 | 27.1 | 27.1 | 63.2 | 56.1 | 55.9 | 94.7 | 90.1 | 90.1 |
| 1990 | 22.3 | 20.0 | 19.3 | 34.4 | 28.7 | 25.5 | 23.8 | 20.4 | 18.7 | 28.7 | 26.1 | 26.1 | 58.7 | 51.5 | 51.3 | 94.5 | 89.4 | 89.4 |
| 1991 | 20.5 | 18.4 | 17.7 | 35.5 | 28.9 | 25.8 | 20.5 | 17.4 | 16.2 | 26.5 | 24.0 | 24.0 | 55.8 | 49.3 | 49.1 | 94.2 | 89.3 | 89.3 |
| 1992 | 20.1 | 17.8 | 17.3 | 31.7 | 26.4 | 23.7 | 18.0 | 15.3 | 14.4 | 24.6 | 22.2 | 22.2 | 51.9 | 46.6 | 46.4 | 94.4 | 89.8 | 89.8 |
| 1993 | 20.1 | 17.8 | 17.3 | 28.9 | 24.6 | 22.1 | 17.0 | 14.5 | 13.8 | 22.3 | 20.4 | 20.4 | 51.0 | 45.7 | 45.5 | 94.5 | 89.9 | 89.9 |
| 1994 | 19.6 | 17.6 | 17.1 | 23.9 | 20.4 | 18.8 | 18.6 | 16.4 | 15.3 | 20.6 | 18.7 | 18.7 | 50.6 | 45.1 | 44.8 | 93.6 | 88.7 | 88.7 |
| 1995 | 20.4 | 18.3 | 17.9 | 24.8 | 21.3 | 19.9 | 19.4 | 17.5 | 16.2 | 18.5 | 17.2 | 17.1 | 47.1 | 42.1 | 41.9 | 94.2 | 90.0 | 90.0 |
| 1996 | 19.9 | 18.0 | 17.7 | 22.2 | 20.8 | 19.6 | 18.5 | 16.7 | 15.5 | 18.0 | 16.9 | 16.9 | 44.3 | 39.6 | 39.6 | 94.7 | 89.6 | 89.5 |
| 1997 | 23.4 | 21.5 | 21.0 | 22.2 | 19.8 | 18.6 | 16.0 | 14.1 | 14.0 | 18.6 | 17.4 | 17.4 | 42.8 | 38.6 | 38.6 | 94.4 | 89.9 | 89.8 |
| 1998 | 25.3 | 23.2 | 22.5 | 22.2 | 19.7 | 18.8 | 14.9 | 13.3 | 13.2 | 20.4 | 19.0 | 19.0 | 42.1 | 38.2 | 38.2 | 94.1 | 89.4 | 89.3 |
| 1999 | 26.4 | 24.3 | 23.6 | 18.3 | 16.3 | 15.7 | 13.2 | 12.0 | 11.9 | 20.4 | 19.0 | 19.0 | 39.6 | 35.9 | 35.8 | 93.5 | 89.4 | 89.4 |
| 2000 | 26.7 | 24.5 | 23.7 | 20.0 | 18.1 | 17.5 | 13.2 | 12.1 | 12.0 | 19.5 | 18.3 | 18.3 | 38.9 | 35.1 | 35.1 | 93.8 | 90.2 | 90.1 |
| 2001 | 28.0 | 25.6 | 24.8 | 20.1 | 19.1 | 18.6 | 13.9 | 13.2 | 13.1 | 18.2 | 17.2 | 17.2 | 37.5 | 33.6 | 33.6 | 97.1 | 83.9 | 83.8 |
| 2002 | 28.3 | 25.8 | 25.0 | 21.6 | 21.0 | 20.6 | 14.0 | 13.2 | 13.2 | 18.8 | 17.9 | 17.9 | 37.6 | 33.7 | 33.7 | 93.6 | 90.7 | 90.6 |
| 2003 | 26.2 | 23.8 | 23.3 | 22.3 | 22.2 | 22.0 | 12.6 | 12.1 | 12.1 | 22.7 | 22.1 | 22.1 | 37.8 | 35.6 | 35.6 | 91.9 | 88.1 | 88.0 |
| 2004 | 26.8 | 24.0 | 23.7 | 22.0 | 21.9 | 21.8 | 12.7 | 12.0 | 12.0 | 20.8 | 20.3 | 20.3 | 37.2 | 35.3 | 35.3 | 90.9 | 86.9 | 86.8 |
| 2005 | 24.8 | 22.4 | 22.2 | 21.6 | 21.6 | 21.5 | 13.2 | 12.4 | 12.4 | 21.5 | 21.0 | 21.0 | 35.3 | 34.4 | 34.4 | 88.2 | 83.8 | 83.8 |
| 2006 | 26.8 | 24.3 | 24.2 | 20.3 | 20.2 | 20.2 | 17.9 | 17.4 | 17.4 | 19.9 | 19.6 | 19.6 | 32.6 | 32.3 | 32.3 | 87.2 | 86.0 | 86.0 |
| 2007 | 23.1 | 22.7 | 22.6 | 21.1 | 21.0 | 21.0 | 16.8 | 16.6 | 16.6 | 21.4 | 21.2 | 21.2 | 31.6 | 31.4 | 31.4 | 87.8 | 86.8 | 86.8 |
| 2008 | 23.2 | 23.0 | 22.9 | 19.1 | 19.1 | 19.1 | 17.3 | 17.3 | 17.3 | 21.3 | 21.0 | 21.0 | 30.2 | 30.1 | 30.0 | 87.9 | 87.1 | 87.1 |
| 2009 | 29.6 | 29.4 | 29.3 | 20.8 | 20.7 | 20.7 | 21.0 | 21.0 | 21.0 | 24.4 | 24.3 | 24.3 | 31.1 | 31.1 | 31.1 | 84.0 | 84.0 | 84.0 |

Source: Calculated from PROWESS, CMIE.

Note: **WM** denotes without merger; WC denotes without cross-border merger; All denotes the overall.

Table6.5B Concentration levels for leading 10 with and without merged (and cross-border merged) firms (in percent)

| Top 10 | Chemicals | | | Drugs, Pharmaceutical | | | Food, Food Products | | | Machinery | | | Metals | | | Petroleum Products | | |
|---|---|---|---|---|---|---|---|---|---|---|---|---|---|---|---|---|---|---|
| | WM | WC | All | WM | WC | All | WM | WC | All | WM | WC | All | WM | WC | All | WM | WC | All |
| 1989 | 46.8 | 42.1 | 40.7 | 66.9 | 57.1 | 50.9 | 45.0 | 38.7 | 35.0 | 44.9 | 41.3 | 41.3 | 78.2 | 69.4 | 69.2 | 99.8 | 95.0 | 95.0 |
| 1990 | 42.8 | 38.4 | 37.2 | 61.3 | 51.2 | 45.6 | 43.8 | 37.6 | 34.5 | 45.3 | 41.1 | 41.1 | 73.6 | 64.6 | 64.3 | 99.7 | 94.4 | 94.4 |
| 1991 | 38.7 | 34.7 | 33.4 | 59.2 | 48.2 | 43.0 | 40.7 | 34.5 | 32.0 | 43.2 | 39.0 | 39.0 | 69.5 | 61.3 | 61.1 | 99.8 | 94.6 | 94.6 |
| 1992 | 38.8 | 34.4 | 33.3 | 52.1 | 43.5 | 38.9 | 35.7 | 30.3 | 28.5 | 39.5 | 35.7 | 35.7 | 67.1 | 60.2 | 60.0 | 99.6 | 94.7 | 94.7 |
| 1993 | 37.4 | 33.1 | 32.2 | 50.1 | 42.7 | 38.3 | 34.2 | 29.3 | 27.8 | 36.3 | 33.2 | 33.2 | 65.9 | 59.1 | 58.9 | 99.6 | 94.7 | 94.7 |
| 1994 | 35.9 | 32.3 | 31.4 | 42.4 | 36.3 | 33.3 | 34.0 | 29.9 | 27.9 | 34.1 | 31.0 | 31.0 | 63.4 | 56.4 | 56.1 | 99.5 | 94.3 | 94.3 |
| 1995 | 35.5 | 31.9 | 31.2 | 41.0 | 35.4 | 32.9 | 33.1 | 30.0 | 27.7 | 32.2 | 29.8 | 29.8 | 59.5 | 53.2 | 52.9 | 99.4 | 95.1 | 95.1 |
| 1996 | 35.0 | 31.8 | 31.2 | 40.0 | 34.3 | 32.4 | 31.9 | 28.8 | 26.7 | 30.3 | 28.4 | 28.4 | 56.9 | 50.9 | 50.8 | 99.2 | 93.9 | 93.8 |
| 1997 | 37.1 | 34.1 | 33.3 | 39.8 | 35.4 | 33.3 | 31.2 | 27.6 | 27.4 | 31.7 | 29.7 | 29.7 | 55.2 | 49.7 | 49.7 | 99.2 | 94.5 | 94.4 |
| 1998 | 39.8 | 36.4 | 35.4 | 40.1 | 35.6 | 34.1 | 28.5 | 25.5 | 25.2 | 34.6 | 32.2 | 32.2 | 55.9 | 50.9 | 50.8 | 99.2 | 94.1 | 94.1 |
| 1999 | 40.2 | 37.1 | 36.0 | 34.3 | 30.5 | 29.4 | 25.6 | 23.3 | 23.0 | 33.1 | 30.8 | 30.8 | 53.3 | 48.3 | 48.2 | 99.3 | 95.0 | 94.9 |
| 2000 | 40.1 | 36.8 | 35.6 | 36.6 | 33.1 | 32.0 | 26.3 | 24.1 | 23.8 | 31.9 | 29.9 | 29.9 | 53.7 | 48.6 | 48.5 | 99.2 | 95.4 | 95.4 |
| 2001 | 41.4 | 37.7 | 36.6 | 36.5 | 34.6 | 33.7 | 24.8 | 23.5 | 23.4 | 30.2 | 28.5 | 28.5 | 54.0 | 48.5 | 48.4 | 99.4 | 85.8 | 85.8 |
| 2002 | 41.0 | 37.4 | 36.2 | 38.8 | 37.7 | 36.9 | 26.5 | 24.9 | 24.9 | 30.3 | 28.8 | 28.7 | 53.3 | 47.8 | 47.7 | 99.4 | 96.4 | 96.3 |
| 2003 | 39.6 | 36.1 | 35.2 | 39.7 | 39.4 | 39.2 | 23.3 | 22.4 | 22.4 | 34.1 | 33.1 | 33.1 | 52.3 | 49.2 | 49.2 | 99.2 | 95.1 | 95.1 |
| 2004 | 41.0 | 36.7 | 36.2 | 37.8 | 37.6 | 37.4 | 23.5 | 22.2 | 22.2 | 32.2 | 31.3 | 31.3 | 53.2 | 50.5 | 50.4 | 99.2 | 94.8 | 94.7 |
| 2005 | 39.5 | 35.7 | 35.3 | 37.2 | 37.1 | 37.1 | 23.9 | 22.4 | 22.4 | 33.2 | 32.3 | 32.3 | 52.4 | 51.1 | 51.1 | 99.1 | 94.3 | 94.3 |
| 2006 | 41.3 | 37.4 | 37.3 | 36.5 | 36.3 | 36.3 | 27.1 | 26.4 | 26.4 | 32.2 | 31.7 | 31.7 | 49.8 | 49.3 | 49.3 | 99.3 | 97.9 | 97.9 |
| 2007 | 35.3 | 34.6 | 34.5 | 36.5 | 36.3 | 36.3 | 27.8 | 27.5 | 27.5 | 33.1 | 32.8 | 32.8 | 49.5 | 49.2 | 49.2 | 99.3 | 98.2 | 98.2 |
| 2008 | 35.6 | 35.4 | 35.2 | 34.9 | 34.8 | 34.8 | 28.0 | 27.9 | 27.9 | 34.2 | 33.8 | 33.8 | 47.9 | 47.7 | 47.7 | 99.2 | 98.3 | 98.3 |
| 2009 | 44.8 | 44.5 | 44.4 | 37.1 | 37.0 | 37.0 | 33.1 | 33.1 | 33.1 | 36.9 | 36.7 | 36.7 | 47.8 | 47.7 | 47.7 | 99.1 | 99.1 | 99.1 |

Source: Calculated from PROWESS, CMIE.

Note: WM denotes without merger; WC denotes without cross-border merger; All denotes the overall.

Table 6.5C Concentration levels for leading four with and without merged firms (in percent)

| Top 4 | Automobiles | | Footwear | | Paper, Printing | | Rubber, Plastic | | Textiles | | Wood and Furniture | | Non metallic Minerals | |
|---|---|---|---|---|---|---|---|---|---|---|---|---|---|---|
| | WM | All | WM | All | WM | All | WM | All | WM | All | WM | All | WM | All |
| 1989 | 46.9 | 46.2 | 100.0 | 100.0 | 41.4 | 37.1 | 51.4 | 48.0 | 24.5 | 22.1 | 57.1 | 56.2 | 37.1 | 34.1 |
| 1990 | 47.5 | 46.5 | 96.9 | 96.9 | 38.5 | 35.5 | 48.6 | 45.1 | 25.1 | 22.8 | 53.2 | 53.2 | 43.9 | 40.6 |
| 1991 | 45.2 | 44.4 | 96.6 | 96.6 | 35.2 | 32.7 | 39.9 | 36.4 | 18.0 | 16.5 | 49.0 | 49.0 | 38.2 | 35.6 |
| 1992 | 46.8 | 46.0 | 89.3 | 89.3 | 39.5 | 37.6 | 42.3 | 38.6 | 17.9 | 16.5 | 52.8 | 52.8 | 41.2 | 38.2 |
| 1993 | 44.9 | 44.1 | 85.7 | 82.8 | 41.4 | 39.3 | 41.5 | 38.6 | 16.9 | 15.6 | 51.6 | 51.6 | 39.3 | 36.7 |
| 1994 | 46.3 | 45.5 | 66.8 | 65.1 | 39.1 | 36.8 | 35.9 | 33.5 | 16.4 | 15.7 | 48.3 | 48.3 | 37.0 | 34.5 |
| 1995 | 49.0 | 48.2 | 55.2 | 54.3 | 36.3 | 34.2 | 32.1 | 30.3 | 15.2 | 14.6 | 41.3 | 41.3 | 36.8 | 34.6 |
| 1996 | 51.6 | 50.6 | 50.4 | 49.6 | 35.2 | 33.5 | 35.5 | 33.6 | 14.6 | 13.9 | 39.3 | 39.3 | 35.3 | 33.2 |
| 1997 | 53.5 | 52.8 | 49.7 | 48.8 | 32.1 | 30.4 | 37.6 | 35.5 | 15.0 | 14.2 | 41.8 | 41.7 | 36.0 | 33.8 |
| 1998 | 48.5 | 48.0 | 55.5 | 54.8 | 22.9 | 21.6 | 37.0 | 34.9 | 15.6 | 14.8 | 34.4 | 33.4 | 34.5 | 32.2 |
| 1999 | 43.4 | 42.8 | 56.4 | 55.7 | 31.5 | 29.5 | 32.9 | 31.1 | 14.5 | 13.9 | 37.6 | 36.8 | 35.6 | 33.2 |
| 2000 | 38.9 | 37.5 | 55.5 | 54.7 | 25.3 | 23.6 | 34.0 | 32.2 | 15.2 | 14.6 | 40.9 | 39.5 | 35.4 | 32.2 |
| 2001 | 39.0 | 37.3 | 56.6 | 56.6 | 29.9 | 26.7 | 32.6 | 30.9 | 13.0 | 12.5 | 46.1 | 45.2 | 34.4 | 31.7 |
| 2002 | 41.9 | 41.4 | 58.7 | 58.7 | 28.7 | 28.3 | 31.3 | 29.6 | 9.4 | 9.0 | 30.7 | 30.0 | 32.3 | 30.0 |
| 2003 | 38.9 | 38.3 | 46.4 | 46.4 | 25.6 | 23.8 | 35.3 | 34.7 | 10.9 | 10.4 | 27.4 | 26.9 | 31.9 | 30.0 |
| 2004 | 38.5 | 38.1 | 46.6 | 46.6 | 25.9 | 25.6 | 34.4 | 33.8 | 12.0 | 11.5 | 39.8 | 38.8 | 33.6 | 31.5 |
| 2005 | 39.8 | 39.5 | 43.4 | 43.4 | 24.7 | 24.6 | 33.4 | 33.0 | 13.3 | 13.0 | 42.1 | 41.5 | 33.1 | 31.3 |
| 2006 | 39.3 | 39.0 | 42.1 | 42.1 | 24.0 | 23.9 | 33.7 | 33.4 | 12.7 | 12.4 | 45.1 | 45.1 | 31.3 | 29.4 |
| 2007 | 38.0 | 37.8 | 44.3 | 44.3 | 25.8 | 25.7 | 33.3 | 33.0 | 12.9 | 12.9 | 47.2 | 47.2 | 36.0 | 34.9 |
| 2008 | 36.7 | 36.7 | 44.0 | 44.0 | 26.9 | 26.9 | 32.6 | 32.6 | 12.6 | 12.5 | 51.6 | 51.6 | 32.7 | 32.1 |
| 2009 | 39.1 | 39.1 | 47.2 | 47.2 | 26.8 | 26.8 | 34.7 | 34.7 | 13.9 | 13.8 | 49.5 | 49.5 | 31.2 | 30.8 |

Source: Calculated from PROWESS, CMIE.

Note: WM denotes without merger; All denotes the overall.

Table 6.5D Concentration levels for leading 10 with and without merged firms (in percent)

| Top 10 | Automobiles | | Footwear | | Paper & Printing | | Rubber & Plastic | | Textiles | | Wood & Furniture | | Non metallic Minerals | |
|---|---|---|---|---|---|---|---|---|---|---|---|---|---|---|
| | WM | All | WM | All | WM | All | WM | All | WM | All | WM | All | WM | All |
| 1989 | 69.6 | 68.5 | 100 | 100 | 67.6 | 60.6 | 79.3 | 74.1 | 43.1 | 38.9 | 91.5 | 90.0 | 55.1 | 50.6 |
| 1990 | 70.8 | 69.4 | 100 | 100 | 65.3 | 60.2 | 77.2 | 71.7 | 41.0 | 37.2 | 85.1 | 85.1 | 60.2 | 55.7 |
| 1991 | 66.3 | 65.1 | 100 | 100 | 59.4 | 55.1 | 68.4 | 62.5 | 31.7 | 29.1 | 77.7 | 77.7 | 54.7 | 50.9 |
| 1992 | 66.6 | 65.4 | 100 | 100 | 62.2 | 59.3 | 68.7 | 62.6 | 31.0 | 28.5 | 80.6 | 80.6 | 56.6 | 52.6 |
| 1993 | 63.9 | 62.8 | 100 | 97.2 | 62.4 | 59.3 | 65.2 | 60.6 | 30.2 | 28.0 | 75.2 | 75.2 | 54.7 | 51.1 |
| 1994 | 65.3 | 64.2 | 83.2 | 81.1 | 59.8 | 56.3 | 60.1 | 56.1 | 28.2 | 26.9 | 69.2 | 69.2 | 54.6 | 51.0 |
| 1995 | 67.3 | 66.3 | 74.4 | 73.2 | 55.2 | 51.9 | 54.1 | 51.1 | 26.6 | 25.4 | 64.2 | 64.2 | 53.4 | 50.3 |
| 1996 | 67.1 | 65.7 | 72.0 | 70.9 | 54.6 | 52.0 | 56.7 | 53.5 | 26.9 | 25.7 | 65.4 | 65.4 | 51.8 | 48.7 |
| 1997 | 66.4 | 65.4 | 71.9 | 70.6 | 51.4 | 48.8 | 58.3 | 55.0 | 26.7 | 25.3 | 63.9 | 63.8 | 53.6 | 50.3 |
| 1998 | 66.2 | 65.4 | 76.2 | 75.2 | 45.1 | 42.5 | 56.6 | 53.4 | 27.5 | 26.1 | 69.5 | 67.4 | 52.6 | 49.2 |
| 1999 | 62.5 | 61.6 | 79.4 | 78.4 | 51.7 | 48.4 | 51.3 | 48.5 | 26.2 | 25.1 | 65.6 | 64.2 | 51.6 | 48.1 |
| 2000 | 58.8 | 56.6 | 78.2 | 77.1 | 46.3 | 43.2 | 53.3 | 50.5 | 26.2 | 25.3 | 68.4 | 66.1 | 50.7 | 46.1 |
| 2001 | 59.2 | 56.7 | 78.0 | 78.0 | 50.5 | 45.1 | 50.0 | 47.3 | 23.8 | 22.9 | 70.4 | 69.1 | 51.7 | 47.6 |
| 2002 | 61.3 | 60.5 | 82.3 | 82.3 | 46.4 | 45.8 | 47.9 | 45.3 | 20.5 | 19.7 | 59.9 | 58.6 | 48.5 | 45.1 |
| 2003 | 60.2 | 59.2 | 67.0 | 67.0 | 45.1 | 41.9 | 50.3 | 49.4 | 21.6 | 20.7 | 57.3 | 56.0 | 48.0 | 45.1 |
| 2004 | 58.8 | 58.2 | 70.7 | 70.7 | 42.2 | 41.6 | 49.7 | 48.9 | 23.3 | 22.3 | 65.3 | 63.6 | 50.1 | 47.0 |
| 2005 | 60.2 | 59.7 | 67.7 | 67.7 | 42.0 | 41.8 | 49.8 | 49.1 | 24.5 | 23.9 | 66.7 | 65.6 | 48.9 | 46.3 |
| 2006 | 59.9 | 59.5 | 68.8 | 68.8 | 40.1 | 39.9 | 50.9 | 50.4 | 24.6 | 24.2 | 68.4 | 68.3 | 47.9 | 45.0 |
| 2007 | 59.4 | 59.0 | 74.3 | 74.3 | 43.1 | 43.1 | 51.0 | 50.5 | 24.5 | 24.4 | 67.1 | 67.1 | 53.1 | 51.4 |
| 2008 | 59.7 | 59.7 | 74.0 | 74.0 | 43.5 | 43.5 | 51.4 | 51.4 | 24.3 | 24.2 | 70.4 | 70.4 | 51.1 | 50.3 |
| 2009 | 62.4 | 62.4 | 79.5 | 79.5 | 44.5 | 44.5 | 54.2 | 54.2 | 26.3 | 26.2 | 70.8 | 70.8 | 49.1 | 48.5 |

Source: Calculated from PROWESS,CMIE.

Note: **WM** denotes without merger; **All** denotes the overall.

Tables 6.5A–D and Figure 6.3, the following observations can be made. In chemicals sector, the overall concentration in terms of leading four firms was 22.3 in 1989, which increased to 25.7 due to the disappearance. Similarly, the leading ten firms' ratio increased to 47 from 41. The difference in the ratios was even higher in the case of drugs and pharmaceuticals sector. In this sector, the shares of the leading four firms increased to 38 from 29, and that of leading ten firms increased to 67 from 51 due to disappearance since 1989. However, during the post-2000 period, the graphs with and without mergers are converging; this is mainly because of the addition of shares of the disappeared firms to the surviving firm; consequently, the sample without merged firms resembles the sample with mergers or overall case. Here also, the inclusion of more leaders almost doubles the concentration levels. In the food sector, initially, the four-firm concentration ratio increased to 26 percent from 20 percent due to the disappearance of the merged firms. The corresponding figures for the leading ten firms are 35 percent and 45 percent respectively. This trend continued into the early part of 2000s. Metals and metal products also have a similar story. It is one of the highly-concentrated sectors. However, overall concentration has declined over the years. In 1989, 56 percent of the sales was controlled by leading four firms, which went up to 63 percent due to disappearance, while the same figure for leading ten firms is 78 percent from 69 percent. Most interestingly, the petroleum sector has shown very high variation with and without merged firms. This sector is highly concentrated due to the regulations prevailed earlier.[16] Ninety percent of the shares was controlled by the four leading firms, which increased to 95 percent in the absence of merged firms. Similarly, the leading ten firms' ratio was 95, which went up to 99.8 percent in the absence of disappeared firms. Two important mergers in this sector involve two central government undertakings, Bongaigaon Refinery and Petrochemicals Ltd with the Indian Oil Corporation Ltd. and Kochi Refineries Ltd with Bharat Petroleum Corporation Ltd, which strengthened the domain of the merging firms to a great extent.

*Table 6.6* Impact of mergers on disappearance and market concentration (C4 and C10 together)

| Disappearance rate | Change in Market Power | High | Medium | Low | Nil |
|---|---|---|---|---|---|
| High | | Petroleum, pharmaceutical chemicals, food and food products | Non-metallic; machinery | | Automobiles |
| Medium | | Metals and metal products | | Rubber & plastic | |
| Low | | | | Paper; textiles | Footwear; wood & furniture |

Source: Calculated from PROWESS, CMIE.

Thus, from the foregoing analysis, it is clear that size wise, survival probability is higher for mega-sized firms. In four sectors, that is, petroleum, pharmaceuticals, chemicals and food, the disappearance rate as well as the changes in market concentration were high owing to mergers.

### 6.4.3 Implications of cross-border deals

As discussed earlier, the implications of disappearance may be important if it is a cross-border deal,[17] since it can lead to the creation of a foreign monopoly. It is feared that it may lead to the creation of global monopolies with the help of the already established subsidiaries. As mentioned earlier, for many foreign firms, consolidation provides easy entry into India's vast consumer market. Once they enter with their well-equipped sales and distribution network strategies, advertising capacity along with the unbeaten technical capability, it may enable them to create market power and may drive out domestic firms. It is also possible that they "cherry pick" the domestic firms, which means they may be more cautious in selecting the target. They also see to it that the partner company has well established strategic assets. Therefore, we assume that the degree of market power they earned through mergers might be substantial, especially in sectors where the overall concentration ratios have changed because of mergers. For this, we have taken only those sectors in which concentration ratios have changed substantially due to the disappearance of firms. Out of the five sectors in which concentration changed substantially due to mergers—petroleum, metals and metal products, drugs and pharmaceuticals, food and food products and chemicals—it is seen that petroleum and metals have not experienced any change because of cross-border deals. For petroleum sector and the metals and metal products sector, it is due to the low intensity of cross-border deals.[18] In the case of chemicals, too, it shows a very small change because of cross-border deals. Thus, it is not due to the low intensity of cross-border deals since it is only 24 percent (28 deals). However, the market share seems to increase when we compare the leading ten firms with the leading four firms. The effect of cross-border mergers is most noticeable in drugs and pharmaceutical industry. A similar trend can be noticed in food and food products also. In the case of drugs and pharmaceutical industry, in the year 1989, the concentration ratio of the leading four firms was 32.5 percent (57 percent for leading ten) in the absence of merged cross-border firms from 29 percent (51 percent for leading ten). Thus, the contribution of cross-border deals in the overall change in concentration is 39 percent[19] for leading four firms and 37.5 percent for leading ten firms. The cross-border intensity[20] in this sector is 30 percent. Similarly, in the food and food products sector, the corresponding figure in concentration is 22 from 20 percent for leading four firms and 39 from 35 percent for leading ten firms. Thus, the contribution of cross-border deals in the overall change in concentration in the food sector is 33.3 percent for leading four firms and 40 percent for leading ten firms. In

*Table 6.7* Impact of cross-border mergers on disappearance and market concentration (C4 and C10 together)

| Cross-border Intensity | Change in Market Power | High | Low | Nil |
|---|---|---|---|---|
| High | | Drugs & pharmaceutical | Chemicals | |
| Low | | Food & food products | | Petroleum, metals & metal products |

Source: Calculated from PROWESS, CMIE.

this sector, the cross-border intensity is very low at 6.25 percent. Even with this low cross-border intensity, the market shares appear to be responding to mergers. Out of the eight cross-border mergers covered in this sample, six are owned by the Unilever Group. Unilever has undertaken several mergers, not only in the food sector, but also in other sectors such as soaps and detergents, chemicals, and metals. Even the former market leader, Brooke Bond Lipton India Ltd, has been acquired through this process. Moreover, as discussed earlier, in both sectors, many 1989 leaders have disappeared because of mergers. Most of them were cross-border deals. The absence of these firms will substantially increase the market power of the existing leaders. Table 6.7 summarises the above results for four-firm and ten-firm concentration ratios. These observations are very important since it is occurring in two consumer goods sectors, which has serious implications for consumer welfare.

### 6.4.4 *Product level analysis of two sectors*

One of the major problems facing the above analysis is that it does not take homogeneous products into account since we have undertaken the analysis at the two-digit level. As mentioned earlier, it is because of the nature of the information we have. However, we have tried to concentrate on this issue by focusing on the food and the pharmaceuticals sectors, which are highly responsive to mergers, especially cross-border deals. Though an attempt has been made to delve into the product level, an important point to be noted is that many firms produce multiple products. And, we have only been able to capture their major product lines. According to National Industrial Classification(NIC) classification, there are 38 product lines within the food and food products sector, and in the pharmaceuticals sector, it is 51. We have calculated the disappearance due to mergers in each of these product lines and selected the major product line based on the disappearance rate. We have seen that within the pharmaceuticals sector, 55 percent of all mergers (numbers: 34/62) occurred in the drug formulations subsector. Similarly, in the food sector, 33 percent (40/121) of mergers occurred in the beer & alcohol subsector, and another 24 percent (29/121) were among the tea and coffee producing firms (see Table 6.8). Therefore, we have selected these three sectors for a more disaggregated level of analysis. Here we have repeated the earlier analysis of changes in concentration with and without the merger.

The results are shown in Table 6.9. It can be seen that in all sectors, the effect of mergers is very high, compared to the two-digit industry level. Within the food sector, the concentration ratios of both divisions'—beer & alcohol and tea & coffee—increased more than 100 in the absence of merged firms, which merely shows that in these cases, too, leaders (both top four and 10) have disappeared through mergers. Here cross-border deals also show similar impact in the case of tea & coffee, but its impact has been almost absent in the case of beer & alcohol. In the case of drug formulations also, the impact is highly noticeable. However, it is less as compared to the former two. Cross-border deals in the formulation had an impact on the overall concentration. From this it is clear that at the disaggregated level, sectors/products with relatively high merger rates are likely to be affected by consolidation.

*Table 6.8* Disaggregated level of merger activity (number of firms)

| Industry | Economic Activity | Number of Firms | | Share (percent) | |
|---|---|---|---|---|---|
| | | Non-merging | Merged | Total | Merged to Total |
| 1. Drugs and pharmaceutical | Penta-erythritol | 0 | 2 | 2 | 100 |
| | Sulphamethoxazole | 3 | 1 | 4 | 25 |
| | Pharmaceutical products, nec | 22 | 4 | 26 | 15.4 |
| | Drug formulations | 278 | 34 | 312 | 10.9 |
| | Drugs, medicines & allied products | 172 | 20 | 192 | 10.4 |
| | Antibiotics | 9 | 1 | 10 | 10.0 |
| | Others | 99 | 0 | 99 | 0.0 |
| | *Total* | *583* | *62* | *645* | *9.6* |
| 2. Food and food products and beverages | Tea | 184 | 25 | 209 | 13.6 |
| | Colza oil; Cotton seed oil; different types of oil | 324 | 19 | 343 | 5.9 |
| | Beer | 24 | 19 | 43 | 79.2 |
| | Country liquor | 40 | 16 | 56 | 40.0 |
| | Sugar | 137 | 14 | 151 | 10.2 |
| | Ethyl alcohol | 31 | 5 | 36 | 16.1 |
| | Coffee | 17 | 4 | 21 | 23.5 |
| | Cereal roasted products, etc. (snacks & namkin) | 22 | 3 | 25 | 13.6 |
| | Fish | 97 | 2 | 99 | 2.1 |
| | Milk | 23 | 2 | 25 | 8.7 |
| | Others | 311 | 12 | 323 | 3.7 |
| | *Total* | *1210* | *121* | *1331* | *10* |

Source: Calculated from PROWESS, CMIE.

Table 6.9 Changes in concentration: disaggregated level (in percent)

| Year | Top 10 | | | | | | | | | Top 4 | | | | | | | | |
|---|---|---|---|---|---|---|---|---|---|---|---|---|---|---|---|---|---|---|
| | Beer & Alcohol | | | Tea and Coffee | | | Drug Formulations | | | Beer & Alcohol | | | Tea and Coffee | | | Drug Formulations | | |
| | All | WM | WC | All | WM | WC | All | WM | WC | All | WM | WC | All | WM | WC | All | WM | WC |
| 1989 | 81 | 170 | 83 | 83 | 183 | 132 | 57 | 75 | 64 | 58 | 122 | 59 | 62 | 137 | 99 | 35 | 45 | 39 |
| 1990 | 82 | 173 | 84 | 78 | 143 | 110 | 51 | 69 | 57 | 65 | 137 | 66 | 54 | 98 | 76 | 30 | 41 | 33 |
| 1991 | 81 | 212 | 82 | 74 | 135 | 103 | 48 | 65 | 53 | 56 | 149 | 57 | 51 | 94 | 72 | 29 | 39 | 32 |
| 1992 | 77 | 214 | 78 | 73 | 127 | 100 | 46 | 60 | 51 | 52 | 145 | 53 | 51 | 90 | 70 | 28 | 37 | 31 |
| 1993 | 77 | 200 | 77 | 73 | 132 | 102 | 45 | 59 | 50 | 52 | 135 | 52 | 52 | 95 | 73 | 26 | 34 | 29 |
| 1994 | 81 | 201 | 81 | 72 | 135 | 114 | 41 | 53 | 45 | 58 | 146 | 59 | 54 | 101 | 86 | 24 | 30 | 26 |
| 1995 | 77 | 162 | 78 | 76 | 141 | 121 | 41 | 52 | 45 | 52 | 110 | 53 | 61 | 113 | 97 | 25 | 31 | 27 |
| 1996 | 74 | 164 | 75 | 76 | 138 | 121 | 40 | 49 | 42 | 53 | 116 | 53 | 61 | 110 | 96 | 24 | 30 | 26 |
| 1997 | 81 | 253 | 82 | 73 | 84 | 76 | 40 | 48 | 42 | 55 | 174 | 56 | 50 | 58 | 52 | 23 | 27 | 24 |
| 1998 | 73 | 185 | 74 | 69 | 81 | 73 | 41 | 49 | 43 | 50 | 125 | 50 | 48 | 57 | 51 | 23 | 27 | 24 |
| 1999 | 66 | 140 | 67 | 66 | 81 | 72 | 37 | 43 | 38 | 45 | 94 | 45 | 46 | 57 | 50 | 20 | 23 | 20 |
| 2000 | 66 | 141 | 67 | 63 | 74 | 68 | 39 | 45 | 40 | 45 | 96 | 45 | 44 | 51 | 47 | 21 | 24 | 22 |
| 2001 | 65 | 92 | 65 | 58 | 65 | 60 | 41 | 45 | 43 | 40 | 57 | 40 | 34 | 38 | 35 | 23 | 25 | 24 |
| 2002 | 64 | 92 | 64 | 67 | 70 | 67 | 45 | 47 | 46 | 34 | 49 | 34 | 51 | 54 | 51 | 25 | 26 | 26 |
| 2003 | 63 | 71 | 65 | 60 | 64 | 60 | 48 | 48 | 48 | 38 | 43 | 39 | 41 | 44 | 41 | 27 | 27 | 27 |
| 2004 | 62 | 75 | 63 | 54 | 58 | 54 | 47 | 48 | 47 | 36 | 44 | 37 | 32 | 34 | 32 | 27 | 28 | 28 |
| 2005 | 66 | 81 | 66 | 54 | 57 | 54 | 47 | 48 | 47 | 39 | 48 | 39 | 33 | 35 | 33 | 27 | 28 | 27 |
| 2006 | 68 | 75 | 68 | 58 | 59 | 58 | 46 | 46 | 46 | 47 | 52 | 47 | 38 | 38 | 38 | 26 | 26 | 26 |
| 2007 | 73 | 81 | 73 | 61 | 62 | 61 | 47 | 47 | 47 | 52 | 57 | 52 | 39 | 39 | 39 | 27 | 27 | 27 |
| 2008 | 71 | 78 | 71 | 64 | 64 | 64 | 45 | 45 | 45 | 48 | 53 | 48 | 41 | 41 | 41 | 25 | 25 | 25 |
| 2009 | 79 | 87 | 79 | 63 | 63 | 63 | 47 | 47 | 47 | 58 | 64 | 58 | 41 | 41 | 41 | 27 | 27 | 27 |

Source: Calculated from PROWESS, CMIE.

Notes: 1. WM denotes without merger; WC denotes without cross-border merger; All denotes the overall. 2. Values can be more than 100, which we have explained in the text.

### 6.4.5  On surviving firms in the sample

The following observations emerge from the foregoing discussion. In several industries, firms that merged/disappeared were strong enough to change the share of the existing leaders. When we include more leaders, the degree of their influence on concentration also increases since the successive leader is also involved in several deals. In the case of cross-border deals, its impact is currently noticeable only in certain sectors such as drugs and pharmaceutical and food. So far, we have focused on disappearing firms. But, an important point to be mentioned here is the "invisibility" of the merged firms. In actuality, they do not disappear; rather, they only become invisible during the post-merger period because they add their market shares to the surviving firms in the process of competition. Now, the issue is whether these firms add their values to the leaders or the low-ranking firms in the respective sectors. If it is the first case, the concentration ratio[21] will increase since the disappeared firms are added to the existing leaders. In the second case, the leader's share need not rise, but competition increases, as the low-ranked firms are now better-off due to the addition of these firms.[22]

We have attempted to understand this by examining mergers undertaken by the leading ten firms in the drugs and pharmaceutical industry. It will help us identify where the disappeared firms have added their shares. We have selected this industry because of its importance in general as well as for its cross-border deals, as seen from the analysis. It is interesting to see that the leading ten firms in this industry have undertaken 38.3 percent of all mergers[23] in this industry; this is in addition to the fact that the number of acquisitions is very high compared to the number of mergers. For this analysis, we have taken only mergers due to data limitations. However, from our earlier discussion it is seen that in general, merger intensive sectors are also acquisition intensive. So, these results also indicate the presence of acquisitions. The number one ranking firm Cipla Ltd has not engaged much in consolidation activities except for a few deals made recently. But the followers are actively involved in consolidation activities. Ranbaxy, Sun Pharmaceuticals, Piramal Healthcare, GlaxoSmithKline are well known in the field of M&As. They have also undertaken cross-border transactions. Ranbaxy's consolidation spree can be understood from its initial takeover by the Japanese manufacturing firm, Daiichi Sankyo Ltd and later by Sun Pharma in 2015.[24] The findings based on the ranking and market share analysis of the leading firms are given below.

### 6.4.6  Ranking and market share of the surviving leaders

It is noted that many of the big businesses use consolidation strategy to expand their market and widen their operations. In most sectors, the leaders are engaged in multiple consolidation activities. And, most of the leading firms are owned by big business groups which rely on M&As as their growth strategies in all areas of operation so as to expand their domains, reduce risk

*Table 6.10* Market share of leader ten firms in the pharmaceutical sector

| | Dr. Reddy | Ranbaxy | Lupin | Aurob | Sun | Piramal | Glaxos | Cadila | Matrix |
|------|------|------|------|------|------|------|------|------|------|
| 1989 | | | | | | 0.6 | 7.0 | | |
| 1990 | 0.6 | | | | | 0.7 | 8.0 | | |
| 1991 | 1.1 | | | | | 1.2 | 8.6 | | |
| 1992 | 1.7 | | | | | 1.4 | 8.1 | | |
| 1993 | 1.7 | 6.0 | | 0.3 | | 1.2 | 7.2 | | |
| 1994 | 1.9 | 6.5 | 0.0 | 0.4 | 0.6 | 1.4 | | | 0.1 |
| 1995 | 1.7 | 6.0 | 0.3 | 0.7 | 0.7 | 1.3 | 6.6 | | 0.1 |
| 1996 | 1.6 | 6.3 | 0.4 | 0.9 | 0.8 | 1.3 | 6.5 | | 0.1 |
| 1997 | 1.6 | 6.7 | 0.4 | 1.4 | 1.1 | 3.3 | 4.6 | 1.4 | 0.1 |
| 1998 | 1.9 | 7.1 | 0.5 | 1.7 | 1.5 | 3.1 | 4.4 | 1.7 | 0.2 |
| 1999 | 2.0 | 5.2 | 0.5 | 2.5 | 1.6 | 2.0 | 4.0 | 1.6 | 0.2 |
| 2000 | 2.0 | 6.8 | 0.3 | 3.1 | 2.0 | 2.0 | 3.7 | 1.8 | 0.2 |
| 2001 | 3.8 | 6.8 | 3.1 | 3.8 | 2.1 | 2.2 | 3.7 | 1.9 | 0.3 |
| 2002 | 5.4 | 6.6 | 3.0 | 3.5 | 2.3 | 3.2 | 3.8 | 1.9 | 0.4 |
| 2003 | 4.7 | 9.2 | 3.0 | 3.5 | 2.3 | 3.4 | 3.4 | 2.9 | 1.2 |
| 2004 | 4.2 | 9.3 | 2.9 | 3.2 | 2.1 | 3.4 | 2.9 | 2.7 | 1.3 |
| 2005 | 3.8 | 8.9 | 2.8 | 2.7 | 2.4 | 3.0 | 3.4 | 2.6 | 1.5 |
| 2006 | 4.2 | 6.5 | 3.4 | 2.9 | 2.7 | 3.0 | 3.1 | 2.6 | 1.5 |
| 2007 | 6.5 | 5.6 | 3.2 | 3.1 | 2.7 | 2.7 | 2.7 | 2.4 | 1.2 |
| 2008 | 4.8 | 4.9 | 3.6 | 3.2 | 3.3 | 2.7 | 2.4 | 2.4 | 1.3 |
| 2009 | 5.6 | 4.9 | 3.7 | 3.6 | 3.5 | 2.9 | 2.2 | 2.2 | 1.9 |

Source: Calculated from PROWESS, CMIE.

Note: Shaded points show the year of merger.

and derive synergies. The same group owns more than one firm in the same sector, under different names and with small changes in product profile. Some of the consolidation intensive groups are Tata, Unilever, Murugappa Chettiar, Thapar, and RPG Enterprises. However, we are not going into the details since it is not a subject matter of our analysis. Our examination of the changes in the ranks based on the sale values of the leading ten firms immediately after a merger shows that firms could graduate to relatively better positions immediately after a merger. For example, Ranbaxy ranked number one in the year 1997, immediately upon its merger with Crosslands Research Laboratories Ltd in 1996 (from rank 2). The ranking of Matrix Laboratories Ltd changed from 85 in 2001 to 21 in 2003 with two mergers in 2002; it ranked 10 in 2009.[25] Similar observations can be made in the case of Piramal Healthcare Ltd, Dr Reddy's Laboratories Ltd, etc. There is also evidence for group consolidation, which helped improve the rankings; for instance, Lupin Laboratories Ltd moved up to the sixth position in the year 2001 from 83 upon merging with Lupin Ltd.[26]

When we analyse the market shares of disappeared firms, we can see a clear increase in the shares of the surviving firms immediately after undertaking merger. It can be seen from Table 6.10 that immediately after undertaking merger, the surviving firms were able to expand their shares in all cases.

For example, before entering a merger with American Remedies Ltd and Cheminor Drug Ltd., Dr Reddy's Laboratories Ltd held only 2 percent of the market shares in 2000, which increased to 3.8 percent in 2001. Similar observations can be made in the case of all other leading firms. It can be seen that in the case of Lupin Laboratories Ltd., there was a shift in the market share from 2001 onward, which is mainly due to its internal merger. However, in some cases, the firms could not sustain their increased market shares in the long run. Why it happened is an interesting question. Here, we shall refer to the findings from Chapter 5, in which we have observed that efficiency declines after getting into the merger.

By using different indicators such as concentration ratios and ranking of firms, from the forgoing discussion we have seen that the *disappeared* firms played an important role in deciding the market structure of various sectors, while the *surviving* firms used merger as an important growth strategy. The limitation of this analysis is that it does not take trade effects into account.

## 6.5 Concluding observations

In this chapter, an attempt has been made to explore whether the merger strategy followed by firms in the Indian manufacturing sector has changed the structure of the industries, as indicated by the theoretical literature on M&As. We have seen that a large number of firms have disappeared from the manufacturing sector, and the disappearance rate is substantial since it has changed the concentration ratios in the respective sectors. The survival probability of big firms is relatively higher than that of small firms; however, there are sectoral variations. The sectors, which are more affected by the occurrence of mergers is chemicals, drugs and pharmaceuticals, food and food products, metals and petroleum products. Amongst these, the petroleum sector is most influenced by mergers. It seems that the change in concentration levels is moving in tandem with the disappearance rate, which indicates that the entry of new firms is inadequate to overcome the effect of disappearance through mergers. It is also evident that the emergence of more leaders increases concentration. Though we understand that the Indian scenario is not completely comparable with the international experience due to differences in policy regimes and the stages of development, our findings are in accordance with the findings of some earlier studies in the international context, such as that of Weiss's. In the case of cross-border deals, the effect is visible in drugs and pharmaceuticals and food and food products sectors, while the chemicals sector is not much affected. High frequency of cross-border deals in some sectors (such as the pharmaceutical sector) reflects the buyers' and sellers' preferences to invest in attractive sectors. Moreover, it also reflects the changes made in the Foreign Direct Investment (FDI) policy over time. We also examined the product level impact on three sectors selected on the basis of the earlier analysis. We found that when further disaggregated, the impact of mergers increases. Consolidation leads to the invisibility of the disappeared firms as part of the surviving firms, which requires examining, whether the disappeared firms are adding their shares to the leaders or those at the lower end. We have examined this by taking the case of drugs and pharmaceuticals sector. The study found that the top ten leaders in this sector are involved in a substantial proportion of deals. Also, their ranks have improved compared to the pre-merger phase. We have also noted that many of the 1989 leaders either disappeared or lost their market shares substantially, whereas the 2009 leaders have increased their market shares. The data shows that in many cases, the disappearance of leading firms is due to mergers, along with that of exit other than merger.[27] Many of the leaders are owned by big business groups, which are engaged in consolidation activities. They have not only consolidated their subsidiaries and affiliates but also consolidated those firms which are unrelated to the management.

In short, in most of the merger-intensive sectors, firms that have disappeared through mergers have been strong enough to influence the concentration ratios. However, in the case of surviving firms, the increase in market shares is not sustained in the long run as was expected. This may indicate the absence of adequate synergy creation to the expected levels for further strengthening the market position. In this regard, we shall refer to the efficiency analysis carried out in Chapter 5, in which we have observed that efficiency declines upon entering into M&As (Saraswathy, B, 2015). There is the need for further inquiry into the reasons for the declining efficiency.

## Notes

1  The normal profit is included in the cost curve.
2  Shift from competitive conditions to monopoly.
3  Merger waves in USA are: (1) 1890s–1905, (2) 1920s–1930, (3) 1950s–mid 1970s, (4) 1980s and (5) 1990s. In the case of the UK, the merger waves are (1) 1920s small wave, (2) 1960s–1970s, (3) 1980s–1989 and (4) 1990s (see Owen, 2006 for details).
4  "Majors" means top ranking or leading firms.
5  In other words, not much increase in concentration.
6  This definition of internal growth is given by Ijiri and Simon. However, in our study, we define growth by M&As as external growth, as is done by other studies.
7  Here, the contribution of the merger is higher than that of the total change. It is because of the presence of displacement factor, which exerts negative pressure on the total change in concentration.
8  In other words, it is the differential growth rates.
9  See Baldwin, J. and Paul Gorecki (1998), and Curry and George (1983) for a detailed discussion of different measures.
10  There is no exact rule to decide upon the actual number of firms in the n-firm concentration ratio. We have taken the leading four and ten firms.
11  Thus, the chemical sector in the study excludes pharmaceutical firms.
12  This analysis is restricted to this period because from 2011 is when the CCI regime started, which makes the sample deal different.

13 The unbalanced panel has been used for this analysis since we are dealing with the mergers. The total number of firms from each sector used for this can be seen from Table 6.2.

14 To illustrate, when survival probability equals to one, it implies that the number of surviving firms is equal to the number of firms in the industry and vice versa for the disappearance.

15 These figures may be a little different from the overall disappearance rate we have discussed in Table 6.2 since here we had to classify firms according to their size. In some cases, it is missing.

16 Recently, the government deregulated the sector. Earlier, FDI was permitted up to 26% in public sector units (PSUs), another 26 percent the PSUs were holding and the rest 48 percent of the public (Government of India, 2003). Now the FDI limit has been raised to 49 percent. But automatic approval will not be available for the refining; rather, it will be through the Foreign Investment Promotion Board (FIPB). In the case of private Indian companies, 100 percent FDI is now allowed through the automatic route (GOI, 2008). However, most of the leaders in this sector are PSUs.

17 Cross-border deals are defined as deals which involve foreign firms.

18 In the petroleum sector, there is only one cross-border deal, while in the metal and metal products sector there are seven deals, based on the sample used for this analysis.

19 This is calculated as the percentage of change in concentration in the absence of cross-border deals to the change in concentration in the absence of all deals.

20 Cross-border intensity is the presence of cross-border deals in the overall deals.

21 An increased concentration ratio sometimes undermines the actual degree of concentration. For example, it can lead to increased concentration within the major four firms, in which case the ratio may rise, but the extent of competition will be greater than the pre-merger scenario.

22 It need not always be "better off," since the deal may prove unsuccessful in the long run.

23 Twenty-three mergers are covered in the sample.

24 In India, Ranbaxy was operating under the same name when it was acquired by Daiichi. In March 2015, Ranbaxy was acquired by Sun Pharma.

25 It is also involved in other deals post-2002.

26 Upon merger, the name Lupin Laboratories Ltd was changed to Lupin Ltd.

27 The exit of firms may be either due to merger or due to other reasons. Here we have captured exit through mergers only.

## References

Aaronovitch, S. and Malcom, C.S. (1975). Mergers, Growth and Concentration. *Oxford Economic Papers, New Series,* 27(1), pp. 136–155.

Baldwin, J. and Paul G. (1998). *Dynamics of Industrial Competition: A North American Perspective.* Canada: Cambridge University Press.

Beena, P.L. (2008). Trends and Perspectives on Corporate Mergers in Contemporary India. *Economic and Political Weekly,* 43(39), pp. 48–56.

Cook, P.L. (1954). Review. *The Economic Journal,* 64(255), pp. 586–588.

Curry, B. and George, K.D. (1983). Industrial Concentration: A Survey. *Journal of Industrial Economics,* 31(3), pp. 203–255.

Demsetz, H. (1973). Industry Structure, Market Rivalry, and Public Policy. *Journal of Law and Economic,* 16(1), pp. 1–9.

Desvousges, W.H. and Micheal, J.P. (1979). The Effect of Large Mergers on Concentration Trends in Petroleum Production, 1955–1975. *Southern Economic Journal,* 46(2), pp. 615–622.

Dhall, V. (2007). *Competition Law Today: Concepts, Issues and the Law in Practice.* New Delhi: Oxford University Press.

Evely and Little (1960). Concentration in British Industry: An Empirical Study of Industrial Production 1935–51. Cambridge University Press, UK.

Farrell and Shapiro., 1990. Horizontal Mergers: An Equilibrium Analysis. *The American Economic Review,* 80(1), pp. 107–126.

Federal Trade Commission Report (1948). *The Merger Movement, A Summary Report.* Washington: Princeton University Press.

George, K.D., (1975). A Note on Changes in Industrial Concentration in the UK. *Economic Journal.* 85(337). pp. 124–28.

George, K.D. (1972). The Changing Structure of Competitive Industry. Economic Journal, March Supplement, 82: 353–68.

Glais, M. (2000). Merger Control Laws in European Union, In: J. Kraft, ed., *The Process of Competition.* UK: Edward Elgar. pp. 165–187.

Government of India (2003). *Manual on Foreign Direct Investment in India (FDI): Policy and Procedure.* Secretariat of Industrial Assistance, Department of Policy and Promotion. New Delhi: Ministry of Commerce and Industry.

Government of India (2008). *Petroleum and Natural Gas Sector Foreign Direct Investment (FDI) Policy.* New Delhi: Ministry of Petroleum and Natural Gas.

Hall, M. and Tideman, N. (1967). Measures of Concentration. *Journal of the American Statistical Association,* 62, 162–168.

Hanna, L. and Kay, J.A. (1977). The Contribution of Mergers to Concentration Growth: A Reply to Professor Hart. *Journal of Industrial Economics,* 29(3), pp. 305–313.

Hart, P.E. (1960). Business Concentration in the United Kingdom. *Journal of the Royal Statistical Society,* 123, Series A, Part 1.

Hart, P.E. (1979). 'On Bias and Concentration', Journal of Industrial Economics, (28)3, pp. 211–216.

Hart, P.E. (1957). *On Measuring Business Concentration.* Bulletin of the Oxford Institute of Statistics, 19 (3). pp. 225–248 (Reprinted 1975)

Hart, P.E and Clarke, R. (1980). Concentration in British Industry 1935–75. NIESR. Cambridge University Press. Cambridge.

Hart, P.E. and Prais, S.J. (1956). The Analysis of Business Concentration: A Statistical Approach. *Journal of the Royal Statistical Society, Series A,* 119, pp. 150–191.

Hart, P.E, Utton, MA and Walshe, G (1973). Mergers and Concentration in British Industry. National Institute of Economic and Social Research. Occassional Papers 26. Cambridge University Press: London.

Ijiri, Y. and Herbert, A.S. (1971). Effects of Mergers and Acquisitions on Business Firm Concentration. *The Journal of Political Economy,* 79(2), pp. 314–322.

Moody, J., 1904. The Truth about the Trusts, Moody Publishing Company, New York.

Motta, M. (2004). *Competition Policy: Theory and Practice.* Cambridge: Cambridge University Press.

Mueller, J. (1976). The Impact of Mergers on Concentration: A Study of Eleven West German Industries. *The Journal of Industrial Economic,* 25(2), pp. 113–132.

Nutter, G.W. (1954). Growth by Merger. *Journal of the American Statistical Association,* 49(267), pp. 448–466.

Owen, S. (2006). *The History and Mystery of Merger Waves: A UK and US Perspective.* Working Paper No. 2006-02. Australia: The University of New South Wales.

Saraswathy, B. (2010). "Cross-Border Mergers and Acquisitions in India: Extent, Nature and Structure". Working Paper No. 434. Thiruvananthapuram, India: Centre for Development Studies.

Saraswathy, B. (2015). *Production Efficiency of Firms with Mergers and Acquisitions in India.* Working Paper No. 299. New Delhi: Indian Council for Research on International Economic Relations, June.

Stigler, G.J. (1950). Monopoly and Oligopoly by Merger. *The American Economic Review,* 40(2), pp. 23–34.

Stigler, G.J. (1956). The Statistics on Monopoly and Mergers. *Journal of Political Economy,* LXIV(1), pp. 33–40.

Utton, M.A. (1971). The Effect of Mergers on Concentration: UK Manufacturing Industry 1954–1965. *The Journal of Industrial Economics,* 20(1), pp. 42–58.

Weiss, L.W. (1965). An Evaluation of Mergers in Six Industries. *The Review of Economics and Statistics,* 47, May, pp. 172–181.

Weston, J.F. (1953). *The Role of Mergers in the Growth of Large Firms.* California: University of California Press.

# 7 The post-merger integration
Some ignored dimensions

From the previous chapters, the study reached the following broad conclusions. Even though the mergers & acquisitions (M&As) increased the spending on technology in terms of research & development (R&D) and payments for royalties and technical knowhow, it is not leading to the expected synergies as it was evident from the efficiency analysis. Overall, the technical efficiency of the firms declined during the post-merger period, which raised the issue of market power since the occurrence of M&As is considered to be against the assumptions of perfectly competitive market conditions; this is in addition to the fact that the tendency of oligopolistic competition is increasing in the present market scenario owing to several reasons such as the opening of market and disappearance of the domestic market boundaries. However, the study found that even though the monopoly elements increased immediately after the merger as shown by the increased market share of the surviving firms after a merger, the incidence of it is disappearing as time passes. In other words, the increase in the market shares of the firms had been a short or very short run phenomenon after consolidation. Nevertheless, the disappearance of firms through a merger is significantly contributing to the present market structure itself. For instance, many of the old market leaders disappeared in the process of mergers, and the entry of new leaders in many cases has been facilitated by merger, not the fresh entry *per se*. Thus, our study is in agreement with the earlier studies (e.g. Meeks, 1977; Singh, 1971; Ravenscraft and Scherer, 1989; Beena, 2000; Beena, 2008), which observed that *merger weakens the performance of firms*, which necessitates us to think why it is occurring so, even though mergers are expected to remove the inefficient managers through the hostile takeover threat. However, as mentioned earlier, there are many other issues such as overpayment, or over expectation from the deal, low capacity utilisation and governance issues such as the absence of proper post-merger integration may contribute to the post-merger performance. In this section, we shall try to bring out certain post-merger integration issues arising from consolidation, which is less discussed in the existing literature on M&As in India though they are very important. However, our attempt is only an initial step in this direction.

## 7.1  Mergers and acquisitions as a governance issue

Under corporate setting, there are many stakeholders such as shareholders, the board of directors, management, creditors etc. Each of these stakeholders has their own personal goals. Therefore, the corporate governance plays a key role in promoting the interests of the stakeholders and to establish the relationships among these stakeholders. The divergence in goals leads to the conflict of interest among different groups, which is known as the Agency problem or the Principal Agent Theorem in the literature.[1] Agency Theory predicts the managers act largely out of self-interest unless they are closely monitored by a large block of shareholders (Demsetz, 1983; Shleifer and Vishny, 1997; Walsh and Seward, 1990; as in Lane et al. 1998). The agency approach emphasises that when the firms grow, it becomes inevitable to separate the ownership from control. The classical economists from Adam Smith (1776) to Berle and Means (1932) were dealing with the separation of ownership and control that is the relationship between the principal (that is, owners, who are outsiders) and the agent (that is, managers, who are insiders). In this process, it is important to ensure that the agents act according to the interest of principal.

The occurrence of mergers and acquisitions (M&As) are usually treated as a governance strategy to replace the inefficient management, which will bring more efficient operation of the firm, which is more important in the case of hostile deals. However, managers can use M&As as a tool to improve or weaken the system. For example, undertaking a less prosperous deal may undermine the performance of the company, which will weaken the shareholders' returns also. On the other hand, a well-motivated deal can increase the value of the company and thereby help the shareholders as well. Berle and Means (1932) observed that firms, which are characterised by multiple goals, will not allow the firm to realise the maximum potential output. When the managers of these firms face competition, they try to avoid competition through interpersonal relations. Here a merger or takeover offered prospects for high profitability either through a reduction in the cost of production or improved trading of the combined firm (as in Meeks, 1977).

When we include cross-border deals into the scenario, the implications again change, because of the governance rules and structure changes according to the nationality of the firm. Acquisitions made by the firms from countries with better governance considered to bring better performance post merger. Shareholders' protection varies according to countries. Within this, the minority and majority shareholders' issue comes in (Bris and Cabolis, 2004).

## 7.2  Integration issues: evidence with an illustrative case study

There have been hundreds of M&As occurring every year, and a good proportion amongst them are resulting in losses or are not in a position to gain the expected benefits from the deal, and it leads to the deterioration in the value of the firm rather than the value creation. The present study also observed that the surviving firms are not generating the expected synergies, though their disappeared counterparts were strong in many instances,[2] this has been evident in almost all the indicators used in the study. This raises concern regarding the reasons for the worsened performance. In this context, it should be realised that each merger and acquisition is a separate event. The uniqueness of each and every deal makes the reason for the successes and failures also different. Some studies such as Gadiesh and Ormiston (2002) examined the reasons for the failure of mergers and found that five factors such as mismatch of cultures, difficulties in communicating and leading the organization, poor integration planning and execution, paying too much for the target company and poor strategic rationale as the major reasons for this (as in McDonald et al., 2005). Kautzsch and Thormahlen (2007) points out that "no other managerial project is as complex as post-merger integration and poses such a high-risk error. Not even every second acquisition succeeds in generating its expected synergies and creating additional value". A survey conducted by the Business Week among the merger seasoned managers in the United States observed that more than 40 percent of them blamed the post-merger integration (PMI) process for the transaction's failure, whereas only 27 percent faulted the price of the acquisitions (as in Wyman, 2008). In this context, it is important to assess how far the merged firms could integrate their operations during the post-merger period. Even though the governance part of merger literature is somewhat rich,[3] the post-merger integration issues are less discussed in the merger literature, especially in the studies on industrial organisation. Here our attempt is to understand the major issues related to post merger integration. Though we have decided to investigate the integration issues in a wider context by undertaking a survey of firms, which recorded poor performance, the response of these companies was extremely poor. The only alternative was to rely on the response of a major consolidation intensive firm's perception on the importance of integration in determining the success of deals. We have undertaken an interview with a top company official who is an expert in the area of integration and is involved in monitoring M&As to understand the dynamics of integration. This company is selected based on the deal history and the intensity of the deals along with the involvement in cross-border deals. We are not divulging the name of the company for keeping the information confidential, as suggested by the top officials of the company.

This company is incorporated in the mid-1940s as a steel trading company, which entered the automotive manufacturing after two years. It has operations in more than 18 key sectors such as agribusiness, automotive components, construction equipment, consulting services, industrial equipment, information technology, leisure and hospitality, logistics, real estate, retail, two wheelers and so on. Globally, it has expanded in more than 100 countries. This company is one of the leading Indian automobile manufacturers and is within our sample deals. We have also used information from different websites to understand the details of the deals. In the initial years themselves, this company had a different mode of agreements with other companies, including foreign. It involved in all types of deals, which we had been dealing earlier, including cross-border deals. It has undertaken more than 8 mergers and 27 acquisitions and it has been involved in several strategic alliances. The strategy of the company was to make strategic alliances with the companies in foreign locations, which helps to adapt production to the local conditions. In addition to this interview, we have also traced some of the deals in the Indian and global consolidation scenario to portray the importance of integration issues. We have observed that the consolidation strategy followed by this company through mergers, acquisitions and joint ventures enabled it to fill the weakness at different levels of operation, which converted it as one of the big Indian multinational firms. The consolidation history of this company is certainly a 'guide' for the other companies, who are facing the need for strategic assets, technological capabilities, efficiency enhancement and market expansion. In this context, we will discuss the possible major issues related to the post-merger integration and the perception of this particular firm towards these issues, and some such evidence from the consolidation scenario.

### 7.2.1 Post merger integration (PMI) issues

The integration issues can be broadly classified into those related to human resource, cultural integration and the integration of physical assets (see Figure 7.1). Human resource integration is influenced by the cultural integration and *vice versa*. Cultural issues further consist of issues relating to national and organisational culture. However, most studies dealing with culture treat it as an aggregate term rather than making such a distinction (Anderson and Maja Karlsson de la Rosa, 2006). The physical assets integration issues include marketing, manufacturing and financial integration issues. Human resource and cultural integration are considered to be most important since it has a bearing on all other departments, which involves in the assets integration. We shall discuss below the important aspects on each of these issues from the Indian consolidation scenario. Further, integration issues accruing to each industry, firm and each deal will be different. Therefore, one cannot talk about all these issues with the same firm or same deal. And in the Indian case, discussion on such issues are constrained by the availability of specific information. Moreover, at least some of the integration issues such as relating to technological integration are new, yet to occur since the technology motive through M&As itself is still evolving in India. Therefore, we have also used some of the deals occurred globally to portray these issues.

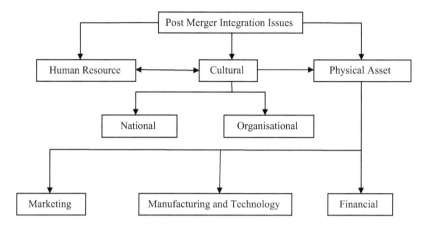

*Figure 7.1* Categorisation of post merger integration issues.
Source: Authors' compilation.

### 7.2.1.1 Human resource integration

Human resource is an integral part of any firm. Any disorder in this will result in collapsing the entire operation of the firm. Therefore, human resource
integration is the major task to be carried out after the deal. Otherwise, the
expected synergies through the cost reduction in marketing, technology and
market expansion plan of the firm will be adversely affected. Thus, integrating
human resource influences the performance of all other departments of the firm
indirectly. Therefore, separating human resource integration from other integration issues such as technology, marketing, cultural integration is impossible.

The employees play a key role in producing the outcome in the case of any
firm. Any dispute with the employees creates organisational inertia and negative impact on the performance of the firm. When the merger occurs, one
important issue that arises is the "me issues" as mentioned by Bruner (2004);
this is related to the employees and captured by the following questions.
"Will I have a job? Will my pay and benefits change? Whom will I report
to? Will I have to move? What will 'they' be like to work for? How will my
status and title change?" These issues are highly distractive and affect the
productivity of the employees. Delay in responding to the "me issues" are
costly in organisational terms since it may result in losing the highly tal-
ented employees. Thus, the post-merger integration should be done at different levels, first among the top-level managers and others and then spread
across the employees and again to the customers of the product. The speed
within which the integration achieved is also important. In sectors such as
banking, this will have important implications. These issues deserve special
attention in the labor-intensive industries rather than that of the capital-
intensive sectors (Borghese and Borgese, 2001).

The discussion with the top official of the Indian company also underlines the above-mentioned facts. According to him,

> the issues relating to human resource integration deserve special attention, while undertaking deals. Each and every employee is an actor in the system, which in turn can influence the success of each department and ultimately the performance of the firm. There is urgent need to integrate each and everyone into the system.

He stressed that their company gives importance to the 'communication' among the partners to make the deal successful. From the Indian consolidation scenario, the recent problem with the Air India due to the merger with Indian Airlines makes the above-mentioned issues relevant. Even though it occurred in the aviation sector, it gives a good lesson for all other firms across all sectors.

*Case I, Air India and Indian airlines merger:* The Government of India approved the merger between Air India and Indian Airlines, on 1st March 2007 in order to synergies the operation of the two national carrier's airlines. Accordingly, the National Aviation Company of India Limited (NACIL) formed on 30th March 2007. Post merger, the newly formed company is known as "Air India" with retaining 'Maharaja' as the mascot. The merger was intended to derive synergy through route rationalisation, fuel procurement, stores and inventory purchase both aircraft and non-aircraft, insurance benefits, handling of flights and employee productivity (Public Enterprises Survey 2010–11). However, the NACIL reported a loss of Rs. 2226 crore on a turnover of Rs. 13638 crores in the year 2007–08 with a net worth of Rs. 5813 crore. The company experienced a severe cash crunch, which resulted in delaying the salary payment for June 2009, for the first time in the history of Air India (Venkatesan, 2009). The cumulative loss of the firm was calculated to be Rs. 22165 crores along with a debt of Rs. 22000 crores (The Hindu, 17th August 2011). According to the Public Enterprises Survey 2010–11, for the year 2009–2010, NACIL registered a net loss of Rs. 5552.44 crores from the 2007–08 figures of Rs. 2226.16 crores.[4]

From the media reports, Air India could not bring the expected synergies from the deal. The market share declined to 16 percent in 2016 compared to 35 percent at the time of the merger, which essentially indicates the strong rivalry from the other airlines.[5] It is important to recall the employee strike occurred during the phase of acute financial crunch. It seems the Air India could not establish proper post merger integration with the earlier Indian Airlines human resources, which ultimately led to the strike by the erstwhile Indian Airlines pilots asking for salary parity with the Air India employees, since both of them were undertaking a similar activity. As per media reports, RN Pathak, the former director with the Indian Airlines said,

> pilots of erstwhile Indian Airlines are angry for not getting the same pay as their colleagues of Air India for doing the identical job and working

in the same organization. Some top officials including the chief operating officer Gustav Baldauf have quit because of that.

He also mentions,

> ...the immediate cause of the trouble can be traced to the senseless merger of the two wings of the airline....it is not that the country does not have the experience of airline merger business. The Indian Airlines Corporation had its initial teething problems, but then the merger plan was so meticulously worked out that all issues of integration got sorted out in a couple of years and the new-born airline took wings smoothly.

Further, "...the present amalgamation of the two wings of the national airline was done hastily and defied the recommendations of several committees..." (News One, 16 August 2011). Moreover, there has been cut in the number of operations owing to the huge losses, which again reduces the salary of the pilots.[6]

*Case II, Glaxo-Wellcome-Burrough:* Another example for the human resource issue is the case of the merger of Glaxo-Wellcome-Burrough, which was one of the most celebrated deals in the pharmaceutical sector. Globally, these firms have decided to merge in the year 1996. However, the deal materialised in India only after nine years of global implementation (in 2004) due to the existence of high pay difference between the employees of Glaxo and Wellcome in India. Even though the workers of Wellcome offered a one-time compensation of Rs. 2 lakhs in 1998, which has not been accepted by the employees. Further Voluntary Retirement Scheme (VRS) launched by the firm evoked a very tepid response. Since 1997, the firms have been operating as independent subsidiaries in India (Pareek, 2012; Business Line, 2004).

### 7.2.1.2 Cultural integration: organisational and national culture

According to Weber and Camerer (2003), culture is usually thought of as a generally shared social understanding, resulting in commonly held assumptions and views of the world among organisational members. Culture is developed in an organisation through joint experience over a long period of time. It allows the members of an organisation to coordinate the activity tacitly without having to reach agreement explicitly in every instance. Language in the form of codes, symbols, anecdotes, and rules about appropriate statements play an important role in the organisational culture of the firms. Organisational culture is different from the national culture (Sarala, 2008). National culture has been defined as the collective programming of the mind acquired by growing up in a particular country (Hofstede, 1991, as in Sarala, 2008); this is reflected in the fact that even though the organisational characteristics are the same, each actor in an organisation will have national cultural uniqueness. For example, the organisations in the Germany and Netherlands may look increasingly similar from the outside, whereas both of them continue to behave differently within their organisations (Sarala, 2008). Organisational culture is changed especially since the firm is undergoing changes in the management after the deal. Often, consolidation leads to the reduction in the workforce as well as re-design of the existing organisational set up. The impact of this will be strong on those who perceive that they lack control over the firms new setup. This generates considerable pressure on the performance of those involved (Fried et al., 1996 as in de Sousa, 2006).

National cultural differences are very important for cross-border deals. In the case of some deals, the bidder gives full freedom to the target firm to keep their traditions and culture, and in some other instance, the bidder changes the culture and traditions of the target firm completely, which ultimately affects the performance of the firm after the deal. A study by the researchers of Bain and Company found that in many cases, the merging firms impose their business culture on the target firms. This is the case especially in the scale driven deals.[7] Whereas in the scope driven cases,[8] they keep the culture of the merged entity separate and make it completely new (Till Vestring et al., 2003, as cited in Bruner, 2004). However, post-merger integration is very much inter-firm phenomenon since it can vary according to the firms and also across the deals. The size of the firms involved in the deal is an important factor, which can lead to the integration issues. The approach of the surviving firms towards a small sized target may be different from that to a medium or large sized target firm. However, for a successful deal maker, differences in size and strength of the firm will not make any difference in the dealings with the target. Otherwise, it leads to integration issues and ultimately leads to the unscrambling of the deal after a period. According to Borghese and Borgese (2001), in many cases, employees are unaware of their cultural strength and how it impacts their daily activities. Therefore, it is important for administrators to follow the following steps while undertaking deals. (1) to allow cultural differences to play a part in determining the deal's value, (2) to realize that both companies' cultures are important, (3) to admit that it is not in either company's interest to maintain both companies' cultures and (4) to combine the two cultures in a way that it will prevent the deal from exploding.

According to the top official of the company we interviewed, cultural differences are obvious and existed in their consolidation experience also. They tackled it successfully by taking the positive elements from the disappeared firm and by integrating them into the bidder. According to him, "a deeper understanding in using the own strength of the disappeared firm is important while undertaking deals. Identifying the areas of integration is unavoidable under all circumstances". Further,

> cultural integration often requires communication, meetings, plant visit, performance management system etc. Since all these involve

different layers of employees as it takes time to settle down. Sometimes it may take one to two years to integrate the whole system after the deal. Thus it is a long term affair.

Thus, like the human resource integration, cultural integration requires communication, especially the unofficial communication, which is vital in tackling all issues.

*Case III, Daimler-Chrysler deal:* The best example for the issues relating to the cultural integration is the Daimler-Chrysler deal—an American-German deal in the automobile sector at the global level. It was considered as a 'merger of equals', and after that, there was a great expectation that the merger would be successful. It was expected to derive synergies from the strength and capabilities of the two firms, which will render mutual benefits. However, the performance after the merger was entirely different from the expectation, particularly the Chrysler division. This company began to experience losses shortly after the deal and was expected to continue to do so for several years. There was also significant layoff at Chrysler following the deal. It has been found that the major reason for this has been the cultural difference between the two firms. Operations and managements were not integrated as of 'equals', due to the differences in the operation of the Americans and Germans. Daimler's culture was a more formal and structured management style, but the others' was more relaxed, freewheeling style. The views on pay scales and travel expenses were also different. Gradually, the German firm started dominating over Chrysler, and consequently, the employee performance of the American firm began to worsen. And the Daimler became increasingly dissatisfied with the performance of the other firm (Finkelstein, 2002).

*Case IV, General motors—Electronic Data Systems deal:* Another example of the cultural conflict has been the purchase of Electronic Data Systems (EDS), a computer service giant by the automakers General Motors (GM) for $2.5 billion made in the year 1984. It has been expected that the cost of production will decline and the market share of GM increase after the deal. Following the deal, GM became world's number one data processing company. However, the high-tech dream was never materialised. One of the major reasons behind this was the differences in the corporate culture and management style. GM's management culture was more bureaucratic, centralised style, whereas that of EDS was more entrepreneurial and customer driven approach. From the start, the data processing subsidiary's unique status as an independent company within GM doomed the merger itself. EDS' founder Ross Perot, given a seat on the GM Board of Directors clashed publicly with the GM chairman Roger Smith, the man who engineered this deal, over his role in the combined entity. GM silenced its most vocal critic in 1986 by buying back its stake. After 12 years, in 1996, GM spun off EDS as an independent, publicly traded company (as in Borghese and Borgese, 2001).

The above experiences underline the need to address the cultural issues adequately.

### 7.2.1.3 Manufacturing, technology and marketing integration

Integration issues related to manufacturing and marketing raises mainly because of the product profile of the bidder and target. It is obvious that if both the firms are engaged in the production of the competing brands, it may lead to 'ego' and inferiority complex. This is important even in the case of 'equal deals' since the possibility of 'ego clash' is higher in this case. Evidence suggests that sometimes, it may lead the firms to deny the sharing of the marketing outlets, which may spread to the other aspects of employee relation and ultimately on the performance of the firms. Therefore, identifying this issue, right from the beginning is very important.

***Technological integration***: Technology is an important area where a divergence of views emerges, especially because it involves the sharing of tacit knowledge, which may be the outcome of a long year of trial and error by the firms involved. It has been pointed out that the Multinational Companies (MNCs) prefer to locate their R&D centres in their headquarters in order to keep their technology safe, even though they have technical collaborations with the firms in other countries. Similar issues may arise in the context of consolidation through M&As as well. Narula's discussion about the Rational Risks in the alliance capitalism can be applied here (see Narula, 2003). Rational Risks arise when one or more partners in the alliance are unwilling to work towards the mutual interest of the partnership. They may not be sharing the required inputs to the partners as prescribed. In the merger context, sometimes the bidder may not be disclosing the critical knowledge to the target, while they may be using the targets' capabilities; this ultimately exploits the target, while the bidder will improve its product profile. This may create disappointment among the employees of the bidder firm, which may lead to the differences in the views and ultimately the poor performance. The cross-border firms involve nationality feelings as well. Adding to this, a large number of qualified human resources is an essential condition for monitoring the externally acquired knowledge (through consolidation) and converts it into productive activities. Therefore, it involves the integration of not only different firms but also the involvement of a large number of human resources in the innovation department. The current stage of technological development of the firms involved is also important, especially for those deals which are aiming at the derivation of synergies in innovation efforts. If the target is in the initial stages of innovation, it may not be able to adapt to the superior technology of the surviving firm, which may create serious integration issues. It also involves a great deal of challenges, when the firm is converted from the traditional system to a consolidated entity. Holweg et al. (2004) mention in the context of the supply chain collaborations that in reality, it is a difficult task to link the externally acquired information with that of the firm. Large MNCs usually do not use firm collaborations to fine tune their day to day operations. The joint operation also brings issues regarding the ownership, when the firm succeeds to generate Intellectual Property Rights and such other technology outcomes. If the target is not getting the adequate appreciation for their involvement and ideas, it creates integration issues. It is also possible that the consolidated foreign firm export the entire products made in the domestic country to their home country and take benefit of the low-cost production and technology locations in the developing countries. Berggren (2001) says from the ABB Group experience that technical integration of the two systems after the deal may be costly since it involves the development of a unified platform, which means all the new products generated must be compatible 'backwards' to all the existing machinery. Similarly, matching of design after consolidation is also important because it will influence the suppliers, plant tooling spare parts, systems, and the large array of service shops.

In the case of the present company under study, while reviewing the history of the firm we have observed that consolidation enabled them to bridge the lacking technological capabilities. According to the top official we have interviewed, they *give importance to identifying the own strength of the firms involved.* Technological capability of the target is given importance and is used along with that of the bidder. Gaining from the complementarities through the acquired assets have been very important in the case of the company considered.

*Case V, Daimler—Chrysler deal:* This case is an example of manufacturing, technology and marketing related integration issues as well. It has been pointed out that Daimler was not ready to share its marketing and manufacturing locations to Chrysler. The logic for this being that Chrysler wants to protect the sanctity of the Mercedes-Benz as the hallmark of its uncompromising quality; this adversely affected the market penetration of Chrysler in Europe. Further, regarding production and technology, the Daimler was always more oriented towards "quality at any cost", with the disciplined German engineers with uncompromising quality, whereas Chrysler was focusing on the price targeted production (Finkelstein, 2002). It became very clear that both the firms could not integrate their technological skills. Instead, they were trying to compete with each other's brands even after the deal became effective. These issues ultimately led to the demerger of the newly created firm.

Thus, changes or up gradation in technology also has implications on matching the entire system and the consumer preferences.

### 7.2.1.4 Financial integration

Financial integration is an important part of the value creation of the firm. Usually, the target firm's shareholders will be gaining less relating to the bidder firms. The unequal distribution of the financial benefits decided during the pre-merger period may lead to integration issues. At the time of consolidation, firms have to value the assets, liabilities, intangible assets etc., which is mostly done through consensus, and it is a due diligence time affair rather than the post-merger time. However, if the target feels that, they have not received adequate compensation, this may lead to issues in the future course. When the firms go for consolidation, the financial services of the two companies become part of the consolidated entity's capital base. Consequently, the financial allocation for different activities will be undertaken by the newly created firm, which may create issues. In this context, it is also possible that the minority and majority shareholders' issue may come in.

JianHua (2007) discussed different areas of financial integration. Defining and integrating the goal of financial management in terms of profit maximisation and or value maximisation is important. The financial management system should take the entire group's benefits and the strategic plan after M&As. Its content of integration includes the integration of investment system, financing system, distribution system, credit management system, financial risk management system etc. Another important area is the integration of accounting system. Sometimes there are differences in the accounting practices of both the parties to the combination, which needs to be appropriately integrated. Proper accounting enables to understand the extent of synergies generated through cost saving, which is extremely important in identifying the areas, which needs more attention. Next in importance is the integration of the financial structure, which involves the integration of both storage quantity property and integration of debt. Amongst this, the integration of storage quantity property includes the integration of tangible and non-tangible assets. The integration of debts includes the merge of financial reports. Finally, there should be achievement appraisal system during the post deal performance, which is essential in policy formulation (see JianHua, 2007).

The top official of the company we interviewed also said that identifying the problem from the beginning is very important. And the capabilities of the target should be adequately valued. Otherwise, it will create post-merger integration issues.

*Case VI: ABB-Flakt deal:* This case is an example of the financial integration issues. The firm ABB is created through the cross-border merger between ASEA AB of Sweden and BBC Brown Boveri of Switzerland in 1988. In that year itself, the consolidated firm again acquired Flakt AB, Sweden. In India also their subsidiaries became consolidated following the parental operations. However, the studies were done on the financial performance after the deal revealed that the gain from this deal was less than the capital market Bombay Stock Exchange Sensitive Index (BSE SENSEX) growth. The shareholders of the erstwhile Flakt India lost heavily. The main reason for this was the bias in swap ratios.

Therefore, the expected synergies could not be realised (Ray, 2004; as in Ray, 2010).

These are the major issues related to post-merger integration. Even though all these issues are equally important both for the domestic and the cross-border deals, it brings more concerns for the latter especially due to the foreign national content of the deals. From the cases we have cited, it is also clear that even the cross-border deals occurring at the headquarters level (as the parent company) are different from that of the deals between different subsidiary firms. During the subsidiary integration times, new issues are being generated. It also involves the differences in language, nationality and culture among the employees of the firms involved in the deals, which creates risks. Appropriate due diligence process can take care these issues to a great extent. Another complexity arises when the firms go for the multiple deals, which is a common phenomenon at present. Most of the top firms have undertaken more than two deals. Each merger cannot be separately seen. Thus, the bidder is not a single firm; rather a group of firms, which go for the deal. It raises the need for integration within each bidder. In the absence of proper coordination among the bidder firms, it is worthless to talk about the integration with the newly acquired target firm. In some cases, the target may be made of the consolidation with some other firms, which will bring the similar issues to the target as well. This necessitates the need for broader integration first among the bidder firms, then among the target firms and finally between the target and the bidder firms. Vayudoot's deal with Air India is an example to this.

A successful manager will be the one who can handle all the above-mentioned agency issues such as human resources, cultural, manufacturing and marketing among others. From the discussion with the top official of the company, it is clear that the firms face different issues while undertaking the deals. Those who want to become successful through consolidation should realise the importance of it while undertaking the deal. According to the top official we have interviewed,

> the culture and communication play serious roles in the integration of firms after the deal. The firms, which are undertaking the deal, need to understand the areas where integration is necessary. Each firm consists of different actors and different departments with conflicting interests such as financing, manufacturing, human resource (including different vendors). A proper integration of each of these actors is necessary.

These issues are important in determining the performance of the deal. As mentioned earlier, the present firm has been undergoing a large number of consolidation activities. And in the view of the respondent, the above-mentioned integration strategies followed by the firm helped it to make overall success in deal making and performance through these deals. The consolidation strategy followed by this firm has been a major driver in many crucial product lines of this company, not only within the Indian market but also in the overseas market. One important speciality of the deals of this company has been that in many cases, the firm started with a lesser degree of relationship such as alliances, joint ventures, which in many cases led to the acquisition and then to mergers. It may be an indication that the company could integrate the acquired assets on the right direction during the post deal period.

## 7.3 Conclusion

In this chapter, our attempt has been to give one line of explanation to the varying performance of firms which are going for M&As. Globally, many of the studies found that *merger undermines the performance of firms.* In other words, the post-merger period is associated with deteriorated performance in terms of various performance indicators. The present study in the Indian context also reached an almost similar conclusion. In this context, our aim in this chapter has been to portray one of the less discussed but very important issues in determining the post-merger performance that is the role of integration issues. The agency issues are important in determining the performance of firms even without a merger. A merger brings new actors into the front and thereby new issues as well. The cross-border content of deals may again aggravate integration issues as the culture of both the firms may be entirely different. There are three major types of post-merger integration issues identified, such as human resource, cultural and physical assets. We have attempted to explain this with the help of M&As occurred. Along with this, we have attempted to capture the views and perception of one top official of a consolidation intensive Indian company regarding the above-mentioned areas of integration. This company's product market and the geographic market has been widely expanded by engaging in consolidation strategies. We have been trying to inquire their views.

It is evident from the study that the firms which are undertaking consolidation should give special emphasise on the post-merger integration. Human resource integration is the most important, which will have an impact on all other areas of integration. Communication and meetings have very important role in achieving human resource integration, which the future deals may give emphasise. Differences in culture and tradition should be viewed with dignity, and it should be integrated with mutual understanding. Similar is the case with the extent of quality in production, manufacturing, and all other areas of operation. Identifying the areas of integration is important. Even though the cross-border deals bring additional complexities, the mode of integration is not much different from that of domestic deals. Even though post-merger integration is vital for the success of the deals, the adequate importance is not given now, which has led to the unsuccessful operation. It seems the decline in post-merger efficiency and the not so remarkable increase in market power after consolidation, especially in the long run may be the outcome of inadequate integration of the firms after merger along with other issues such as over payment for the deal.

## Notes

1 See Bruner (2004) for a detailed discussion on Principal Agent Model.
2 See Chapter 6 for details.
3 There are many studies, which dealt with the valuation issues and the shareholders' wealth creation through mergers (see for instance Sudarsanam et al., 1996; Mandelkar, 1974; Dodd, 1983; Asquith and Kim, 1982; Asquith, 1983; Kumar and Paneerselvam, 2009).
4 Air India experienced an operating profit in fiscal 2016 for the first time in nine years since the merger.
5 Balachandran, M (2016), "9 Years and Rs. 30000 crore later, Air India is finally set to make some money", Quartz India, 16th March, Accessed on 30th April 2017.
6 This was reported by a pilot of the Indian Commercial Pilots Association (ICPA) while announcing their strike. Available at http://www.rediff.com/business/report/air-india-cmd-writes-open-letter-ahead-of-stir/20110307.htm, Accessed on August 17th 2011.
7 Cases where the deal aims at the efficiency enhancement.
8 Such as to broaden the product lines etc.

## References

Anderson. and Maja, Karlsson de la Rosa., (2006). *Cross-border and Corporate Aspects on Culture in Mergers and Acquisitions.* Bachelor Thesis. Department of Business Studies, Uppsala University.

Asquith, Paul. and Han. E. Kim., (1982). The Impact of Merger Bids on the Participating Firm's Security Holders. *Journal of Finance,* 37(5):1209–1227.

Balachandran, M (2016), "9 Years and Rs. 30000 crore later, Air India is finally set to make some money", Quartz India, 16th March, Accessed on 30th April 2017.

Beena., (2000). An Analysis of Mergers in the Private Corporate Sector in India. Working Paper No: 301. Thiruvananthapuram: Centre for Development Studies.

Beena., (2008). Trends and Perspectives on Corporate Mergers in Contemporary India. *Economic and Political Weekly,* 43(39):48–56.

Berle, A. A. and G. C. Means., (1932). *The Modern Corporation and Private Property.* New York: Macmillan.

Berggren, C. (2001). Mergers, MNEs and Innovation—The Need for New Research Approaches. In: ESRC Transnational Communities. Conference on Multinational Enterprises. Warwick, Sweden, 6–8 September.

Borghese, R. J. and Paul, F. Borgese., (2001). M&A From Planning to Integration. Mc-Graw Hill. New York.

Bris, A. and Cabolis, C. (2004). *Adopting Better Corporate Governance: Evidence from Cross-Border Mergers.* USA: Yale School of Management, January.

Bruner, R.F. (2004). *Applied Mergers and Acquisitions.* UK: John Wiley and Sons.

Business Line, (2004). GSK, Burroughs Wellcome boards clear Merger-Share swap at 14:10. Business Line, Available at http://www.thehindubusinessline.

com/2004/03/18/stories/2004031802660100.htm. [Accessed on 8th October, 2015].

Demsetz, H., (1983). The Structure of Ownership and the Theory of the Firm. *Journal of Law and Economics,* 26: 375–390.

Dodd, P., (1980). Merger Proposals, Management Discretion and Stockholder Wealth. *Journal of Financial Economics,* 8(2):105–137.

Fried, Y. Tiegs. R.B., Naughten, T.J. and Ashford, B.E., (1996). Managers Reactions to a Corporate Acquisition: Test of an Integrative Model. Journal of Organisational Behaviour, 17: 401–427.

Hofstede, G. (1991). *Culture and Organisations: Software of the Mind.* London: McGraw Hill.

Holweg, M., Disney, S.M., Holmstrom, J. and Smaros, J. (2004). *Supply Chain Collaboration: Making Sense of the Strategy Continuum.* Available at: http://lrg.tkk.fi/logistics/publications/collaboration_strategy_continuum.pdf. [Accessed on 19th July 2012].

JianHua, W. (2007). *Post Merger Financial Integration of the Enterprises.* School of Economics and Management. China: Henan Polytechnic University. Available at: http://www.seiofbluemountain.com/upload/product/200910/2007glhy06a5.pdf. [Accessed on 3rd October 2012].

Kumar, and Paneerselvam (2009). Mergers, Acquisitions and Wealth Creation: A Comparative Study in the Indian Context. IIMB Management Review, 21(3):222–244.

Lane, A., Cannella, J.R. and Micheal, H. Lubatkin., (1998). Agency Problems as Antecedents to Unrelated Mergers and Diversification: Amihud and Lev Reconsidered. Strategic Management Journal, 19(6): 555–578.

Mandelkar, G., (1974). Risk and Return: The Case of Merging Firms. Journal of Financial Economics, 1(4): 303–335.

McDonald, Jarrod. Max. Coulthard. and Paul, de Lange., (2005). Planning for a Successful Merger or Acquisition: Lessons from an Australian Study. *Journal of Business and Technology,* 1 (2).

Meeks, G. (1977). *Disappointing Marriage: A Study of the Gains from Merger.* Cambridge: Cambridge University Press.

News One (2011). http://www.inewsone.com/2011/05/08/air-india-crisis-a-carefully-crafted-design-comment/48957. [Accessed on 16th August].

Pareek, R., (2012). Amalgamation and Merger— Issues and Problems. Variorum, Multi-Disciplinary e-Research Journal, 2(3). Available at: http://ghrws.in/charity/Variorum/Variorum%20Vol.-02%20Issue%20III,%20February%202012/1%20Dr.%20Dani.pdf. [Accessed on 17th October 2016].

Ravenscraft and Scherer, F.M., (1989). The Profitability of Mergers. *International Journal of Industrial Organisation,* 7(1):101–116.

Vaara, E. Sarala, R. Stahl. and Bjorkman (2012). The Impact of Organisational and National Cultural Differences on Social Conflict and Knowledge Transfer in International Acquisitions: Domestic and Foreign Acquisitions of Finnish Companies. *Journal of Management Studies,* 49(1):1–27

Shleifer, A. and Vishny, R.W. (1997). A Survey of Corporate Governance. *Journal of Finance,* LII(2), pp. 737–783.

Singh, A., (1971). *Takeovers: Their Relevance to the Stock market and the Theory of the Firm.* Cambridge: Cambridge University Press.

Smith, A., (1776). *An Inquiry into the Nature and Causes of Wealth of Nations.* Harvard Publishing: UK.

Sudarsanam, S., Peter, H. and Avo, S (1996). Shareholder Wealth Gains in Mergers: Effect of Synergy and Ownership Structure. *Journal of Business Finance and Accounting,* 23(6).

The Hindu, 17th August 2011.

Till, V., King, B., and Rouse, T. (2003). Should You Always Merge Cultures? *Harvard Management Update*, May 2003, Page 10; As cited in Bruner, F. (2004).

Venkatesan, R. (2009). Should the Air India Maharaja be Awarded his Privy Purse. *Economic and Political Weekly*, XLIV(32), pp. 33–37.

Walsh, J. P. and J. K. Seward., (1990). On the Efficiency of Internal and External Corporate Control Mechanisms. Academic Management Review, 15:421–458.

Weber, R.A. and Camerer, C.F. (2003). Cultural Conflict and Merger Failure: An Experimental Approach. *Management Science*, 49(4), pp. 400–415.

Wyman, O. (2008). Post Merger Integration: A Tailored Approach to Sustainable Transaction Success. Available at: http://www.oliverwyman.com/media/Post_ Merger_Integration_en.pdf. [Accessed on 8th July 2012].

# 8 Conclusions and policy inferences

Like the global scenario, the Indian corporate sector too experienced a boom in M&As led restructuring strategies especially after liberalisation, which is mainly due to the increasing presence of subsidiaries of big MNCs here as well as due to the pressure exerted by such strategies by the domestic firms. Besides, many MNCs realised the fact that the Indian market is a big consumer base to meet their desired objectives such as market creation, efficiency enhancement, strategic assets creation etc. Thus, the entry into the Indian market is unavoidable. Mergers, acquisitions and similar other strategies are an easy way of accessing the big Indian market without much cost of time and effort compared to the Greenfield mode of entry. In order to facilitate globalisation, the Indian government also implemented various policies which marked a paradigm shift in the operation of the domestic firms as it removed the patronage enjoyed by the domestic firms under the assumptions like Infant Industry argument and exposed them for the free play of market forces. More importantly, globalisation reduced the product life cycles, and the firms began to bring out new products quickly to the market as compared to the past. The computer aided manufacturing helped to reduce the time needed for production. Shortened product life cycles meant high R&D intensity, and this has to be recouped before the technology becomes obsolete, which becomes especially important if a rival firm succeeds to bring out a new generation product. These factors are equally important for the domestic firms. These circumstances prompted firms to engage in various kinds of agreements to reduce the high risk associated with innovation and to become successful through the sharing of tangible and intangible assets. Given this broad context, our attempt has been to analyse the changing nature of foreign investment in the form of M&As vis-à-vis the domestic deals. The absence of data prevented many scholars from making detailed studies. More specifically, our aim is to understand whether the strategy of M&As adopted by the firms helped them to achieve their desired objectives in terms of improvement in technology, enhancement of efficiency and market power in the context of the increasing M&As in India since the introduction of market oriented policies in the 1990s.

The study also gains importance in the context of the new Competition Act (CA), which aims at maintaining competition and protect the consumers' interests without harming that of producers along with their innovation efforts. However, the new Act faces a dilemma whether to allow the firms to become 'bigger' and permit them to exercise their monopoly power in future. The size effect through a merger is expected to enable firms to undertake costly innovations. Here the interaction of Intellectual Property Rights (IPR) and CA also gains significance. Though the IPR aims at providing temporary monopoly power to the inventor, the CA aims at creating and sustaining competition. If the costly innovation effort is unprotected, the innovation creation in future will be adversely affected. However, the relationship between technological performance and M&As has not been adequately addressed in the literature, because it was not a major concern during the initial merger scenario. It became important especially in the context of increasing competition, and thereby the firms started to use consolidation strategies to become more competitive. In India too, initially, M&As were mainly intended to enhance efficiency and market power. However, in the context of fast moving innovation effort, consolidation is also aimed to achieve fast moving technological advancement. The study examined these issues in the Indian manufacturing sector. The study consists of eight chapters. After outlining the broad context and issues in the first chapter, the second chapter introduced the major concepts, evolution and policy points associated with M&As. The third chapter portrayed the nature, extent and structure of M&As occurred in India and abroad, in the context of the global scenario. The subsequent chapters addressed the issues regarding technology, production efficiency as well as market concentration arising out of M&As in a comparative framework involving the ownership categories such as cross-border and domestic and compared this with their own pre-merger period. The major analysis is restricted to the cross-border and domestic deals occurred within India. Major findings from the study are discussed in the following sections.

Globally, in general, the number and value of cross-border M&As are increasing year after year. There is a gradual shift in organic ways of foreign investment to inorganic means of brownfield investment. Like the case of overall FDI, there has been a high national difference in attracting Brownfield FDI, which is very much evident from the fact that the top ten purchasers in the world constitute more than 70 percent of the value of cross-border transactions. It is evident that the world FDI flows are moving in tandem with the movement of cross-border M&As. Further, M&As are again moving in line with the movement of the service sector M&As. Thus, it becomes clear that the service sector M&As are the major force behind the world FDI during the study period.

Despite the recent surge in cross-border deals, the Indian cross-border M&As scenario is still in a nascent stage. However, its share FDI increased to 17 percent in 2014 from the meagre share of 2 percent in the 1990s. Around

35 percent of the M&As occurred in India during 1978 to November 2007 were cross-border deals. It has significantly increased only after mid-1990s. The industrialised countries such as UK, USA and Germany are the most common dealmakers in India. Most of the top valued M&As are occurring in technology intensive sectors such as drugs and pharmaceutical, telecom, petroleum, power generation etc. and there is high occurrence of horizontal and vertical deals. Prior to mid-1990s the M&As scenario in India was dominated by domestic deals, followed by an increasing presence of cross-border deals from the mid-1990s. The recent surge in overseas acquisitions is the post-2000s phenomenon. Many of the overseas deals were partial deals for getting strategic assets such as brand names and assets. Brand names acquisition was mainly in the Drugs and Pharmaceutical sector, whereas that of the plant and other assets acquisitions were resorted to for capacity expansion. Here also the service sector firms dominated the entire deals. Needless to say, in many instances, foreign acquisitions helped the Indian firms to become world leaders through altering the capacity and thereby market power.

By examining the trends and patterns of M&As, we felt the need to examine the earlier mentioned hypothesis on technology, efficiency, and market concentration arising out of consolidation. Technology becomes important since it is seen that the industrialised nations such as the UK, the USA and Germany are the most common dealmakers in India and the occurrence of top valued deals in more technology intensive sectors are expected to improve the technological performance of surviving firms, which may further lead to higher efficiency. The high intensity of horizontal deals further demands the inquiry into the market structure.

Specifically, on the issue relating to technological performance, an attempt has been made to analyse whether this has actually led to the expected increase in technological performance during the post-M&As period and whether it changes according to the nature and structure of deals. The inter-firm variations in performance are measured by using two major input measures of technology such as R&D intensity and payments made for royalties and technical know-how. The study observed that the R&D intensity of majority of the firms increased or remained the same during the post-M&As period. Payments for royalties remained constant for the majority of the firms. Major observation from the cross-border and domestic classification is that R&D intensity of domestic firms is higher than the cross-border deals in more technology and consolidation intensive sectors. Whereas, cross-border firms are more technology import intensive than in-house R&D intensive. Thus, the dependence of the cross-border M&A firms on the import of technology is clearly noticed. Nevertheless, before reaching any conclusion, we should also realise the fact that in India, consolidation strategies are of recent origin unlike the US or UK experience. India's initial phase of M&As activity is comparable to the fourth and fifth merger waves of UK and USA. Consolidation was a market expansion strategy rather than a technology driver until recently. Even though an increasing number of firms are using it and deriving technological synergies, it is very difficult to capture the technological outcome simply through the spending on R&D. The patent is another such outcome variable of technological progress, but in the case of developing countries such as India, it is too inappropriate to depend on patents also. Information on M&As related patents is also scanty. Such incremental additions to knowledge will be reflected in the overall performance of the firms in the form of increased efficiency. At present, it is not sure whether the increased spending on technology that is through R&D investment as well as import of technology is leading to the efficient utilisation of the resources, which forms the core of our next chapter.

Production efficiency can be increased through increased capacity utilisation (that is, through deriving economies of scale and scope) and through cutting down multiple expenses. Besides, a number of studies suggest that M&As in general changes inefficient managers and exert pressure on the existing non-merging firms to restructure their operations in order to strengthen themselves. There will be a significant difference in the post deal productivity of firms involved in cross-border deals and domestic deals. Cross-border deals assume to have more efficient utilisation of resources. However, it may be more affected from the issues such as differences in culture, language etc. Nevertheless, we expect the type of integration would have a greater say in productivity and efficiency.

After consulting the other techniques in the relevant literature, the study used stochastic frontier production function along with inefficiency effects introduced by Battese and Coelli (1995). The study found that the post consolidation technical efficiency of the firms involved in M&As declined for the majority of the firms and M&As has not significantly contributed to reducing the inefficiencies except for 1994 deals. In the previous chapter, it is observed that the spending on R&D and royalties increased after getting into M&As. However, from the efficiency analysis, it becomes clear that the increased spending on technology is not used to its full potential. The decline in technical efficiency for the post-M&As period is true for sector-wise analysis also. Reading from the results, we can argue that the negative pressure exerted by M&As is not enough to overcome the production inefficiencies in general. Technical efficiency of both horizontal, as well as vertical deals, declined during the post-merger period. It was expected that for these deals the synergy creation is more and thereby the efficiency enhancement will be higher. Added to this, the elasticity of factor inputs shows that post-M&As period is associated with the more efficient use of labour. The contribution of capital is the lowest in the overall changes in total output. This may be reflecting that during the post-M&As period, firms are unable to derive the expected synergies in capital usage. Thus, it appears that M&As is leading to the underutilisation of capital. Even better utilisation of labour is not enabling to overcome the inefficiencies associated with production. Examination of the profitability and cost of production per unit of output also show that there is substantial reduction in the former and expansion in the latter after entering into M&As; this is also true for both cross-border and domestic deals. This result is in consensus with the earlier findings on post-M&As profitability of the firms both in the Indian and international context. The reason for this may be due to the increasing cost of M&As or due to the acquisition of loss making counterpart, lack of proper integration of the firms during post-M&As period or it may be reflecting the increased interest payments after undertaking huge investment for M&As. As mentioned earlier, another side of efficiency gains is the implications on market structure, specifically, whether the strategy of M&As is leading to changes in industrial structure in the respective sector, as proposed by the theoretical literature on M&As. We have addressed this issue in the next chapter.

The study observed that there is the disappearance of a large number of firms from the manufacturing sector and found that, the disappearance process is substantial since it is changing the concentration ratios in the respective sectors. The survival probability of the big firms is relatively higher than that of the small firms. However, there are sectoral variations. The sectors, which experienced high intensity of mergers are chemicals, drugs and pharmaceutical, food and food products, metals and petroleum products. It seems that the change in concentration levels is moving in tandem with the disappearance rate. It is also evident that the inclusion of more leaders increases the concentration; this is in accordance with the findings of some earlier studies in the international context, such as Weiss. In the case of cross-border deals, the effect is seen in the drugs and pharmaceutical and food and food products sector, while the chemical sector is not much affected. We have also examined the product level impact on three sectors selected on the basis of the earlier analysis. From this, we have seen that the impact of mergers is even strong when we disaggregate the sectors. Consolidation is leading to the invisibility of the disappeared firms as part of the surviving firms. This requires us to examine, whether the disappeared firms are adding their share to the leaders or at the lower end. We have examined this, by taking the case of drugs and pharmaceutical sector. The study found that the top ten leaders in this sector are undertaking a substantial proportion of the deals. It is also important to note that they are engaging in multiple numbers of deals. Our examination of the top ten leaders proved that their ranks (based on market shares) are better off compared to the pre-merger phase. Many of the 1989 leaders either disappeared or lost their market share substantially, whereas that of 2009 leaders have increased their market shares. In many cases, the disappearance of leading firms is due to mergers.[1] Many of the leaders are owned by big business groups, which are engaged in consolidation activity. They have not only consolidated their subsidiaries and affiliated group firms but also consolidated the firms, which belong to totally unrelated management. An examination of the top Indian players in global market also revealed that they are using consolidation strategy for growing fast.

In short, in most of the intensive merger sectors, the disappeared firms through merger have been strong enough to influence the prevailing concentration ratios. However, in the case of surviving firms, the increase in market shares is not sustained in the long run as expected. Further, the profitability performance of the surviving firms is declining after getting into consolidation. Here a relevant question would be what makes the firms unable to derive the expected synergies? The literature suggests a number of reasons—from the future expectations to the high-interest payments in determining the post-merger performance. One important factor, which is less discussed in the economic literature on M&As is the agency issues arising out of M&As such as the issue of post-merger integration. This is very important in the context of M&As since it involves the matching of two entirely different cultures. From the literature, it is evident that it is evident that there are three types major types of post-merger integration issues identified, such as human resource, cultural and physical assets. We have attempted to explain this with the help of different consolidation instances occurred in and outside India. The absence of human resource integration creates unnecessary tensions, which leads to the worsened performance of firms, during the post-merger period. If asset integration is not taking place as expected, it will affect capacity utilisation, which in turn affects efficiency. The involvement of cross-border deals further complicates the scenario since it further brings the issues on language, working culture etc. The study also captured the views and perception of one top official of a consolidation intensive company, which also highlighted the need for proper post-merger integration to become successful after consolidation. Thus, from the producers' point of view, there should be the proper mechanism with which the acquired firms are integrated properly in order to derive the maximum potential out of the deal. If the firms could derive the actual synergies, the effect of consolidation on market concentration would have been even higher.

## 8.1 Outcome of the study and the Competition Act

The important factor considered by the competition authority in determining the approval of a deal is the effects of the deal on technology, efficiency and its trade off with the market power creation. Even though the consolidation strategies are often defended in terms of its welfare enhancing effects, the study found that the expected efficiency generation is not taking place after getting into consolidation. Rather, there is a possibility for market concentration to increase since the disappeared firms have been playing a major role in keeping the market competition alive during the pre-merger period. After the deal, the invisibility of them in the surviving firms in general and big business groups, in particular, provide them ample opportunities to exercise monopoly power. It can also lead to different forms of collusion enhancing effects (that is the pro-collusion effect of the merger), which the regulators may not be even able to recognise in right time. However, at present, it is not creating any visible adverse effect on competition since the surviving firms are not generating expected synergies.

In the technology front, even though it is evident that firms are increasing their spending on R&D after the deal, this is mainly contributed by the domestic deals. Still, the cross-border firms are technology import intensive, which may not be bad *per se*. However, when we take the 'nationality' content similar to the case of direct foreign investment, we can say that the *in-house R&D creation has been still away from the foreign firms' research agenda. Most of them are still depending on the foreign headquarters for this.* Now the question here is that, whether this will really increase the spillovers to the domestic counterparts, without direct involvement in research activities. Thus, the study points to the need to rethink the 'technology spillover defence', especially arising from the cross-border deals to a certain extent. However, there has been an improvement in spending on technology after getting into the deals. This improved spending on technology is not translated into the higher efficiency and consequently to the firm's market share in the long run. The effect of mergers on market power creation would have been much higher if the firms were deriving the expected synergies. Effective synergy creation depends on the proper post-merger integration, which involves the inclusion of each agents starting from the owners to the managers and further to the employees. Here the integration issues in the cross-border cases need special mention as it involves additional complications.

Currently Competition Commission of India deals with the antitrust issues. The quality of implementation of Competition Act in any nation indirectly depends on the quality of competition assessment. It appears that given the babyhood of the Commission, compared to the grand old competition regulators abroad, it has been effectively intervening in implementing Competition Act in India. India, being a sovereign country with its own peculiarities in terms of the stage of economic development, a direct comparison with its well off counterparts is unnecessary. The following section presents certain factors where the Commission can think of improvements.

*Relevant Product Market and Relevant Geographic Market:* The first and foremost part of competition assessment is the definition of the relevant market, which consists of both relevant product market as well as relevant geographical market. Most often, the firms are multi product, engaged in the business of many products. However, the usual practice is to examine the products for which horizontal/vertical overlap exists. In this case, the decision is taken without consulting whether the other products (hereinafter "non-overlapping products") are important for the domestic consumers. Normally, the product-wise details on revenue generated and the significance of the party in the 'non-overlapping product market' is not considered while assessing the competition. It is obvious that the companies dismantle production of less-profitable or insignificant revenue generating products after combination. These insignificant products to the parties may be significant from the consumer's point of view. In other words, the withdrawal of the party from the 'non-overlapping product market' may affect competition in that segment post combination; this is more important when the deal has cross-border content[2] since the possibility of dismantling less-profitable products is more.

Though our competition regime has the right to enquire into the deals entered outside India, if it is likely to create competition concern in India, the Act does not give any special emphasise on the nationality' content of the deals while assessing competition. In other words, deals between domestic companies are treated same as those involving foreign firms while assessing competition. While defining the geographic market during prima facie stage, the main consideration given is the direct or indirect presence or absence of the parties to the combination in the Indian market. If it is not present in India, most often the deal is sanctioned saying that it will not affect the Indian market. However, this needs to be further scrutinised. In many cases, foreign firms are attracted to the Indian firms, not to make the domestic firm efficient, but because they want to extract the cheap factors of production from the domestic market, both human and physical. The cheap factors of production will enable them to compete internationally. Under this scenario, the possibility to discontinue or lower the production of the overlapping products of domestic firm's (which are often less priced compared to the acquirer's price) products is high. Foreign firms can simply export the products from the domestic market to the high paid foreign locations, which ultimately lead to the price rise in the domestic market in the long run, especially in the absence of close substitutes. Consequently, the domestic firm, with its long years of experience in the domestic market is being acquired by the foreign counterparts and they can benefit from the low cost of production facilities existing in the Indian market (Saraswathy, B., 2016). These issues are crucial in sectors like pharmaceutical, where the patients' life itself may be affected due to the non-availability of appropriate medicines.

It is also important to recognise the need for adequate human resources from various disciplines to handle various relevant product markets. For example, while defining the relevant market for the pharmaceutical industry, an economist or lawyer cannot understand the drug composition in a particular drug, which is a very much-specialized area. This is applicable for all the sectors. This has to be read with the confidentiality provisions since the Commission is bound to ensure confidentiality of information submitted by the parties to the combination. It requires the establishment of an expert division from various disciplines, which should provide technical help on various matters. This division can be centrally governed to cater to the needs of various Ministries or departments whenever required.

Mostly, the party to the combination is only a subsidiary of a firm, which concentrates on particular products. However, the group may be diversified, engaged in the business of the acquirers' products as well, which makes the definition of relevant market complicated. When it comes to the relevant geographic market also, there is confusion for different products. Here the point made by Joseph, K.J. (1991), regarding the regional market segmentation taking the television receivers as a case study becomes important. The study found regional market concentration exists even though the industry appeared to be highly competitive at the national level measured in terms of four firm concentration ratios. It is to be highlighted that the Commission normally define the relevant geographic market as 'India', rather than regional level. Even if it is defining the regional geographic boundary as the relevant geographic market, it is not necessary that the data on competition pertaining to the relevant region is available. Parties cannot be blamed for this since it is not the party alone determine competition, rather it is also the totality of other firms operating in the relevant geographic market which determines the competition. Normally data on this is not available for all the companies across various products.

*Data availability*: At present, most of the companies are not reporting product-wise financial information on sales, export etc., in their Annual Report. In the absence of it, the available firm level database like PROWESS database of Centre for Monitoring Indian Economy (CMIE) will not report data beyond a four-digit level of industrial classification. However, the Commission's definition of relevant product market is much more disaggregated, depending on the cases. Even though the Commission has administrative power to ask for such information from the parties, it is not necessary or possible that the parties submit information on their competitors, substitutes etc. For deciding the level of competition, it is very important to get information on the product wise details on production and trade related aspects of the competitors. However, since this information is kept in high confidence by the companies, the parties to the combination may not be able to access such information. The clear-cut decision of the Commission depends on the accuracy of information. The absence of information makes the whole analysis based on numbers, which are unreal. Time series data availability is another issue. Short period data may be very much influenced by the seasonality elements, which is not at all taken into account in the analysis. Thus, in the wake of the current Competition Act, there is an urgent need for the government to ask the listed and unlisted firms to periodically report the product-wise financial information, which can be effectively used by the Commission while assessing the competition. The same data can also be used for coordinating the functioning of other government organisations.

*Efficiency-Concentration Trade-off:* While including various aspects of competition and concentration, it is not clear, how the Commission takes into account the potential efficiency generation; this has to be discussed in the background that the merger regulations are *ex ante* in nature. An exact measurement of synergies needs expertise, not only in the market dynamics but also on the application of statistical and econometric tools. It is also not clear which measure of market concentration is the standard economic tool adopted by the Commission. As we discussed in the previous chapters, the economic concept of competition and the reliability of each of the meas-ures of competition are still undergoing debate. Currently, the Commis-sion stresses the availability of product substitutes, import competition and export potential, entry barriers, the possibility of innovation, failing firm hypothesis and existing market shares, while assessing the competition. However, in most of the cases, economic assessment is done in terms of the market share only. The rigorous analysis of the above variables requires quantitative as well as qualitative information on each of the product line of the parties involved in the deal and their competitors.

*Threshold Limit:* As discussed earlier, the parties to the combination shall file notice with the Commission, if it is coming under the prescribed thresh-old limit based on assets and turnover. Then the Commission will come up with the *prima facie* report on the possibility of an adverse effect on the competition. However, if the firms are not meeting the threshold, it will not come under the provision of the Act. Though the competition assessment at present is limited to the relevant product market, the threshold is not based on the relevant product market alone. In highly capital-intensive sectors, the capital base will be higher than that of the other sectors. The Commission has fixed common threshold, irrespective of the sector to which it belongs. Thus, even though a firm is the leader in a particular relevant market, it may not come under the provision of the Act It leaves room for the future threat of competition. To give an example, despite affecting approximately 100 Million active users,[3] the acquisition of Whats App by Facebook did not come under the purview of the Commission due to the limited turn-over of Whats App from India. As per newspaper reports, in the unpaid mobile messaging segment, Facebook owned 'Facebook Messenger' and 'Instagram' were competing with Whats App. In a way, the deal has resulted in removing a strong competitor from the market. In short, even though the Competition Act calls for a similar asset/turnover limit for all firms, in certain sectors, it may not be necessary that the firm needs to cross that cat-egory to exercise monopoly power. Sector specific fixation of asset/turnover limits and application of more than one criterion such as consumer base and market share for merger scrutiny are required.

*Post Combination Surveillance:* There should be an appropriate mech-anism to examine, whether the proposed deal is actually bringing efficien-cies, technical know-how and ultimately the consumer satisfaction since the merger control laws are *ex ante* in nature. This is especially important for those deals, which were sanctioned based on the efficiency defence. Similarly, if an approved deal is creating market distortions in the form of market power creation, how the CCI handle such issues are not clear. One possibility is to regulate it under the abuse of dominance or anti-competitive agreements again, which dilutes the purpose of the regulation. In light of the findings of the study, it seems there should be periodic review of the approved deals that it is generating efficiency or not creating a threat to the competition as the case may be at least for the past three years of the deal.

*Advocacy Initiatives and Regional Representation:* The Approach Paper to the Eleventh Five Year Plan rightly recognised that the *'successful implementation of the Competition policy and law largely depends upon its acceptance by the people.'* India is a vast country with diverse languages and culture across regions. Competition issues are created at the regional level and spread across. However, the Commission is located in Delhi. In order to file a case from the southern end of the nation, the party (or representative) has to spend a lot of money, time and effort for travel alone. This is important given the mandatory time limit for filing the notice and other documents. Though the Commission is undertaking advocacy initiative in various states and institutions, that is not effectively reaching the public. As per the Annual Report of the Commission, consumers are the least beneficiaries of the advocacy initiatives (see Figure 8.1) for whom only 3 percent of the initiatives targeted during the period 2011–2012 to 2013–2014. In absolute terms, only 6 out of 189 events conducted among consumers. Even that may be mainly conducted among the consumer organisations or its representatives, who are only a minor fraction of the ordinary consumer base in India.

It is important to have regional level offices not only to create awareness among the public but also to identify and report regional level competition issues to the Commission. Regional level offices will reach out the public in a better way since it can take care of language differences. The recently started online filings is a notable step in this direction as a short run

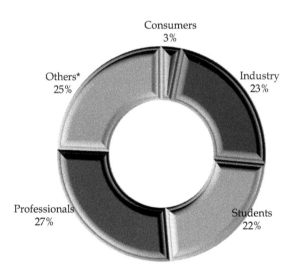

*Figure 8.1* Advocacy initiatives of the commission (2011–2012 to 2013–2014).

Source: Calculated from Annual Report (2014), Competition Commission of India, Government of India.

Note: *Others constitute multiple stakeholders including market studies/sectoral/regulatory impact assessment studies and capacity building initiatives etc; Professionals include bar associations and government officials.

measure, which will reduce the unnecessary hassle confronted by the parties to meet the deadlines. At present, the competition issues affecting the lower strata of the population are not getting adequate attention because they are not aware of reporting these issues to the Commission. The establishment of regional offices will address this issue, and it will become the competition watchdog in the real sense. The commission should also encourage the public to report competition issues directly through the website, social media and free SMS facilities, which will make it more consumer friendly.

*Coordination with other Agencies in and outside India*: It is also important to establish proper coordination among different government agencies (such as sectoral regulators such as Telecom Regulatory Authority of India (TRAI) Central Electricity Regulatory Commission, Petroleum and Natural Gas Regulatory Board, Insurance Regulatory Development Authority; Department of Consumer Affairs, Foreign Investment Promotion Board), and the Commission while approving the cases. Delineating the 'competition' boundaries from the issues dealt by the sectoral regulators and the other government agencies will become important in the coming years.

Similarly, in the backdrop of the increasing significance of cross-border deals,[4] it is also important to have a strong international tie-up with competition regulators of other jurisdictions. From the available information, Commission is now successfully interacting with other agencies especially for knowledge building. However, it is also important to have such exercises while assessing various cases involving foreign firms. It will help to prevent the international cartels, collusion etc., effectively. In this context, it is important to mention the preliminary discussions made on the formation of the International Competition Policy.[5] However, the economic nationalism followed by the countries may prevent them from the successful introduction of competition provisions across countries.

In short, during the last four years of implementation of the Combination Regulation in India, the CCI has become an important regulator within the economy as well as in the international realm compared to the counterparts in developing nations. However, in future, it has to take up more challenging cases. In that direction, the creation of a knowledge base in terms of both competition issues as well as sectoral expertise is inevitable. Rather than focusing on the short run, it should focus on the long run with a clear understanding of the macroeconomic dimensions of the economy. Data is still a bottleneck for assessing the competition, which is the backbone of regulation. Beyond all, the successful implementation of the Competition Act depends on the acceptance of it by each and every common citizen of India, who are affected by antitrust issues. Hence, post combination surveillance and involving the public through free SMS and email facilities should be encouraged. There should be a more appropriate mechanism to take care of the competition issues arising at the regional level. Apart from this, greater cooperation with the national and international agencies are also vital.

## Notes

1 The exit of firms may be either due to a merger or due to other reasons. Here we have captured exit through M&As.
2 In other words, combinations involving foreign companies.
3 As per the newspaper reports, during the time of the deal, the active Facebook users in India were around 93 Million, and that of Whats App was 40 Million. We assume that a good proportion of the Whats App users may be using Facebook as well (see Bose, A (2014), "Why India's Antitrust Body should Scrutinise the WhatsApp Buy", Business Standard, 2nd March).
4 See Saraswathy, B (2013) and Beena, (2014) for details.
5 See Utton (2008) for details.

## References

Beena, P.L., 2014. "Mergers and Acquisitions: India under Globalisation". India: Routledge.

Joseph, K.J. (1991). *Indian Electronics Industry: A Study of Growth and Structural Change in the Eighties.* Ph.D. Jawaharlal Nehru University, Centre for Development Studies.

Saraswathy, B. (2013), 'Global Trends in Cross-border Mergers and Acquisitions,' in K.R. Chittedi (Ed.) *The Economic and Social Issues of Financial Liberalisation: Evidence from Emerging Countries,* New Delhi: Bookwell Publishing, pp. 26–40.

Saraswathy, B., (2016), "An Assessment of Foreign Acquisitions in India", Working Paper No. 193, Institute for Studies in Industrial Development, New Delhi.

Utton, M. (2008). "International Competition Policy: Maintaining Open Markets in the Global Economy". UK: Edward Elgar Publishing.

# Bibliography

Aaronovitch, S. and Malcom, C.S. (1975). Mergers, Growth and Concentration. *Oxford Economic Papers, New Series,* 27(1), pp. 136–155.

Agarwal, M. (2002). *Analysis of Mergers in India.* M. Phil. Delhi School of Economics.

Agarwal, M. and Aditya, B. (2006). Mergers in India: A Response to Regulatory Shocks. *Emerging Markets Finance and Trade,* 42(3), pp. 46–55.

Agarwal, M. and Aditya, B. (2008). Are Merger Regulations Diluting Parliamentary Intent? *Economic and Political Weekly,* XLII(26–27), pp. 10–13.

Ahluwalia, I.J. (1991). *Productivity and Growth in Indian Manufacturing.* New Delhi: Oxford University Press.

Ahuja and Katila., (2001). Technological Acquisitions and the Innovation Performance of Acquiring Firms: A Longitudinal Study. Strategic Management Journal. 22(3):197–220.

Aigner, D., Lovell, C.A.K., and Schmidt, P. (1977). Formulation and Estimation of Stochastic Frontier Production Function Models. *Journal of Econometrics,* 6, pp. 21–37.

Anderson, M. and Maja, K. (2006). *Cross-Border and Corporate Aspects on Culture in Mergers and Acquisitions.* Bachelor Thesis. Department of Business Studies, Uppsala University.

Angwin, D. (2001). Mergers and Acquisitions across European Borders: National Perspectives on Pre-acquisition Due Diligence and Use of Professional Advisors. *Journal of World Business,* 36(1), pp. 32–57.

Angwin, D., ed. (2007). *Mergers and Acquisitions.* Malden Blackwell Publishing.

Ansoff, H.I. and Weston, J.F. (1962). Merger Objectives and Organizational Structure. *The Quarterly Review of Economics and Business,* 2(3), p. 49.

Asquith, P. (1983). Merger Bids, Uncertainty and Stockholder Returns. *Journal of Financial Economics,* 11(1–4), pp. 51–83.

Asquith, P. and Han. E.K. (1982). The Impact of Merger Bids on the Participating Firm's Security Holders. *Journal of Finance,* 37(5), pp. 1209–1227.

Bain, S.J. (1956). *Barriers to New Competition: Their Character and Consequences in Manufacturing Industries.* Cambridge: Harvard University Press.

Balachandran, M., 2016. "9 Years and Rs. 30000 crore later, Air India is finally set to make some money", Quartz India, 16th March, Accessed on 30th April 2017.

Balakrishnan, P. (2004). Measuring Productivity in Manufacturing Sector. *Economic and Political Weekly,* 39(14–15), pp. 1465–1471.

Balakrishnan, P. and Pushpangadan, K. (1994). Total Factor Productivity Growth in Indian Industry: A Fresh Look. *Economic and Political Weekly,* 29(31), pp. 2028–2035.

Balakrishnan, P. and Pushpangadan, K. (1995). Total Factor Productivity Growth in Manufacturing Industry. *Economic and Political Weekly,* 30(9), pp. 462–464.

Balakrishnan, P. and Pushpangadan, K. (1996). TFPG in Manufacturing Industry. *Economic and Political Weekly,* 31(7), pp. 425–428.

Balakrishnan, P. and Pushpangadan, K. (1998). What Do We Know about Productivity Growth in Indian Industry? *Economic and Political Weekly,* 33(33–34), pp. 2241–2246.

Balakrishnan, P., Pushpangadan, K., and Suresh, B. (2002). *Trade Liberalization, Market Power and Scale Efficiency in Indian Industry.* Working Paper No. 336. Thiruvananthapuram: Centre for Development Studies.

Baldwin, J. and Paul G. (1998). *Dynamics of Industrial Competition: A North American Perspective.* Cambridge: Cambridge University Press.

Basant, R. (1997). Technology Strategies of Large Enterprises in Indian Industry: Some Explorations. *World Development,* 25(10), pp. 1683–1700.

Basanth, R. (2000). Corporate Response to Economic Reforms. *Economic and Political Weekly,* 35(10), pp. 813–22.

Battese, G.E. and Coelli, T.J. (1995). A Model for Technical Inefficiency Effects in a Stochastic Frontier Production Function for Panel Data. *Empirical Economics,* 20, pp. 325–332.

Baumol, William, J. (1959). *Business Behavior, Value and Growth.* New York: Macmillan.

Beena, P.L. (2000). *An Analysis of Mergers in the Private Corporate Sector in India.* Working Paper No. 301. Thiruvananthapuram: Centre for Development Studies.

Beena, P.L. (2001). Intangibles and Finance: Motives and Consequences of Mergers in the Indian Corporate Sector. In: P. Banarjee and F.J. Richter, ed., *Intangibles in Competition and Co-operation: Euro-Asian Perspectives.* London: Palgrave.

Beena, P.L. (2004). *Towards Understanding the Merger Wave in the Indian Corporate Sector: A Comparative Perspective.* Working Paper No. 355. Thiruvananthapuram: Centre for Development Studies.

Beena, P.L. (2008). Trends and Perspectives on Corporate Mergers in Contemporary India. *Economic and Political Weekly,* 43(39), pp. 48–56.

Beena, P.L. (2011). *Financing Pattern of Indian Corporate Sector under Liberalisation: With Focus on Acquiring Firms Abroad.* Working Paper No. 440. Thiruvananthapuram: Centre for Development Studies.

Beena, S. (2006). *Mergers and Acquisitions in the Indian Pharmaceutical Industry: An Analysis.* M. Phil. Jawaharlal Nehru University.

Beena, S. (2008). Concentration via Consolidation in the Indian Pharmaceutical Industry: An Inquiry. *The ICFAI Journal of Mergers and Acquisitions,* 5(4):51–70.

Beena, S. (2009). *Mergers and Technological Performance: An Inquiry into the Indian Manufacturing Sector.* In: Institute for Studies in Industrial Development. National Conference. New Delhi, 27–28 March.

Behrman, J.N. (1972). *The Role of International Companies in Latin America: Autos and Petrochemicals.* Lexington, MA: Lexington Books.

Berggren, C. (2001). Mergers, MNEs and Innovation—The Need for New Research Approaches. In: ESRC Transnational Communities. Conference on Multinational Enterprises. Warwick, Sweden, 6–8 September.

Berle, A.A. and Means, G.C. (1932). *The Modern Corporation and Private Property.* New York: Macmillan.

Bhattacharjea, A. 2003. "India's Competition Policy: An Assessment". *Economic and Political Weekly,* XVIII(34), pp. 3561–3574.

Bhattacharjea, A. 2010. "Of Omissions and Commissions: India's Competition Law". *Economic and Political Weekly,* XLV(35). pp. 31–37.

Bladwin, W.L. (1964). The motives of Managers, Environmental Restraints, and the Theory of Managerial Enterprises. *Quarterly Journal of Economics,* 78, pp. 236–258.

Boone, J. (2008). A New Way to Measure Competition. *The Economic Journal,* 118(531), pp. 1245–1261.

Borghese, R.J. and Paul, F.B. (2001). *M&A from Planning to Integration.* New York: McGraw-Hill.

Brahmananda, P.R. (1982). *Productivity in the Indian Economy: Rising Inputs for Falling Outputs.* Mumbai: Himalaya Publishing House.

Bresman, H., Birkinshaw, J. and Nobel, R. (1999). Knowledge Transfer in International Acquisitions. *Journal of International business Studies,* 30(4), pp. 439–462.

Bris, A. and Christos, C. (2004). *Adopting Better Corporate Governance: Evidence from Cross-Border Mergers.* New Haven.: Yale School of Management, January. Bruner, R.F. (2004). *Applied Mergers and Acquisitions.* New York: John Wiley & Sons.

Business India (2005). Tonning up Glaxo. June.

Business Line, 2004. GSK, Burroughs Wellcome boards clear Merger-Share swap at 14:10. Business Line, Available at http://www.thehindubusinessline.com/2004/03/18/stories/2004031802660100.htm. [Accessed on 8th October 2015].

Calvet, A.L. (1981). A Synthesis of Foreign Direct Investment Theories and Theories of the Multinational Firm. *Journal of International Business Studies, 12*(1), Tenth Anniversary Special Issue (Spring-Summer), pp. 43–59.

Cantwell, J. and Grazia, S. (2002). Mergers and Acquisitions and the Global Strategies of TNCs. *The Developing Economies,* XL(4), pp. 400–434.

Carlton, D.W. (2009). *Why We Need to Measure the Effect of Merger Policy and How to Do It.* Working Paper No. 14719. Cambridge: National Bureau of Economic Research.

Cassiman, B. and Massimo, G.C. (2008). *Mergers and Acquisitions: The Innovation Impact.* Cheltenham: Edward Elgar.

Centre for Monitoring Indian Economy (CMIE), Size and Market Shares. New Delhi. Various Issues.

Centre for Monitoring Indian Economy (CMIE), Monthly Review of the Indian Economy. New Delhi. Various Issues.

Centre for Monitoring Indian Economy (CMIE). M&A Database, New Delhi. Various Issues.

Chari, A.S.R. (1972). Monopolies and the Public Policy. In: *A Round Table Discussion Organised by the Society for Democracy, Monopolies and the Public Policy.* New Delhi. People's Publishing House.

Chaudhury, S. (2005). *WTO and India's Pharmaceutical Industry: Patent Protection, TRIPS and Developing Countries.* New Delhi: Oxford University Press.

Chaudhury, S. (2012). Multinationals and Monopolies: Pharmaceutical Industry in India after TRIPS. *Economic and Political Weekly,* XLVII(2):46–54, March 24.

Chen, C. and Findlay, C. (2002). A Review of Cross-Border Mergers and Acquisitions in APEC. *Asian-Pacific Economic Literature.* 17(2): 14–38.

Chilosi, A. and Mirella, D. (2007). Stakeholders vs. Shareholders in Corporate Governance. Munich Personal RePEc Archive MPRA, [online]. Available at: http://mpra.ub.uni-muenchen.de/2334/ [Accessed on 25th June 2011].

Clark, J.M. (1961). *Competition as a Dynamic Process.* Washington, DC: Brookings Institution.

Coelli, P.R., Donnel, C.J. and Battese, G.E. (2005). *An Introduction to Efficiency and Productivity Analysis.* New York: Springer.

Coelli, T.J. (1996). *A Guide to FRONTIER Version 4.1: A Computer Programme for Stochastic Frontier Production and Cost Function Estimation.* CEPA Working Papers No. 7. University of New England, Australia.

Company Secretaries of India (2008). *Handbook on Mergers, Amalgamations and Takeovers.* New Delhi: ICSI.

Competition Commission of India (2010). *Competition Law in the Indian Pharmaceutical Industry.* New Delhi: Centre for Trade and Development.

Congress House Senate Committee on the Judiciary (US) (1964). Subcommittee on Antitrust and Monopoly. *Economic Concentration.* Hearing. Washington, DC.

Cook, P.L. (1954). Review. *The Economic Journal,* 64(255), pp. 586–588.

Curry, B. and George, K.D. (1983). Industrial Concentration: A Survey. *Journal of Industrial Economics,* 31(3), pp. 203–255.

Cyert, R.M. and James, G.M. (1963). *A Behavioral Theory of the Firm.* USA: Prentice-Hall.

de Sousa, J.V. (2006). *Post-Acquisition Integration Process of Two Diverse Acquisitions by a Company.* South Africa, Gordon Institute of Business Science: University of Pretoria.

Demsetz, H. (1973). Industry Structure, Market Rivalry, and Public Policy. *Journal of Law and Economic,* 16(1), pp. 1–9.

Demsetz, H. (1983). The Structure of Ownership and the Theory of the Firm. *Journal of Law and Economics,* 26, pp. 375–390.

Department of Industrial Policy and Promotion (2008). *Fact Sheet on Foreign Direct Investment.* New Delhi, Ministry of Commerce and Industry: Government of India.

Department of Industrial Policy and Promotion (2012). *Fact Sheet on Foreign Direct Investment.* New Delhi: Ministry of Commerce and Industry, Government of India.

Dessyllas and Hughes (2005). R&D and Patenting Activity and the Propensity to Acquire in High Technology Industries. Working Paper No. 298. ESRC Centre for Business Research, University of Cambridge.

Desvousges, W.H. and Micheal, J.P. (1979). The Effect of Large Mergers on Concentration Trends in Petroleum Production, 1955–1975. *Southern Economic Journal,* 46(2), pp. 615–622.

Dhall, V. (2007). *Competition Law Today: Concepts, Issues and the Law in Practice.* New Delhi: Oxford University Press.

Dodd, P. (1980). Merger Proposals, Management Discretion and Stockholder Wealth. *Journal of Financial Economics,* 8(2), pp. 105–137.

Downie, J. (1958). *The Competitive Process.* London: Gerald Duckworth.

Dunning, J.H. (1993). *Multinational Enterprises and the Global Economy.* New York: Addison-Wesley Publishing Company.

Ernst and Young (1994). *Mergers and Acquisitions.* New York: John Wiley & Sons.

Eckbo, E. (1983). Horizontal Mergers, Collusion and Stockholder Wealth. *Journal of Financial Economics,* 11(1–4), pp. 241–273.

Erez-Rein, N., Erez, M. and Maital, S. (2004). Mind the Gap: Key Success Factors in Cross-Border Acquisitions. In: A.M. Pablo and M. Javidan, eds., *Mergers and Acquisitions: Creating Integrative Knowledge.* New Jersey: Blackwell Publishing.

European Commission (2016). *Competition Policy Brief: EU Merger Control and Innovation.* Brussels: Competition Directorate General of the European Commission. Available at: http://ec.europa.eu/competition/publications/cpb/2016/2016_001_en. pdf [Accessed on 23rd May 2017].

Evely and Little., 1960. Concentration in British Industry: An Empirical Study of Industrial Production 1935–51. UK: Cambridge University Press.

Evenett, S. (2003). *The Cross-Border Mergers and Acquisitions: Wave of the Late 1990s.* Working Paper 9655. Cambridge: National Bureau of Economic Research.

Farrell and Shapiro., 1990. Horizontal Mergers: An Equilibrium Analysis. *The American Economic Review,* 80(1), pp. 107–126.

Farrell, M.J. (1957). The Measurement of Productive Efficiency. *Journal of the Royal Statistical Society,* 120, pp. 253–281.

Federal Trade Commission Report (1948). *The Merger Movement, A Summary Report.* Washington, DC: Princeton University Press.

Finkelstein, S. (2002). The Daimler Chrysler Merger. *Fortune Magazine,* (e-journal) Dartmouth. July 26, 2010, Tuck School of Business. Available at: http://money.cnn. com/magazines/fortune/global500/2010/countries/India.html. [Accessed on 8th Nov. 2010].

Fransman, M. (1984). *Technological Capability in the Third World.* London: Macmillan.

Fried, Y., Tiegs, R.B., Naughten, T.J. and Ashford, B.E. (1996). Managers Reactions to a Corporate Acquisition: Test of an Integrative Model. *Journal of Organisational Behaviour,* 17, pp. 401–427.

Fujita, M. (2000). Cross-Border Mergers and Acquisitions: Global Trends. United Nations Conference on Trade and Development.

Gadiesh, O. and Ormiston, C. (2002). Six Rationales to Guide Merger Success. *Strategy and Leadership,* 30(4), pp. 38–40.

Galleco, B.C. (2010). Intellectual Property Rights and Competition Policy. In: M.C. Correa, ed., *Research Handbook on the Protection of IPR under WTO Rules,* vol. 1. Cheltenham: Edward Elgar.

Gardiesh, O. and Ormiston, C. (2002). Six Rationales to Guide Merger Success. *Strategy and Leadership,* 30(4), pp. 38–40. Available at: www.privateequityles sons.com/bainweb/PDFs/cms/Public/Benelux_Results_Six_rationales_guide_ merger_success.pdf [Accessed on 18th Oct. 2012].

Gaughan, P.A. (1999). *Mergers and Acquisitions and Corporate Restructuring.* New York: John Wiley & Sons.

George, K.D., 1975. A Note on Changes in Industrial Concentration in the UK. *Economic Journal.* 85(337). pp. 124–28.

George, K.D., 1972. The Changing Structure of Competitive Industry. *Economic Journal,* March Supplement, 82: 353–68.

Gibrat, R. (1931). *Les Inégalités Économiques.* Paris: Librairie du Recueil Sirey.

Gilbert, R.J. (2007). *Competition and Innovation.* Working Paper Series qt9xh5p5p9. UC Berkeley: Institute for Business and Economic Research.

Glair, M. (2000). Merger Control Laws in European Union, In: J. Kraft, ed., *The Process of Competition*. Cheltenham: Edward Elgar.

Goldar, B. (1986). *Productivity Growth in Indian Industry*. New Delhi: Allied Publishers.

Goldar, B. (2004). Indian Manufacturing: Productivity Trends in the Pre and Post Reform Periods. *Economic and Political Weekly*, 35(42), pp. 5033–5043.

Goldberg, A.H. (2007). Merger Control in Competition Law Today: Concepts, Issues and the Law in Practice. In: V. Dhall, ed., *Competition Law Today: Concepts, Issues and the Law in Practice*. New Delhi: Oxford University Press.

Gonzalez, P., Vasconcellos, G.M., Kish, R.J. and Kramer, J.K. (1997). Cross-Border Mergers and Acquisitions: Maximizing the Value of the Firm. *Applied Financial Economics*, 7(3), pp. 295–305.

Government of India (1989). *National Accounts Statistics: Sources and Methods*. New Delhi: Central Statistical Organisation.

Government of India (2003). *Manual on Foreign Direct Investment in India (FDI): Policy and Procedure*. Secretariat of Industrial Assistance, Department of Policy and Promotion. New Delhi: Ministry of Commerce and Industry.

Government of India 2006. Competition (Amendment) Bill 2006, 44th Standing Committee Report. New Delhi: Loksabha Secretariat.

Government of India (2007). *The Competition (Amendment) Act*. New Delhi: Competition Commission of India.

Government of India (2008a). *Input-Output Transaction Table (Ministry of Statistics and Programme Implementation)*. New Delhi: Central Statistical Organisation.

Government of India (2008b). *Petroleum and Natural Gas Sector Foreign Direct Investment (FDI) Policy*. New Delhi: Ministry of Petroleum and Natural Gas.

Government of India 2008. *Eleventh Five-Year Plan (2007–12)*. New Delhi: Planning Commission.

Government of India (2009). *The Competition Amendment Act*. New Delhi: Competition Commission of India.

Government of India (2011). *Procedures in Regard to the Transaction of Business Relating to Combinations*. New Delhi: Competition Commission of India.

Government of India (2012). Fair play. *The Quarterly Newsletter of Competition Commission of India*, vol. 1, April–June.

Government of India, National Accounts Statistics. New Delhi: Central Statistical Organisation. Ministry of Statistics and Programme Implementation, Various Years.

Government of India, Office of the Economic Advisor. New Delhi: Ministry of Commerce and Industry, Various Years.

Goyal, S.K. (1972). Government Policy and Concentration in the Indian Economy. In: *A Round Table Discussion organized by the Society for Democracy, Monopolies and the Public Policy*. New Delhi: People's Publishing House.

Graham, E.M. (1974). *Oligopolistic Imitation and European Direct Investment in the United States*. Ph.D., Harvard Business School.

Green, M.B. and Meyer, S.P. (1997). International Acquisitions: Host and Home Country Explanatory Characteristics. *Human Geography*, 79(2), pp. 97–111.

Greenberg, D. and Guinan, P.J. (2004). Mergers and Acquisitions in Technology Intensive Industries: The Emergent Process of Technology Transfer. In: A.M. Pablo and M. Javidan, eds., *Mergers and Acquisitions: Creating Integrative Knowledge*. New Jersey: Blackwell Publishing.

Greene, W. (2003). *Econometric Analysis.* New Jersey: Pearson Education.

Greene, W. (2004). Fixed Effects and Bias Due to the Incidental Parameters Problem in the Tobit Model. *Econometric Reviews,* 23(2), pp. 125–147.

Greene, W. (2011). *Econometric Analysis,* New Jersey: Prentice Hall International.

Guellec, D. and de la Potterie, B.V.P. (2001). The Internationalisation of Technology Analysed with Patent Data. *Research Policy,* 30(8):1253–1266.

Hagedoorn, J. and Duysters, G. (2000). *The Effects of Mergers and Acquisitions on the Technological Performance of Companies in a High-Tech Environment.* MERIT, Netherlands: University of Maastricht.

Hall, B.H. (1987). The Relationship between Firm Size and Firm Growth in the U.S. Manufacturing Sector. *Journal of Industrial Economics,* 35(4), pp. 583–606.

Hall, M. and Tideman, N. (1967). Measures of Concentration. *Journal of the American Statistical Association,* 62, pp. 162–168.

Hall, R.E. (1986). Market Structure and Macro Economic Fluctuations. *Brooking Papers on Economic Activity,* 2, pp. 91–112.

Hall, R.E. (1988). The Relation between Price and Marginal Cost in US Industry. *Journal of Political Economy,* 96(5), pp. 285–338.

Hannah, L. and Kay, J.A. (1976). *Concentration in Modern Industry: Theory, Measurement and the UK Experience.* London: Macmillan.

Hanna, L. and Kay, J.A. (1977). The Contribution of Mergers to Concentration Growth: A Reply to Professor Hart. *Journal of Industrial Economics,* 29(3), pp. 305–313.

Hannah, L. and Kay, J.A. (1981). The Contribution of Mergers to Concentration Growth: A Reply to Professor Hart. *The Journal of Industrial Economics,* 29(3), pp. 305–313.

Harris, R.S. and Ravenscraft, D. (1991). The Role of Acquisitions in Foreign Direct Investment: Evidence from the US Market. *The Journal of Finance,* XLV(3), pp. 825–844.

Hart, P.E. (1957). *On Measuring Business Concentration, Bulletin of the Oxford Institute of Statistics,* 19 (3). pp. 225–248 (Reprinted 1975).

Hart, P.E. (1960). Business Concentration in the United Kingdom. *Journal of the Royal Statistical Society,* 123, Series A, Part 1.

Hart, P.E. and Prais, S.J. (1956). The Analysis of Business Concentration: A Statistical Approach. *Journal of the Royal Statistical Society, Series A,* 119, pp. 150–191.

Hart, P.E. (1979), 'On Bias and Concentration', *Journal of Industrial Economics,* (28)3, pp. 211–216.

Hart, P.E, Utton, MA and Walshe, G., (1973). *Mergers and Concentration in British Industry.* National Institute of Economic and Social Research. Occassional Papers 26. London: Cambridge University Press.

Hashim, S.R. and Dadi, M.M. (1973). *Capital-Output Relations in Indian Manufacturing (1946–1964).* The Maharaja Sayajirao University Economics, Series No. 2, Baroda, India.

Healy, P. and Palepu, K.G. (1993). International Corporate Equity Acquisitions: Who, Where and Why. In: K. Froot, ed., *Foreign Direct Investment.* Chicago: University of Chicago Press.

Henningsen, A. (2006). Estimating Censored Regression Models in R using the censReg Package. Available at: University of Copenhagen website http://cran.r-project.org/web/packages/censReg/vignettes/censReg.pdf [Accessed on 8th May 2012].

Hindley, B. (1970). Industrial Merger and Public Policy: Institute of Economic Affairs Hobart Papers. 50. London.

Hitt, M. and Pisano, V. (2004). Cross-Border Mergers and Acquisitions: Challenges and Opportunities. In: A.M. Pablo and M. Javidan, eds., *Mergers and Acquisitions: Creating Integrative Knowledge*. New Jersey: Blackwell Publishing.

Hofstede, G. (1991). *Culture and Organisations: Software of the Mind*. London: McGraw-Hill.

Holweg, M., Stephen, D., Jan, H. and Johanna, S. (2004). Supply Chain Collaboration: Making Sense of the Strategy Continuum. Available at: http://lrg.tkk.fi/logistics/publications/collaboration_strategy_continuum.pdf [Accessed on 19th July 2012].

Homburg, C. and Matthias, B. (2005). A Marketing Perspective on Mergers and Acquisitions: How Marketing Integration Affects Post Merger Performance. *Journal of Marketing,* 69(1), pp. 95–113.

Hymer, S.H. (1960). *The International Operations of National Firms: A Study of Direct Foreign Investment*. Cambridge: MIT Press.

Ijiri, Y. and Herbert, A.S. (1971). Effects of Mergers and Acquisitions on Business Firm Concentration. *Journal of Political Economy,* 79(2), pp. 314–322.

Jha, R. (2007). Options for Indian Pharmaceutical Industry in the Changing Environment. *Economic and Political Weekly,* XLII(39), pp. 3958–3967.

JianHua, W. (2007). *Post Merger Financial Integration of the Enterprises*. School of Economics and Management, China: Henan Polytechnic University. Available at: www.seiofbluemountain.com/upload/product/200910/2007glhy06a5.pdf [Accessed on 3rd Oct. 2012].

Jones, G. (2005). *Multinational and Global Capitalism from 19th to the 20th Century*. Oxford: Oxford University Press.

Joseph, K.J. (1991). *Indian Electronics Industry: A Study of Growth and Structural Change in the Eighties*. Ph.D. Jawaharlal Nehru University, Centre for Development Studies.

Kabiraj, T. and Marjit, S. (2003). International Technology Transfer under Potential Threat of Entry: A Cournot-Nash Framework. In: N. Singh and S. Marjit, eds., *Joint Ventures, International Investment and Technology Transfer*. New Delhi: Oxford University Press.

Kalirajan, K.P. and Shant, R.T. (1994). *Economics in Disequilibrium: An Approach from the Frontier*. New Delhi: Macmillan.

Kasey, K., Thompson, S. and Wright, M. (1997). *Corporate Governance: Economic and Financial Issues*. Oxford: Oxford University Press.

Katrak, H. (1997). Developing Countries' Imports of Technology, In-house Technological Capabilities and Efforts: An Analysis of the Indian Experience. *Journal of Development Economics,* 53(1), pp. 67–83.

Katz, M.L. and Howard, A.S. (2004). *Merger Policy and Innovation: Must Enforcement Change to Account for Technological Change?* Working Paper No. 10710. National Bureau of Economic Research.

Kaur, P. (2010). Determinants of Acquisition: Evidence for India. *The Indian Economic Journal,* 58(3), pp. 67–86.

Kay, N. (1993). Merger, Acquisitions and the Completion of the Internal Market. In: S.K. Hughes, ed., *European Competitiveness*. Cambridge: Cambridge University Press.

Kinne, K. (1999). Efficiencies in Merger Analysis. *Intereconomics,* 34(6), pp. 297–302.

Kleer, R. (2006). *The Effect of Mergers on the Incentive to Invest in Cost Reducing Innovation*. BGPE Discussion Paper No. 11, Wuerzburg.

Knickerbocker, F.T. (1974). *Oligopolistic Reaction and Multinational Enterprise.* Cambridge: Harvard Business School.

Kumar, B. and Paneerselvam, S. (2009). Mergers, Acquisitions and Wealth Creation: A Comparative Study in the Indian Context. *IIMB Management Review,* 21(3) September, pp. 222–244.

Kumar, N. (2000a). Mergers and Acquisitions by MNEs: Patterns and Implications. *Economic and Political Weekly,* 35(32), pp. 2851–2858.

Kumar, N. (2000b). Multinational Enterprises and M&As in India: Patterns and Implications. RIS DP# 5–2000.

Kumar, N. (2008). *Internationalisation of Indian Enterprises: Patterns, Strategies Ownership Advantages and Implications.* Discussion Paper No. 140. New Delhi: Research and Information System for Developing Countries.

Kumar, N. and Siddharthan, N.S. (1997). *Technology, Market Structure and Internationalisation: Issues and Policies for Developing Countries.* New York: Routledge.

Kumar, A., 2007. The Evolution of Competition law in India. In: Vinod, Dhall, ed.2007. *Competition Law Today: Concepts, Issues and the Law in Practice.* New Delhi: Oxford University Press.

Lall, S. (1983). Multinationals from India. In: S. Lall, ed., *The New Multinationals: The Spread of Third World Enterprises.* New York: John Wiley & Sons.

Lall, S. (2002). *Implications of Cross Border Mergers and Acquisitions by TNCs in Developing Countries: A Beginners Guide.* QEH Working Paper Series-QEHWPS88. Available at: www3.qeh.ox.ac.uk/RePEc/qeh/qehwps/qehwps88. pdf. [Accessed on 8th October 2014].

Lane, A.A., Cannella, J.R. and Micheal, H.L. (1998). Agency Problems as Antecedents to Unrelated Mergers and Diversification: Amihud and Lev Reconsidered. *Strategic Management Journal,* 19(6), pp. 555–578.

Langetieg, T.C. (1978). An Application of a Three Factor Performance Index to Measure Stockholder Gains from Merger. *Journal of Financial Economics,* 6(4), pp. 365–383.

Lintner, J.A. and Butters, J.K. (1950). Effect of Mergers on Industrial Concentration 1940–47. *Review of Economics and Statistics,* 32, pp. 30–48.

Livermore, S. (1935). The Success of Industrial Mergers. *Quarterly Journal of Economics,* 50(1), pp. 70–71.

Mandelkar, G. (1974). Risk and Return: The Case of Merging Firms. *Journal of Financial Economics,* 1(4), pp. 303–335.

Manthravadi, P. and Vidyadhar, A.R. (2007). Relative Size in Mergers and Operating Performance: Indian Experience. *Economic and Political Weekly,* 42(39), pp. 3936–3942.

Manthravadi, P. and Vidyadhar, A.R. (2008a). Type of Merger and Impact on Operating Performance: The Indian Experience. *Economic and Political Weekly,* 43(39), pp. 66–74.

Manthravadi, P. and Vidyadhar, A.R. (2008b). Post Merger Performance of Acquiring Firms from Different Industries in India. *International Journal of Finance and Economics,* 22, pp. 193–204.

Mark, R. (2003). *Political Determinants of Corporate Governance.* Oxford: Oxford: University Press.

Markham, J.W. (1955). *Survey of the Evidence and Findings on Mergers.* New Jersey: Princeton University Press.

Marris, R. (1964). *The Economic Theory of Managerial Capitalism*. Glencoe: Free Press.

Marshall, A. (1920). *Principles of Economics*. London: Macmillan.

Mattoo, A., Olarreaga, M. and Saggi, K. (2001). *Mode of Foreign Entry, Technology Transfer and FDI Policy*. CEPR Discussion Papers 2870. C.E.P.R. Discussion Papers.

McDonald, J., Max, C. and de Lange, P. (2005). Planning for a Successful Merger or Acquisition: Lessons from an Australian Study. *Journal of Business and Technology*, 1(2), pp. 1–11.

Meeks, G. (1977). *Disappointing Marriage: A Study of the Gains from Merger*. Cambridge: Cambridge University Press.

Meeks, G. and Meeks, J.G. (1981). Profitability Measures as Indicators of Post Merger Efficiency. *Journal of Industrial Economics*, XXIX(4), pp. 335–344.

Meeusen, W. and van den Broeck, J. (1977). Efficiency Estimation from Cobb-Douglas Production Functions with Composed Error. *International Economic Review*, 18, pp. 435–444.

Mehta, M.M. (1950). Measurement of Economic Efficiency. *The Economic Journal*, 60(240), pp. 827–831.

Mishra, P. (2006). Mergers, Acquisition, Market Structure and Industry Performance: Experience of Indian Pharmaceutical Industry. *Review of Development and Change*, 11(2), pp. 135–164.

Mishra, P. (2008). Concentration-Markup Relationship in Indian Manufacturing Sector. *Economic and Political Weekly*, 43(39), pp. 74–81.

Mishra, P. and Tamal, C. (2010). Mergers and Acquisitions and Firms' Performance: Experience of Indian Pharmaceutical Industry. *Eurasian Journal of Business and Economics*, 3(5), pp. 111–126.

Modigliani, F. (1958). New Developments on the Oligopoly Front. *Journal of Political Economy*, 66, pp. 215–232.

Morgan, G. (2007). M&A as Power. In: D. Angwin, ed., *Mergers and Acquisitions*. Malden: Blackwell Publishing.

Morris, S. (1990). Foreign Direct Investment from India: Ownership and Control of Joint Ventures Abroad. *Economic and Political Weekly*, 25(7, 8), pp. M23–M34.

Moody, J., 1904. The Truth about the Trusts, New York: Moody Publishing Company.

Motta, M. (2009). *Competition Policy: Theory and Practice*. Cambridge: Cambridge University Press.

Mueller, J. (1976). The Impact of Mergers on Concentration: A Study of Eleven West German Industries. *The Journal of Industrial Economic*, 25(2), pp. 113–132.

Mukherjee, H. (1972). On the Monopolies. In: A *Round Table Discussion Organised by the Society for Democracy, Monopolies and the Public Policy*. New Delhi: People's Publishing House.

Nagaraj, R. (2006). Indian Investment Abroad. *Economic and Political Weekly*, 41(46), pp. 4716–4718.

Nanaka, I. and Takeuchi, H. (1995). *The Knowledge Creating Company*. New York: Oxford University Press.

Narula, R. (2003). *Globalisation and Technology: Interdependence, Innovation Systems and industrial Policy*. Cambridge: Cambridge Polity Press.

Natarajan, S. and Rajesh, R. (2007). *Technical Efficiency in the Informal Manufacturing Enterprises: Firm level Evidence from an Indian State*. MPRA Working Paper No. 8144. Munich, Germany. Available at: http://mpra.ub.uni-muenchen.de/7816/1/MPRA_paper_7816.pdf [Accessed on 8th October 2008].

Nayyar, D. (2007). *The Internationalisation of Firms from India: Investment, Mergers and Acquisitions.* SLPTMD Working Paper Series No. 004. University of Oxford: Department of International Development.

News One (2011). Available at: www.inewsone.com/2011/05/08/air-india-crisis-a-carefully-crafted-design-comment/48957 [Accessed on 16th August 2012].

Nutter, G.W. (1954). Growth by Merger. *Journal of the American Statistical Association,* 49(267), pp. 448–466.

Odagiri, H. (1992). *Growth through Competition, Competition through Growth: Strategic Management and Economy in Japan.* Oxford: Clarendon Press.

Oliveira, M.J., Stefano, S. and Dirk, P. (1996). *Mark-up Ratios in Manufacturing Industries: Estimates for 14 OECD Countries.* Working Paper No. 162. Paris: Organisation for Economic Co-operation and Development.

Organization of Economic Co-operation and Development (1974). *Report of the Committee of Experts on Restrictive Business Practices.* Paris: OECD.

Organization of Economic Co-operation and Development (2001). *New Pattern of Industrial Globalisation: Cross-Border Mergers and Acquisition and Strategic Alliances.* Paris: OECD.

Organization of Economic Co-operation and Development (2002). *Measurement of Aggregate and Industry-Level Productivity Growth, OECD Manual.* Paris: OECD.

Organization of Economic Co-operation and Development (2007). Dynamic Efficiencies in Merger Analysis. OECD Round Tables. Available at: www.oecd.org/dataoecd/53/22/40623561.pdf [Accessed on 10th Jan. 2008].

Owen, S. (2006). *The History and Mystery of Merger Waves: A UK and US Perspective.* Working Paper No. 2006-02. Sydney: The University of New South Wales.

Parameswaran, M. (2002). *Economic Reforms and Technical Efficiency: Firm Level Evidence from Selected Industries in India.* Working Paper No. 339. Thiruvananthapuram: Centre for Development Studies.

Parameswaran, M. (2010). International Trade and R&D Investment: Evidence from Manufacturing Firms in India. *International Journal of Technology and Globalisation,* 5(1–2), pp. 43–60.

Pareek, R. (2012). Amalgamation and Merger—Issues and Problems. *Variorum, Multi-Disciplinary e-Research Journal,* 2(3):1–12.

Pesendorfer, M. (2003). Horizontal Mergers in the Paper Industry. *The RAND Journal of Economics,* 34(3), pp. 495–515.

Pillai, P.M. (1979). Technology Transfer, Adaptation and Assimilation. *Economic and Political Weekly,* 14(47), pp. M121–M126.

Pillai, P.M. (1984a). *Changing Dimensions of Technology Dependence in India.* Working Paper No. 192. Thiruvananthapuram: Centre for Development Studies.

Pillai, P.M. (1984b). *Multinationals and Indian Pharmaceutical industry.* Thiruvananthapuram: Kerala Sastra Sahitya Parishat.

Pillai, P.M. (1987). *Policy Intervention and Response: A Study of the Pharmaceutical Industry During the Last Decade.* Working Paper No. 218. Thiruvananthapuram: Centre for Development Studies.

Pillai, P.M. and Jaysree, S. (1988). *Multinational Corporations and National Technological Capability.* Ahmedabad: Sardar Patel Institute of Social and Economic Research.

Pillai, P.M. and Sreenivasan, J. (1987). Age and Productivity of Machine Tools in India. *Economic and Political Weekly,* 22(35), pp. M95–M100.

Pitelis, C. (2003). Privatisation, Regulation and Domestic Competition Policy. In: G. Wignaraja, ed., *Competitiveness Strategy in Developing Countries: A Manual for Policy Analysis.* pp. 239–273.

Porter, M. (1985). *Competitive Advantage.* New York: Free Press.

Porter, M. (1998). *On Competition.* Boston: Harvard Business School.

Pradhan, G. and Barik, K. (1998). Fluctuating Total Factor Productivity in India: Evidence from Selected Polluting Industries. *Economic and Political Weekly,* 33(9), pp. M25–M30.

Pradhan, J.P. (2007). *Trends and Patterns of Overseas Acquisitions by Indian Multinationals.* Working Paper No. 10. New Delhi: Institute for Studies in Industrial Development.

Public Enterprises Survey (2010–2011). Government of India. Department of Public Enterprises. Available at: http://dpe.nic.in/newsite/survey0910/Survey01/NewVol2.htm [Accessed on 17th Aug. 2011].

Pushpangadan, K. and Shanta, N. (2009). *The Dynamics of Competition: Understanding India's Manufacturing Sector.* New Delhi: Oxford University Press.

Ramaswamy, K.V. (2006). Competition Policy and Practice in Canada: Silent Features and Some Perspectives for India. *Economic and Political Weekly,* XLI(18), pp. 1903–1911.

Ranbaxy World (2008). Ranbaxy Daiichi Sankyo Partnership: Transformational Growth. July.

Rao, J.M. (1996). Manufacturing Productivity Growth: Method and Measurement. *Economic and Political Weekly,* 31(44), pp. 2927–2936.

Ravenscraft, D.J. and Scherer, F.M. (1987). *Mergers, Sell-offs and Economic Efficiency.* Washington, DC: The Brooking Institution.

Ravenscraft, D.J. and Scherer, F.M. (1989). The Profitability of Mergers. *International Journal of Industrial Organisation,* 7(1), pp. 101–116.

Ray, K.G. (2004). ABB-Flakt Merger: A Case Analysis. In: International Conference of International Association of Science and Technology for Development, MIT, 8–9 November. Cambridge: Massachusetts.

Rowley, C.K. and Peacock, A.T. (1975). *Welfare Economics. A Liberal Restatement.* Oxford: Martin Robertson.

Ryden, B. (1972). *Mergers in Swedish industry. The Industrial Institute for Economic and Social Research.* Stockholm: Almqvist and Wiksell.

Santarelli, L.K. and Roy, T. (2005). Gibrat's Law: An Overview of the Empirical Literature. In: E. Santarelli, ed., *Entrepreneurship, Growth and Innovation: The Dynamics of Firms and Industries.* New York: Springer, pp. 41–73.

Sarala, R. (2008). The Impact of Organisational and National Cultural Differences on Social Conflict and Knowledge Transfer in International Acquisitions: Domestic and Foreign Acquisitions of Finnish Companies. *Journal of Management Studies,* 49(1):1365–1390.

Saraswathy, B. (2010). "Cross-Border Mergers and Acquisitions in India: Extent, Nature and Structure". Working Paper No. 434. Thiruvananthapuram, India: Centre for Development Studies.

Saraswathy, B. (2013). Global Trends in Cross-Border Mergers and Acquisitions. In: K.R. Chitted, ed., *The Economic and Social Issues of Financial Liberalisation: Evidence from Emerging Countries.* New Delhi: Bookwell Publishing, pp. 26–40.

Saraswathy, B. (2015). "Production Efficiency of Firms with Mergers and Acquisitions in India". Working Paper No. 299. Indian Council for Research on International Economic Relations, New Delhi, June. Available at: http://icrier.org/pdf/Working_Paper_299.pdf. [Accessed on 1st January 2017].

Saraswathy, B (2017). Innovation Consolidation Nexus: Evidence from India's Manufacturing Sector. In Siddharthan and Narayanan, K. *Globalisation of Technology.* Springer (forthcoming).

Saraswathy, B. (2016a). "An Assessment of Foreign Acquisitions in India". Working Paper No. 193. Institute for Studies in Industrial Development, New Delhi.

Saraswathy, B. (2016b). "Impact of Mergers on Market Competition in the Indian Manufacturing: An Assessment". Working Paper No. 188. Institute for Studies in Industrial Development, New Delhi.

Sathpathy, C. (2001). Undervalued Imports and Public Interest: Domestic Rulings vis-à-vis GATT/WTO Jurisprudence-II. *Economic and Political Weekly,* 36(5, 6) February 3–10, pp. 445–447.

Scherer, F.M. and Ross, D. (1990). *Industrial Market Structure and Economic Performance.* Boston: Houghton Mifflin Co.

Schiffbauer, M., Iulia, S. and Frances, R. (2009). *Do Foreign Mergers and Acquisitions Boost Productivity.* Working Paper No. 305. Dublin: Economic and Social Research Institute.

Schoenberg, R. (2000). The Influence of Cultural Compatibility within Cross-Border Acquisitions: A Review. *Advances in Mergers and Acquisitions,* 1, pp. 43–59.

Schoenberg, R. (2001). Knowledge Transfer and Resource Sharing as Value Creation Mechanisms in Inbound Continental European Acquisitions. *Journal of Euromarketing,* 10(1), pp. 99–115.

Schoenberg, R. (2004). Management Style Compatibility and Cross-Border Acquisition Outcome. In: C. Cooper and S. Finkelstein, ed., *Advances in Mergers and Acquisitions*, West Yorkshire: Emerald Gropu of Publishing Limited. pp. 149–175.

Schulz, N. (2007). *Review of Literature on the Impact of Mergers on Innovation.* Wuerzburg: University of Wuerzburg.

Schumpeter, J.A. (1950). *Capitalism, Socialism and Democracy.* New York: Harper and Row.

Securities and Exchange Board of India (1997). Takeover Code: (Substantial Acquisition of Shares and Takeovers) Regulations, Government of India.

Securities and Exchange Board of India (2010). Achuthan Committee Report of the Takeover Regulations Advisory Committee, 15th July. Government of India.

Shapiro, C. (2012). Competition and Innovation: Did Arrow Hit the Bull's Eye? In: J. Lerner and S. Stern, eds., *The Rate and Director of Inventive Activity Revisited* National Bureau of Economic Research. Chicago: University of Chicago Press, pp. 361–410.

Shapiro, C. and Robert, D.W. (1990). On the Antitrust Treatment of Production Joint Ventures. *The Journal of Economic Perspectives,* 4(3), pp. 113–130.

Shekhar, C. (1972). Vested Interests Must be Liquidated. In: *A Round Table Discussion Organised by the Society for Democracy, Monopolies and the Public Policy.* New Delhi: People's Publishing House.

Shimizu, H. and Vydyanadh, P. (2004). Theoretical Foundations of Cross-Border Mergers and Acquisitions: A Review of Current Research and Recommendations for the Future. *Journal of International Management,* 10, pp. 307–353.

Shleifer, A. and Vishny, R.W. (1997). A Survey of Corporate Governance. *Journal of Finance,* LII(2), pp. 737–783.

Siegel, D.S. and Simons, K.L. (2006). *Assessing Effects of Mergers and Acquisitions on Firm Performance, Plan Productivity and Workers: New Evidence from Matched Employer Employee Data.* Rensselaer Working Papers in Economics.

Singh, A. (1971). *Takeovers: Their Relevance to the Stock Market and the Theory of the Firm.* Cambridge: Cambridge University Press.

Sjoholm, F. and Lipsey, R.E. (2006). Foreign Firms and Indonesian Manufacturing Wages: An Analysis with Panel Data. *Journal of Economic Development and Cultural Change,* 55(1), 201–221.

Smarzynska, K. Beata and Shang-Jin, W. (2000). *Corruption and Composition of Foreign Direct Investment: Firm-Level Evidence.* NBER Working Papers 7969. National Bureau of Economic Research.

Smith, A. (1776). *An Inquiry into the Nature and Causes of Wealth of Nations.* London: Harvard Publishing.

Srivastava, V. (1996). *Liberalization, Productivity and Competition: A Panel Study on Indian Manufacturing.* New Delhi: Oxford University Press.

Stahl, G.K. and Andreas, V. (2005). Impact of Cultural Differences on Mergers and Acquisition Performance: A Critical Research Review and an Integrative Model. *Advances in Mergers and Acquisitions,* 4, pp. 51–82.

Stigler, G.J. (1950). Monopoly and Oligopoly by Merger. *The American Economic Review,* 40(2), pp. 23–34.

Stigler, G.J. (1956). The Statistics on Monopoly and Mergers. *Journal of Political Economy,* LXIV(1), pp. 33–40.

Subrahmanian, K.K. (1986). Technology Import Regulation Reduces Cost. *Economic and Political Weekly,* XXI(32), 1412–1416.

Subrahmanian, K.K. (1991). Technological Capability under Economic Liberalism: Experience of Indian Industry in Eighties. *Economic and Political Weekly,* XXVI(35), pp. M87–M89.

Sudarsanam, S. (2004). *Creating Value from Mergers and Acquisitions: The Challenges, An Integrated and International Perspective.* Noida: Pearson Education.

Sudarsanam, S,, Peter, H. and Avo, S. (1996). Shareholder Wealth Gains in Mergers: Effect of Synergy and Ownership Structure. *Journal of Business Finance and Accounting,* 23(6), 673–698.

Swaminathan, S. (2002). Indian M&As: Why They have Worked So Far. *Indian Management,* 41 June, pp. 72–77.

The Hindu (2011). 17th August 2011.

The Sunday Guardian. Available at: www.sunday-guardian.com/investigation/vayudoot-employees-complain-against-ial [Accessed on 17th Aug. 2011].

Till, V., Brian, K. and Ted, R. (2003). Should You Always Merge Cultures? *Harvard Management Update,* 8 May, p. 10. As cited in Bruner, F. (2004).

Tirol, J. (2001). Corporate Governance. *Econometrica,* 69(1), pp. 1–35.

Trivedi, P., A. Prakash and D. Sinate (2000), Productivity in Major Manufacturing Industries in India: 1973–74 to 1997–98, Study No. 20, DRG, RBI, August.

Tobin, J. (1958). Estimation of Relationships for Limited Dependent Variables. *Econometrica,* 26(1), pp. 24–36.

Umakrishnan, K.U. (2006). *Intra-Source FDI Differences in Technology Transfer Behaviour.* Ph.D. Thesis. Thiruvananthapuram: Centre for Development Studies.

Vaara, E. Sarala, R. Stahl. and Bjorkman (2012). The Impact of Organisational and National Cultural Differences on Social Conflict and Knowledge Transfer in International Acquisitions: Domestic and Foreign Acquisitions of Finnish Companies. *Journal of Management Studies*, 49(1): 1365–1390.

UNCTAD (1993). *Concentration of Market Power, (through Mergers, Takeovers, Joint Ventures and Other Acquisitions of Control), and Its Effects on International Markets (In Particular the Markets of Developing Countries)*. New York: United Nations.

UNCTAD (2011). Database on Cross-Border Mergers and Acquisitions. Available at: www.unctad.org/fdistatistics [Accessed on 21st April 2011].

UNCTAD, FDI/TNC Database (2011). Available at: www.unctad.org/fdistatistics [Accessed on 21st Apr. 2011].

UNCTAD, 2011. Database on Cross-border Mergers and Acquisitions, Available at www.unctad.org/fdistatistics [Accessed on 7th January 2017].

UNCTAD, FDI/TNC Database, 2011. Available at < www.unctad.org/fdistatistics> [Accessed on 7th January 2017].

Unel, B. (2003). *Productivity Trends in India's Manufacturing Sectors in the Last Two Decades*. Working Paper No. 22. Asia and Pacific Department, Washington, DC: IMF.

Utton, M.A. (1971). The Effect of Mergers on Concentration: UK Manufacturing Industry 1954–1965. *The Journal of Industrial Economics*, 20(1), pp. 42–58.

Utton, M. (2008). *International Competition Policy: Maintaining Open Markets in the Global Economy*. Cheltenham: Edward Elgar Publishing.

Vasconcellos, G.M. and Kish, R.J. (1996). Factors Affecting Cross-Border Mergers and Acquisitions: The Canada-US Experience. *Global Finance Journal*, 7(2). pp. 223–238.

Venkatesan, R. (2009). Should the Air India Maharaja be Awarded his Privy Purse. *Economic and Political Weekly*, XLIV(32), pp. 33–37.

Verbeek, M. (2000). *A Guide to Modern Econometrics*. New York: John Wiley & Sons.

Vermeulen, F. and Barkema, H.G. (2001). Controlling International Expansion. *Business Strategy Review*, 12(3), pp. 29–36.

Vyas, V., Krishnan, N. and Ramanadhan, A. (2012). Determinants of Mergers and Acquisitions in Indian Pharmaceutical Industry. *Eurasian Journal of Business and Economics*, 5(2), pp. 79–102.

Walsh, J.P. and Seward, J.K. (1990). On the Efficiency of Internal and External Corporate Control Mechanisms. *Academic Management Review*, 15, pp. 421–458.

Walshe, G., 1974. Recent Trends in Monopoly in Great Britain, NIESR. Cambridge: Cambridge University Press.

Weber, R.A. and Camerer, C.F. (2003). Cultural Conflict and Merger Failure: An Experimental Approach. *Management Science*, 49(4), pp. 400–415.

Weiss, L.W. (1965). An Evaluation of Mergers in Six Industries. *The Review of Economics and Statistics*, 47 May, pp. 172–181.

Weston, J.F. (1953). *The Role of Mergers in the Growth of Large Firms*. California: University of California Press.

White and Case (2001). *Survey of Worldwide Antitrust Merger Notification Requirements*. Washington, DC.

Williamson, J. (1996). Profit Growth and Sales Maximization. *Economica*, 33, pp. 1–16.

Williamson, O.E. (1963). Management Discretion and Business Behaviour. *American Economic Review,* 53, pp. 1032–1057.

Williamson, O.E. (1968). Economies as an Antitrust Defense: The Welfare Tradeoffs. *The American Economic Review,* 58(1), pp. 18–36.

Williamson, O.E. (1975). *Markets and Hierarchies: Analysis and Antitrust Implications.* New York: Free Press.

Williamson, O.E. (1985). *The Economic Institutions of Capitalism.* New York: Free Press.

Wooldridge, J.M. (2000). *Introductory Econometrics: A Modern Approach.* United States: South Western College Publishing.

World Investment Report (2000). *Cross Border Mergers and Acquisitions and Development.* New York and Geneva: UNCTAD.

Wyman, O. (2008). Post Merger Integration: A Tailored Approach to Sustainable Transaction Success. Available at: www.oliverwyman.com/media/Post_Merger_Integration_en.pdf [Accessed on 8th July 2012].

# Index

For Product Safety Concerns and Information please contact our EU
representative GPSR@taylorandfrancis.com
Taylor & Francis Verlag GmbH, Kaufingerstraße 24, 80331 München, Germany